To Roberta......,
Kampai! Enjoy with my
best wishes!
Don

CHEF'S
CHOICE

22 Culinary Masters Tell How
JAPANESE
FOOD
CULTURE

Influenced Their Careers
and Cuisine

❖

CHEF'S CHOICE

**22 Culinary Masters Tell How
Japanese Food Culture
Influenced Their Careers and Cuisine**

Saori Kawano & Don Gabor

Conversation Arts Media

BROOKLYN, NEW YORK

Conversation Arts Media
P.O. Box 715
Brooklyn, NY, 11215
www.dongabor.com
www.chefschoicethebook.com

Cover Design Hilary Zarycky

Book Layout © 2014 BookDesignTemplate.com

Book Title/ Chef's Choice: 22 Culinary Masters Tell How Japanese Food Culture Influenced Their Careers and Cuisine / Kawano, Saori & Gabor, Don -- 1st ed.

ISBN 978-1-879834-27-9

❖

Acknowledgements

We want to thank all the participating chefs for their enduring support of this book project. We are honored that many of these chefs are members of The Gohan Society's Board of Directors, Culinary Advisory Board, or Advisory Committee.

We want to express our deepest gratitude to Eileen Cowell for providing editorial polish, clarity, and for her generous help in making this book a reality.

We also thank the following people for their assistance:
Yoshiki Tsuji, Motoatsu Sakurai, Mari Sugai,
Hilary Zarycky, Jeanine Caunt, Nancy Dugan,
Erica Caridio, Brandon Saracco, and Daniel Carman.

In the modern field of gastronomy, mastering Japanese cuisine is more than acquiring the fundamental cooking skills. It also requires a deeper understanding of the historical background of Japanese food culture.

— Yoshiki Tsuji, President of the TSUJI Culinary Institute in Osaka, Japan

❖

CONTENTS

Food culture in the United States has undergone momentous changes in the past three decades. When I first moved to New York City in 1978, Japanese restaurants were small hole-in-the-wall establishments. They served Americanized Japanese food like chicken teriyaki and shrimp tempura, dishes that satisfied a craving for the exotic while still catering to the western palate. Americans were frightened by the idea of eating raw fish, and most restaurant-goers did not appreciate the subtlety of Japanese cuisine.

In this environment, I watched sandwich-eating elementary school students tease my daughter about the lovingly packed bento boxes she brought to school every day. I felt sorry that my daughter was the object of ridicule because of her traditional Japanese lunches. At the same time, I was disheartened by the American public's lack of understanding and appreciation for Japan's proud cuisine and culinary heritage.

At this point, I knew that I wanted to play an active part in transforming America's food culture and to help bridge this culinary gap between the United States and my home country. In 1982 I rented a small space in downtown New York City and founded Korin to introduce to the hospitality industry the exquisite craftsmanship of Japanese tableware and chef knives.

After nearly 25 years of introducing new and traditional Japanese products to western restaurants and chefs, I wanted to share even more of Japan's rich culinary heritage. So in 2005 I founded The Gohan Society, a non-profit organization whose mission is to encourage an understanding and appreciation of Japan's culinary heritage in the United States by reaching out to chefs, culinary arts professionals, and people who admire and enjoy Japanese culture.

The Gohan Society aims to make the knowledge of traditional Japanese ingredients, tools, cooking techniques, and food-related products accessible to the American culinary scene. Gohan's goal is to increase knowledge of Japanese cuisine and culture in the United States. With the encouragement and support of generous chefs, dedicated food professionals, manufacturers, and other organizations, The Gohan Society has expanded its mission by offering professional workshops and demonstrations in New York City and, by funding scholarships for young chefs to study in Japan.

Today in New York City we can find nearly every kind of cuisine, as well as food products and ingredients from most every country. I am proud that Japanese ingredients from miso to dashi are widely used in non-Japanese restaurants, and *umami* is an international culinary term. Chefs from all over are travelling to Japan and then spreading the influence of Japanese cooking techniques and ingredients through kitchens worldwide.

Then in 2013 another exciting event made my heart soar. *Washoku*, or traditional Japanese cuisine, was added to UNESCO's Representative List of Intangible Cultural Heritage, making it the second national cuisine to receive this distinguished honor. We live in a borderless culinary world where food traditions are spread through travel, kitchen experience, literature, and the Internet. I feel privileged to witness such culinary diversity, and I want to support an ongoing exchange of ideas and inspiration. Therein lies my motivation for writing this book.

Over the last thirty years, many accomplished chefs have told me their amazing stories. Time and again I was awestruck by their voracious pursuit of culinary knowledge, perseverance, and determination to succeed in a difficult and demanding business. *Chef's Choice* was written to share these inspirational stories. The introduction, "The Japanese Chef's Way of Thinking," written by Chef Toshio Suzuki, provides a brief historical and cultural context for Japanese cuisine. The essays that follow are based on personal interviews that offer a fascinating look at the careers and culinary decisions made by these dedicated and brilliant chefs. Each essay also explores how Japanese ingredients and products, tools, and cuisine, as well as the merging of western and eastern food cultures, have influenced the individual chef.

I hope that these success stories will inspire aspiring chefs to set and achieve high goals for themselves. No chef begins as a great culinary master. All the chefs in this book started at the bottom of the restaurant business. They scrubbed pots, washed dishes, cut cases of vegetables, and worked tirelessly for years to become the successful chefs they are today. Through this spirit of perseverance and hard work they cultivated excellence and pursued their remarkable careers.

It will give me the utmost joy and satisfaction if readers are inspired to experiment with the Japanese ingredients and cooking techniques mentioned by the chefs in these pages, or are motivated to travel to Japan to discover the rich legacy of culinary tradition in my native country. Finally, I look forward to seeing the evolution of a new generation of chefs who use and share Japan's culinary traditions in the pursuit of their own extraordinary careers.

❖

The Japanese Chef's Way of Thinking

If we don't talk about the fundamentals that inform the way a Japanese chef thinks, then we can't understand how we arrived at Japanese cooking today. It all starts with Japan's location and topography. Japan is made up of about 6,300 islands, including the four main islands of Kyushu, Shikoku, Honshu, and Hokkaido. Ocean currents encircle the islands, running from south to north on one side and from north to south on the other. A mountain range runs north to south along the spine of the islands. When the jet stream from the Himalayas hits the mountain range, it causes rain and snow, and with it the growth of many localized types of vegetation.

I've been living in the U.S. for more than 30 years. Looking from the outside, I can see that the ancient Japanese spirit and ways of thinking still exist in Japan, particularly among Japanese chefs.

The Japanese way of thinking—their outlook and indigenous religious beliefs—is called *Shinto* or *Shintoism*. It was born of the volcanoes, earthquakes, typhoons, and other natural disasters that are particular to this group of islands and topography. Shinto beliefs and ways of thinking are deeply embedded in the subconscious fabric of modern Japanese society, and include feelings of gratitude for all of the blessings that nature provides, as well as the constant fear of fires, floods, and earthquakes. Out of this physical environment came the Japanese people's deepest respect and honor for harmony with nature. They welcome Mother Nature's fury and her bounty. And they believe that all people, animals, plants, and living things are one with nature.

Japanese chefs perform special rituals out of respect for nature's ingredients. For example, by using every scrap of a fish without wasting any part of it, we treat nature's bounty with care. We say *itadakimasu* ("I receive") before eating. In this way, we acknowledge that something that was alive has terminated its life for us. There is an ancient Japanese cooking tradition of cherishing nature and taking great care with our ingredients. We constantly think about how to use every bit of an ingredient—handling it to its best advantage and always considering texture and its seasonality.

Around 1,400 years ago, Japan's ancient ways of thinking about nature expanded with the integration of philosophies and religions that originated in China. Then, around 1333 AD, Dōgen Zenji, a Japanese Zen Buddhist teacher born in Kyōto and founder of the Soutou school of Zen, changed food preparation in Japan. After training as a monk in China, he brought back vegetarianism and other aspects of the *shojin ryori* Buddhist diet to Japan, then incorporated them into principles, or *tanmi*, for the Zen monks. Dōgen Zenji recorded them in his book *Tenzo Kyokun, Instructions for the Cook.*

Some of these principles explained in the book involved *washoku*, which means "harmony of food." One principle of washoku is *takiawase*, sometimes called "kindled vegetables." The vegetables are cooked separately and then assembled on the same plate. In Japanese cooking, takiawase expresses this spirit of unity.

Dōgen Zenji's book also identified other elements, including tastes, cooking methods, and colors. The Five Tastes include salty, sweet, sour, bitter and umami (savory), plus *tanmi*, or the subtle natural flavor of the ingredient. The Five Methods of Cooking—raw, boiled, sautéed, grilled, and steamed—transform flavors. The Five Colors—white, black, red, green, and yellow—serve to balance nutritional content. The book also named five pungent roots to avoid, as well as harsh-tasting foods and strong-smelling foods that are too stimulating to the palate.

During this period, Japanese cuisine continued to change. It became the fashion, particularly in Japan's Imperial Court. Because Japan was never invaded by outsiders and was closed off from the world, its cuisine remained virtually uninterrupted.

Seven hundred years ago, the importance of each ingredient was based on its nature. This reverence for ingredients became the cornerstone of today's *kaiseki ryori*, the traditional multi-course Japanese dinner. Today, specially trained chefs use only the freshest seasonal ingredients, which are prepared to enhance their flavor by balancing taste, texture, appearance, and colors. Dishes are beautifully arranged and garnished on handcrafted tableware, often with real leaves and edible flowers, and are designed to resemble natural plants and animals.

Buddhism also brought a new food culture, as well as utensils, to Japan. Because vegetables were the main dish, knives, tools, and cooking techniques were created as Japan's emerging cuisine developed. The Japanese *hocho*, an all-purpose kitchen knife, is a perfect example of this.

Originally, samurais were in charge of meals in the Imperial Court. They were responsible for the food, but their role also included that of protector. Because it wouldn't do for the emperor to be poisoned, samurais tasted all the food, and they were also in charge of identifying and verifying ingredients. To accomplish this, they read Buddhist texts and medicinal manuscripts and became experts in health, sanitation, and poisonous ingredients.

During the Heian Period (794–1185 AD), a master chef and poet, Yamakage Fujiwara, came to the Imperial Court. By order of the Emperor, he set down rules for using the hocho kitchen knife and the *manaita* cutting board and created the Shijo school. These rules established the knife ceremony and rituals, giving thanks for food and honoring nature's bounty at the Imperial Court. Once the Shijo school of Art established "the way of the knife," other schools began to teach the knife techniques, too, and the art of the knife spread from the Imperial Court to the warrior clans, giving those trained in the military arts even more authority. As a result, the head of the kitchen in each *daimyo* household was schooled in the way of the knife.

The cooks in the Imperial kitchen needed an underlying philosophy, especially when it came to kitchen and food safety. After all, their lives were at stake. If poison was found in the food or if someone became ill because of the food, they would have to commit *seppuku*, or ritual suicide, immediately. No profession at that time could have been more stressful. Being a chef then wasn't like it is today. Now when you make a mistake, you just say, "Oops!"

The powerful clans throughout Japan tried to attract master chefs, since they were a source of pride for a wealthy household. The fine cuisine, the way of the knife, and other cultural arts, such as ceramics, textiles, flower arranging, and the tea ceremony, began to spread across Japan as roads and highways made travel easier. The Edo Period (1603–1868) brought with it the extravagant meal, *rikyu's cha-kaiseki* followed by the *sado* (tea ceremony). These were later unified by the *ryotei* (guest house and restaurant) culture of Kyoto and the Yoshiwara (prostitution/pleasure district) ryotei tradition in Kanto, and eventually developed into contemporary *kaiseki* cuisine. The peak of kaiseki was during the years 1688 to 1704. This period, I believe, was the culmination of the complete arts of Japanese cookery that had begun with the Shijo school of Art.

The Edo Period was a warrior-based, feudal society with a caste system. The warrior was at the top, followed by farmers and artisans. Tradesmen were at the bottom. However, merchants prospered through the distribution of their goods to various destinations despite the limitations of their position in society. Their imagination and creativity with raw ingredients gave rise to *shoyu* (soy sauce) and *shottsuru* (a pungent regional Japanese fish sauce made from the brine of salt-pickled fish). They also made a thin soy sauce called *usukuchi shoyu* from the same brine used to make miso from soybeans.

All of these manufactured foods came to Kanto, the heartland of feudal power. Kanto included the central inland and western coastal region of Honshu, especially the Tokyo-Yokohama areas. Kanto was the dividing point between the cultivation of rice and wheat. The richness of the Tama and Tone Rivers made Kanto a fertile region for growing wheat, which was used to make buckwheat soba noodles.

Originally, shoyu was made only with soybeans, but when shoyu was mixed with wheat, it created a stronger soy sauce that sold like wildfire throughout the Kanto district. In Kanto, there were many shoyu makers. An abundance of shoyu made it possible to develop dishes like *kabayaki* (grilled eel) and the dipping sauce for soba noodles. Wheat also changed how sushi was prepared. Until then, sushi had been pickled in barrels of fermented saké lees. However, by making less-costly vinegar from wheat and saké lees, the merchants of Kanto generated huge profits almost overnight and spread the sushi culture to other areas throughout Japan.

Ieyasu Tokugawa, the founder and first shogun of the Tokugawa shogunate of Japan, also contributed to food use and transportation in Japan. He built an amazing water supply and sewer system around the Tama River. Waterways were used to bring in large volumes of food products and other goods to Edo from all over Japan.

Tokugawa knew about food poisoning and was one of the driving forces behind the successful cultivation and use of wasabi in food as a way to kill bacteria. As a result, the Tokugawa family crest incorporated a plant that resembles the wasabi plant.

Another important product of the Edo period was *nori* (dried seaweed sheets). I believe nori originated in China or possibly Korea. The technique of making nori became popular in the late Edo period, and inlets along the coast near Edo were reclaimed for cultivation. Nori cultivation spread quickly to inlets of other areas. Then, during the Meiji Period (1868–1912), English scientist Kathleen Drew-Baker identified ways to increase seaweed production, and this led to a boost in the Japanese seaweed industry.

The custom of eating rice wrapped in nori (one of the world's first "fast foods") can be traced to the Ginza. During the Edo period, this area was home to many blacksmiths, who, because they were so busy, needed a quick yet nutritious meal. They ate *tekka-maki*. The name tekka-maki (*tekka* means "red-hot iron") was used for the rolled sushi that they could eat quickly and easily. A tekka-maki is just like makimono of today—easily made, filled with vitamins and minerals, and reasonably priced. As a result, tekka-maki grew rapidly in popularity.

Another ingredient that became popular during the Edo period was pickled ginger, or gari. Gari's use was originally medicinal; it was considered a disinfectant for the mouth. Gari was also used to cleanse the palate, preparing it to taste the next dish much in the same way as vinegar, shoyu, and wasabi.

Food fermentation has been part of Japan's food culture in large part because the warm and cold environments, abundant rainfall, humidity, and wide variety of vegetation allow many kinds of microorganisms, fungi, and bacteria to flourish. When chefs and farmers combined rice and soybeans with lactic acid bacilli, they found it was possible to produce miso, saké, shoyu, natto (a sticky soybean paste), tsukemono (pickled vegetables), and other types of fermented foods. The lactic acid bacilli that kill microbes are also used to reclaim clean water from sludge filled with nitrogen. Additionally, lactic acid bacilli destroy the deadly poison tetrodotoxin, which is found in the fugu blowfish liver and other parts of this fish. The liver can then be pickled into tsukemono—it's delicious!

All of these concepts appear in Dōgen Zenji's ancient book, *Tenzo Kyokun, Instructions for the Cook*. Nature makes food for us and no human hand has to touch it. We simply create the opportunity. I see it this way: A chef is like a mediator, or a go-between. What needs to be done in order to bring together this ingredient and that ingredient? It's like matchmaking. I think that's how Japanese chefs approach cooking. They work hard to best utilize each ingredient, often leaving it intact and drawing out the flavor.

I relate this concept to Japanese cooking today. There is a simmered dish called *takiawase*. You don't simmer the ingredients all jumbled together, but one by one. If you have a potato, turnip, and some bamboo shoots, you add some touches to each one, suited to the character of each, so that each ingredient is at its best when combined later. If there is a weak flavor somewhere, you add a little something to it. If something is too strong, you extract some of the flavor, using the concept of "if you add something—take away something." The dish is finished by combining all ingredients together in one stock. I believe this concept of harmony is at the root of Japanese culture and cooking: putting each life to its best use, and treating ingredients with care. Drawing the best flavor out of each individual ingredient is, I think, the fundamental definition of Japanese cooking and at the heart of the Japanese chef's way of thinking.

ONE

ELIZABETH ANDOH

Cookbook Author/Director, A Taste of Culture

Elizabeth Andoh was born and raised in America, although Japan has been her home for more than four decades. Ms. Andoh's formal culinary training was taken at the Yanagihara School of Traditional Japanese Cuisine, in Tokyo. In 1972 she began "A Taste of Culture," a culinary arts program that combines spicy tidbits of food lore with practical tips and skill-building lessons on how to prepare Japanese food. Her programs are conducted in Tokyo and offer a unique opportunity for foreign residents and visitors from overseas to explore and enjoy Japan's culture through its food.

Ms. Andoh is the author of six cookbooks, including the award-winning *Washoku: Recipes from the Japanese Home Kitchen*. She publishes an electronic newsletter about six times a year. Each issue includes a short essay/story focused on some aspect of Japan's food culture. Newsletters include links to photo-illustrated recipes that relate to the chosen theme; those recipes can be downloaded, making it easy for subscribers to take them into the kitchen when they cook. A Taste of Culture's newsletters are free at www.tasteofculture.com.

Influences

I had no experience with Japanese food, so I had nothing to compare it with, which may have been a good thing, because I had no real expectations of how it should taste.

I ended up in Japan by happy accident 40 plus years ago. I was born and raised in New York City. While attending the University of Michigan, I became aware that a scholarship at the Center for Japanese Studies went unclaimed. I applied and landed on the island of Shikoku, which in the mid-1960s was extremely rural. There were no flush toilets. You had to pump water from a well, and there was a small, old-fashioned refrigerator in addition to the icebox.

I stayed with the Andoh family, which is how I got to know the senior Mrs. Andoh (the woman who would become my mother-in-law), and meet (and eventually marry) one of her sons. My husband, Atsunori, is next to the youngest in birth order.

The Andoh household where I stayed had a totally different rhythm than I was used to. Mrs. Andoh was a talented practitioner of *washoku*—a traditional way of preparing Japanese food. Literally, *washoku* means "harmony of food." It is a way of thinking about what we eat and how it can nourish us. Mrs. Andoh ran a large household that included cooking for her husband's factory workers, so her kitchen was like a small restaurant. She had a limited budget, but she purchased and fully used ingredients, preserving their nutrition while coaxing out the very best flavor. She had a real flair for food.

At that time I didn't speak a word of Japanese, so I didn't really understand what was happening, but everyone seemed quite happy about the food they ate, so I figured there had to be something special about it. It was simply up to me to figure out what that was. I had no experience with Japanese food, so I had nothing to compare it with, which may have been a good thing, because I had no real expectations of how it should taste.

In Shikoku, everyone eats udon, the slithery, thick white wheat noodles every day. It's not necessarily served instead of rice—you can also have rice with the noodles. I have always preferred salty food to sweet, so there was something very appealing about pickles and rice. I fell in love with pickled plums—*umeboshi*—especially first thing in the morning. I have never been a donut-and-coffee person.

I decided I wanted to stay in Japan a bit longer, although staying would definitely require that I learn the language. In 1967, I traveled to Tokyo to be part of a pilot program to teach Japanese to those not brought up in Japanese culture. It was a very intensive program.

I was living in a rented room in somebody's house and needed to learn to cook for myself. When I asked Mrs. Andoh for some of her recipes, she said, "Since you are in Tokyo now, you should take lessons from the writer and teacher, Toshio Yanagihara. I'll write him a letter."

Career Path

Mrs. Andoh forgot to mention that I wasn't Japanese, so when I showed up for the interview, Master Yanagihara was a little surprised.

Master Yanagihara was a man with the mindset of the Meiji Period—you know, the turn of the nineteenth century, officially from 1868 to 1912—who appreciated things that were not Japanese. He was such a magnificent writer! He could communicate. He knew exactly what phrase to use and how to describe food so that you could taste it and appreciate it. This experience led me to consider food writing as a career. Master Yanagihara told me, "Hang in there. Basic training at my school is three years. Then you can write about it in English and get the rest of the world excited."

Early into this three-year course, Master Yanagihara came to me and said, "You need to write your own book. Translating my work—nobody's going to get it." In 1972, I queried *Gourmet* magazine as to whether the editors were interested in some pieces on Japanese food culture, and the answer was yes! In 1975 they published my series of six pieces. The rest is history. I served as *Gourmet* magazine's Japanese food correspondent until 2007.

Cuisine

The word "washoku" is a philosophy and a mindset—and it's also the food that's produced when you're in that mindset.

Washoku is Japanese food, but the *wa* character also means "harmony." The Japanese think of themselves and all of the things they do, including their cultural traditions surrounding food, as harmonious. It's a question of achieving balance. The word *washoku* is a philosophy and a mindset—and it's also the food that's produced when you're in that mindset.

I refer to the person who is making the food as the *practitioner*, because he or she practices washoku. It's a very active engagement. There are three groupings of five elements that are important for the practitioner and the person being fed. The three groupings are color, flavor, and what I call *transformation* (as opposed to cooking). If you call it cooking, it implies the application of heat, and sometimes you don't apply heat.

There are five colors: red, yellow, and green, followed by black and white. It's not about equal distribution. It's about balance.

Among these colors, red is the largest category. It includes purple, pink, orange, and even browns. If you know anything about nutrition, you know that red foods are typically rich in polyphenols, and that certain other nutrients appear in leafy greens, so without much effort, if you've got balance of color, you've got nutritional balance. It doesn't require complicated calculations.

The second group is flavor. The big three flavors are sweet, sour, and salty, followed by bitter and spicy. The bitter taste cleanses the palette and helps you to appreciate other flavors. Bitter is used in small amounts to reset your palette. These bitter accents are subtle and spice plays a different role: it is much more about aroma than heat. And when there is heat, it is different. Think of wasabi—it's frontal and nasal, while sansho pepper is tongue-tingling.

So now we come to the third group: transformation. In preparing a meal, ingredients are changed or transformed in some way. The Japanese combine various methods: some foods are simmered, some foods are seared with heat, some foods are steamed (*mushimono)* or fried using a bit of oil, and some foods are eaten raw.

When planning and preparing a meal, you have many things to consider: color, flavor, and the method by which you will transform your ingredient into a finished dish. Combine the elements of five colors, five flavors, and five preparation methods in different ways, and you've got not 15, but three to the fifth power—that's a lot of combinations!

8 · ELIZABETH ANDOH

One concept that's not addressed in the three main groups is "mouth-feel," which is very important to the Japanese.

There are certain textures that the Japanese adore, and the uninitiated may have a hard time appreciating them. For example, the Japanese love *neba neba*, or the slimy, sticky, gooey and stringy texture of boiled okra. *Junsai*, also called "watershield" is another Japanese favorite. The unfurled leaves are covered in a slippery, transparent jelly. It's an alien mouth feel. Forget the taste of it or the smell of it—it's just weird in your mouth! There's a crunch and a slither, and then a briny explosion on your tongue. And it isn't something that happens with other foods—it's a very unusual eating experience.

Another aspect of Japanese food culture is *kansha*, or "appreciation." It compels us to use food and resources fully, not to waste anything—even water. For example, when I was first at the Andoh home in Shikoku, I literally had to go outside and pump water from the well. Pump and schlep. You do not waste water! If you're going to use that water to blanch oily abura-age—a deep-fried tofu pouch—and spinach or some other green vegetable, blanch your greens first.

You need to be mindful. It is not necessarily difficult or more time consuming, but you need to be aware of possible waste and avoid it. This is also part of practicing washoku and kansha.

One style of washoku cooking is taking a single ingredient and making a whole meal with it.

It's funny, because the original *Iron Chef* TV program picked up on that idea, but it's an ancient notion in Japanese cooking. You had a lot of seasonal foods that were locally grown. That was it and probably had to do with necessity in the days before refrigeration and swift transportation. So the really talented chef was not the one who could acquire some exotic or wildly expensive ingredient, but, rather, the person who could take a very simple, humble carrot or daikon and explode the possibilities into a full-course banquet. That notion of taking a very limited item and making various things from it is not unique to the culinary arts. Think about black-and-white brush paintings. You've got a very limited palette, yet can create the impression of varied color. It's about seeing the possibilities in something that has limitations.

Ingredients

Sometimes people were taking Japanese ingredients and using them in ways that the Japanese would not use them.

Today many food critics consider mixing cuisines as fusion. In 1985 I wrote a book, *An American Taste of Japan*, which was about what I called cross-cultural cuisine, and it was far ahead of its time. At that time, I had lived in Japan for almost 20 years, and when I came back to America, I discovered that you could create a Japanese meal anywhere. It had nothing to do with being Japanese and nothing to do with geography. Sometimes people were taking ordinary Japanese ingredients and using them in ways that the Japanese would not use them.

By the mid 1980s, particularly in New York, *shiso*, a perennial herb in the mint family, was beginning to come into popularity. Certainly enoki mushrooms were available. There was wasabi, although it was mostly powder. There were all sorts of foods out there that had not been available 20 years before. People in America began to play with them.

At the same time a new cooking style evolved in Japan when Japanese chefs went to Europe to train and then returned to Japan. Influence and inspiration—and it's inevitable.

Today, Americans no longer assume that cooking with Japanese ingredients is something that only the Japanese do.

Americans are buying Japanese ingredients. People are willing to consider Japanese ingredients as part of their diet and their pantry. This is particularly true among food professionals. But many do not understand the ingredients, and they don't know what they can do and should or should not do.

Enoki mushrooms, for example, don't have to be cooked very long, but a food chemist finally explained to me that there's an enzyme in them that needs to be eliminated. In Japan, cooks usually place enoki mushrooms at the bottom of a bowl and pour hot broth on top. That's all the heat you need to neutralize this enzyme. However, Americans were putting raw enoki mushrooms on salads, as they do with regular mushrooms. Nothing bad happened, but people experienced a slight bit of indigestion.

Another example is wasabi. If you heat wasabi, it does ugly things, so you should add it at the end of the cooking process. Otherwise, it becomes bitter and turns an unappetizing color, especially if you use the powder instead of the real stuff. Frequently Japanese ingredients are used incorrectly.

That's why it's so useful to experience the cuisine and to study how traditional cooks prepare Japanese food. In this way, you can increase your ability to use the ingredients the right way and guide your curiosity in the right direction.

Certainly one kind of miso is not going to be interchangeable with another in any given recipe. It's just not. They're very different.

There were two reasons why I started my tasting programs with Japanese ingredients in the early 1990s. First, no individual is going to go out there and buy 20 different kinds of miso to discover what the range is. If you lived your formative years in Japan or traveled a bit there, you might eventually experience dozens of different kinds of miso without trying.

But if you are living in Chicago or Dallas, it's unlikely that you're going to get a sense of what miso is all about. Yet, certainly one kind of miso is not going to be interchangeable with another in any given recipe. It's just not. They're very different.

On another level, you have something like *kombu*—kelp—which is naturally occurring umami. There are different varieties of kombu kelp and kinds of water (hard or soft) that will influence taste. People in Kansai region Osaka prefer *ma-kombu*, while people in Tokyo prefer *Hidaka kombu*. When I was conducting miso- or kombu-tasting programs, most participants could taste the difference. But those new to ingredients such as miso or kombu had trouble.

Training

The key to understanding the Japanese approach to food preparation is that nothing goes to waste and everything is fully used, appreciated.

At A Taste of Culture I offer different programs for different audiences. The mini-intensives focus on understanding basic ingredients and techniques, and applying them to a wide variety of foods. It's a fast-paced, tightly packed curriculum that appeals to food professionals and serious home cooks.

Because it's important to understand your ingredients, I often include a segment I call "A Peek in the Pantry," in which we sample many varieties of common basic ingredients such as vinegar, miso, and kelp. By exploring the difference between a barley-enriched *mugi* miso and a soybean-only *Hatcho* miso, students gain the basic knowledge and experience they need to successfully experiment with these foods outside the Japanese culinary context.

I was facilitating for several Japanese chefs from Japan in Napa, California at the 2007 Culinary Institute of America's Worlds of Flavor Conference. The Japanese chefs were given huge garbage bags and huge garbage cans, but in the end there was almost nothing in them even though they were making food for 250 people. At the end of filleting the fish, they made *hone sembei*, crisp little bone crackers. And the kombu that was left over from making the dashi stock went into making the food the chefs ate themselves. It's an important culinary skill. An important part of the notion of washoku is kansha (appreciation), which recognizes the potential for fully utilizing ingredients.

I also offer programs in Japan for the ex-pat community, the foreign community whose members typically live there for two to three years because of business.

> *Many don't feel compelled to learn to cook Japanese food because they can go out and eat good Japanese food anywhere, but they want to understand why it tastes great at one restaurant and not at another.*

And often food that is served to them is unrecognizable, and that can cause anxiety. So the goal for many of the people who come into my programs in Japan who are not food professionals is to achieve a certain comfort level with ingredients and dishes that are totally alien to them.

I sometimes structure programs as Kansha Challenges, offering a group only a few ingredients they must share—and use fully—in order to produce a meal. Sometimes, when I travel within the U.S. I ask those in my network (colleagues and volunteers who help me test recipes for my books) to help me put together events in their community. I like to do fundraisers for local groups. I contact a local culinary school and tell them I will teach a class to ten of their students if those students will be my assistants during the fundraiser.

This is a great experience for everyone. The young kids—what enthusiasm! They have no preconceived notions about the preparations. They are very curious and very enthusiastic, so it is a matter of harnessing that energy in a specific way. I taught them how to be my assistants and to help me produce whatever food I was making for the event. They needed to learn how to make stock, but not always in the traditional way. Because I also offered a program that was vegetarian, we used dried shiitake mushrooms instead of fish flakes.

The students had to learn about the order in which certain ingredients are added, because the chemistry of the food wasn't familiar to them.

For example, they learned that saké and sugar go in first, and soy sauce is added only at the very end. They learned the shared traditions handed down and developed over thousands of years, as well as the order and timing necessary in Japanese food preparation. They learned the whole notion that a meal can be served pretty much at room temperature and that it doesn't necessarily require a whole lot of refrigeration. They learned about the rhythm in the kitchen. I kept returning to the rhythm and the pace of the kitchen because it was different from western ways. It was really exciting to see them get it. They were surprised at how complex the flavors were from such straightforward preparations.

A Day in the Life

The training styles and expectations of chefs from Japan and those of culinary students from the U.S. are very different.

A clear example of the differences between Japanese and United States' training styles came to light at the 2007 Culinary Institute of America's Worlds of Flavor Conference. The students assumed that they were going to be able to look over the visiting Japanese chefs' shoulders and ask them questions. They thought that they were going to have conversations and be able to chat. But the training style of Japanese chefs is quite different—it requires students to be patient, remain quiet, and employ keen observational skills.

One does not walk into an exclusive Japanese restaurant like the ones these chefs worked in and simply expect to be shown everything. Students needed to hold their questions until the end. After they had seen the flow of action and had established a context, then they could ask their questions. If they were still puzzled, then that was the time to engage. But some of the culinary students kept asking questions, expecting to be shown everything. One even picked up the Japanese chefs' knives! I thought people were going to be killed!

TWO

MICHAEL ANTHONY

Michael Anthony began cooking professionally in Tokyo where he quickly grew to love the Japanese connection to the changing seasons. Following his time in Japan, Chef Michael moved to France to hone his culinary skills at a number of renowned restaurants. He joined Gramercy Tavern in New York City as the Executive Chef in 2006, and under his leadership the restaurant has earned a number of accolades including a three-star *New York Times* review in 2007 and the James Beard Award for Outstanding Restaurant in 2008. In June 2011, he was named Executive Chef/Partner of Gramercy Tavern. In 2012, Michael Anthony won the James Beard Award for Best Chef in New York City. He is also the author of *The Gramercy Tavern Cookbook*, published by Clarkson Potter in 2013.

Influences

I wanted to experience firsthand what it felt like to work in a Japanese kitchen and try to learn some basics of cooking.

In my family, we celebrated our Italian-American origins, which were humble, during family events that revolved around the dinner table. My grandmother took a lot of pride in her cooking, and we all bragged about it. We ate from the garden, and we realized how wonderful the food was. But it was truly not a very deep gastronomic event—it was fresh and simply prepared. These meals sparked my interest in food. However, I was convinced that going into the restaurant business would crush all of my parents' dreams and hopes for me, so instead I graduated from Indiana University with a degree in French and business, and also a minor in Japanese.

It was only years later in the early 1990s—when I was about 24 and living in Japan—that I decided to pursue the idea of becoming a chef. I made contact with the food critic for the *Harold Tribune* who had been living in Tokyo and told him that I wanted to meet a Japanese chef. He suggested that I contact Shizuyo Shima, an owner chef who ran a restaurant in the Roppongi district in Tokyo. At that time an independent restaurant in Tokyo run by a female chef-owner was not very common. Shima's restaurant had only 18 seats and no counter. She was alone in the kitchen and had one server. It was a very personal style of cooking. She had attended Japanese cooking school, but her professional experience was focused around French training. Her food was a melding of Japanese and French cuisine.

I knew enough Japanese to introduce myself, tell her that I knew some basics of cooking, that I could be useful in the kitchen, and that I wouldn't be a nuisance. My only request was that I wanted to experience firsthand what it felt like to work in her kitchen and to learn some basics of cooking. She wanted to know if I was for real. "I don't want you to waste my time. You can come for one day if you want to watch, but if you really want to learn about cooking, I want to know that you are serious."

Shizuyo Shima had worked for Jean Delaveyne, a famous chef who ran a three-star Michelin restaurant in Paris. He was very old school and had a very archaic way of running a kitchen. He was known for being extremely hard on his chefs, so she learned to be tough, too.

> *My experience working in Shima's kitchen was a turbulent time for me.*

That job tested every notion that I held. "Was this really what I want to do? Had I been honest with this chef? Did I want to learn this business? Was I willing to do whatever it took to answer her questions?" It couldn't have been a more difficult or revealing experience for me. Working with Shizuyo Shima, I finally learned how exciting, how fascinating, and how hard it was to have two people in a small kitchen and make it work so the business thrived and people were impressed. I learned all of those things in that first year.

Career Path

> *Shima taught me how to think logically and organize my kitchen.*

Step one had to be completed in a clean and well-organized way so that I could get to step two. Step two needed to be organized and completed in a clean and logical way so that I could get to step three. That's how I learned to work my way through a recipe, through the prep, through the day, and through to the end result. Every step took the same kind of logical thinking. At the same time, I had to understand step 10 very clearly before I could even begin step one. It was not natural for me, so for me it was work.

Working with Shizuyo Shima was more than a life-altering experience. It was a real exploration in every sense of the word. I always look back on my experience and try to recognize the business value of it and also understand the ego that's involved in having someone watch what you do. She advised me to go to France and attend cooking school, so in 1992 I moved to Paris and enrolled in the culinary school at Le Ferrandi.

My lifeline in the Paris restaurant kitchens where I worked was knowing enough Japanese to communicate with the Japanese chefs.

I moved to Paris to attend cooking school at Le Ferrandi and progressed in my career, advancing from restaurant to restaurant. Working in Paris, I knew for sure that I was in over my head at some of the jobs that I held. I think that is the key to any great learning experience—where you just struggle to barely keep your head above water. All through the 1990s, I saw a huge wave of Japanese chefs moving to France and staying there for two or three years. They often did not get paid any wages and lived together in one apartment. They became a wonderful subculture of the restaurant industry in Paris. My lifeline initially in a couple of the Paris restaurant kitchens that I worked was knowing enough Japanese to communicate with the Japanese chefs. So even if the French chefs were furious at me and ready to kick me out, they would say, "Go tell them that I need this." As far as lifelines go, I was hanging by a thread.

Sometimes on my days off I was invited to my Japanese coworkers' apartment, where we would bring wine for everyone to taste. We barely had enough money to buy a bottle, even though some chefs in this group were working in the very best restaurants in Paris. They would put posters on the wall and break out all their books on wine, and we would taste 10 to 12 wines together. I didn't grasp every nuance of the explanations in Japanese, but I did gain access to drinking great French wine. I certainly didn't have enough money to do that in a restaurant. In fact, I barely had enough money to drink an espresso before I went to work. We got yelled at if we got near the coffee because we were not allowed to drink the espresso in the restaurant or even touch the coffee. So I pieced together pocket change to get an espresso before working an 18-hour day.

After working in some of the best kitchens in Paris I was ready to move on in my career, so I went to New York City to work at Daniel restaurant as a line cook and March restaurant as a sous chef. The next summer, I went back to France to work for Chef Michel Guérard at Le Prés d'Eugénie, and then to upstate New York in 2002 to become the Executive Chef of Blue Hill at Stone Barns. Four years later, I moved to New York City to become the Executive Chef of Gramercy Tavern.

Cuisine

Every chef is yearning for attention and seeking approval. A great chef has something to prove.

What makes our cooking at Gramercy Tavern so special is the personal connection, the improvisation, and the impulsiveness of it. It's an enormous decision to use our resources in that way and to do it without losing our focus. That's not a normal thing for a restaurant of our size. It requires communication, solidarity, and a strong sense of organization. I can work between the two—improvisation and order—as long as they don't collide. I recognize that our chefs need spontaneity and regimentation in order to progress and develop our personal style of cooking. I say "our" because it's not just mine. We have come to Gramercy Tavern to learn about cooking and loosely connect a group of American chefs—not American by nationality, but American by working as chefs in the United States. I think we are all contributing to an interesting progression of "American cooking."

In terms of cooking, both French and Japanese cultures are very committed to form. This is the way you do things, and you don't deviate because if you do you're only asking for trouble. As long as you stick to the agreed-upon form, you will succeed in creating something of quality. When developing a personal style of cooking, we have to break a lot of classic cooking rules that we learned along the way.

At Gramercy Tavern, we are not sacrificing the discipline and persistence that it takes to challenge ourselves to analyze our work. Is it of quality or not? Is it sensible or not? Along the way it's breaking that form. When I say breaking rules, I also mean finding solutions. You don't have to love a dish or have it agree with your palette to find it interesting. This is what assures me that in terms of food, we are on a steep learning curve—one that I would like to cultivate for my own personal development at Gramercy Tavern. I hope that collectively, we can find a sensible way to pursue this.

In Japan, I learned to create meals that are unique to a particular place. Our dishes here should taste unique because they use ingredients that are grown here and are seasonal. For example, a meal in New York in March should taste, look, and feel much different than a meal in early June. A memory of a meal is related exactly to the climate and culture around us.

Uniqueness of time and place is the essence of almost every fine dining experience that I know of in traditional Japanese cooking and other forms of serious cooking. That's the connection.

Our attention has gone beyond the food. Our dishes are now connected with the soil, and we are celebrating all sorts of stories of urban farming, home gardens, the revival of small agriculture in the northeast, our heritage, and heirloom vegetables. However, this is more than a trend—it's a defining moment in our culture. Now more than ever, chefs, educators, restaurateurs and other culinary professionals need to stand up to voice our opinions about our love for and interest in foods of all sorts—especially traditional foods, foods that have inherent flavor, foods grown with care, foods grown on small farms, food products that represent unique and authentic flavors. If we don't stand up now, as food professionals and enthusiastic diners, we may not have the opportunity to enjoy those flavors in the future. For me, this philosophy is what defines what we do at Gramercy Tavern.

Ingredients

We use Japanese ingredients because they taste intriguing.

We use kombu, dried bonito flakes, and shiro dashi, a seasoning agent that's not even that common in Japan. We use certain seasoned fish roe as a textural and aesthetic component. The one menu item that was clearly inspired by Japanese cooking techniques and ingredients is *tsukemono*, or pickles. At first, we offered simple vinegar pickles.

Now, we make a dozen different kinds of new pickles using fermented rice bran, or *nukazuke*, in our own fermentation system.

The idea of natural fermentation, the aroma and the earthiness, piques the curiosity of most customers, but the flavor of the nukazuke pickles is foreign to the American palette. In some cases, without understanding the context, a whiff of the pickles sends the signal, "Something's wrong here!" However, when guests get accustomed to the aroma and then taste the fermented turnips, radishes, sunchokes (also known as "Jerusalem artichokes"), and parsnips, most diners like what they taste. There is pungency but also a surprising crispness in the texture and crunch.

In the end, we are extending the life of our seasonal ingredients by preserving them through natural methods of fermentation. I'd like to think that this is not just me trying to promote the product. The crispy crunch, the interesting graininess of the rice bran, and the inexplicable pungency achieved through natural fermentation all create an irresistible pull to these pickles. It's very hard to stop eating them, even if your palette is initially put off by them.

> *We prepare our dishes with the mentality that everything counts and that not one thing is more important than the other. Doing so presents a unified value from top to bottom.*

Gramercy Tavern has two distinct operations that work simultaneously—it's a dual concept. There is the Tavern in the front room. It has an a la carte menu and is a great expression of seasonal ingredients that are mostly cooked over an open wood fire. We have a sense of casualness with the "no reservation" policy. There is a feeling of, "I can come and go as I please." It's a spontaneous experience, and not a long drawn out, or expensive meal.

The experience in the main dining room, without adding any pretentions, is set up for a more refined meal. As in the Tavern, the main dining room is an expression of seasonal ingredients that are always evolving. But in the main dining room they are introduced in the format of two tasting menus. One is the vegetable tasting menu— not necessarily a vegetarian menu, but one that celebrates vegetables. The other is a seasonal menu. Additionally, there is a collection of dishes that are in a prix-fixe format, with one price for an appetizer, entrée, and dessert in a simple, personable form.

In all these different dishes, vegetables play a very inspired role. Unassuming sunchokes appear harmoniously scattered as if they sailed out of the sky and hit the plate just right. We use sunchokes from farmers' root cellars in the early spring because we want to support the farmers all year long.

We can't ignore the farmers and only buy from them in July and August, when their gardens and farms are exploding. If we don't support them through the cold rainy months, they may not be able to stay in business. So the sunchokes are on the menu.

It makes sense to have good relationships with our growers and to share those stories with our guests, so that they can appreciate the love and the passion that go into bringing our food to the table every day. One of our major goals at Gramercy Tavern is to send folks out saying, "Now I understand a little bit more about your dedication to local ingredients. I learned something about those ingredients."

Training

Internal working relationships are the most important aspect of a restaurant or any business.

At Gramercy Tavern, we extend a sense of high priority to our colleagues so that we place each other in a winning position. The essence of owner Danny Meyer's approach is "Enlightened Hospitality." That is not just a catch phrase. He firmly believes that people work better together when they are self-aware. A large part of my job is to manage how our talented people progress in their careers and how they add interesting ideas to our story.

While generally in the restaurant business, "The guest is king," our number-one tenet is to take care of each other. Look at the track record of Gramercy Tavern. There is a rich story that is still evolving—and it is a wonderful context in which to work. We have attracted the attention of myriad cooks from around the world. We currently have chefs from Tokyo, Kyoto, Copenhagen, London, Paris, and the United States. Channeling all of these different perspectives on food is what makes our kitchen successful.

One of the things that I shattered when I arrived at Gramercy Tavern was the classic hierarchy. Now cooks work their way through our kitchen by bringing natural curiosity and dynamic ideas to the job.

When I started at Gramercy Tavern, it was set up in a very traditional European way. There was a starting point, or boot camp, and you had to prove that you had what it took to work at Gramercy Tavern. If you were good enough, you could make your way into the main kitchen and work through the stations to appetizers, and so on— the roast guys being the most important. All of that was great because it gave line cooks a very clear path: "I know what's in front of me, and I know what I have to do to get there." I tore that process apart because I wanted to give an equal amount of importance to every station in our kitchen.

The moment that a chef puts his or her knife into the radish, turnip or sunchoke, it's as serious and as important as preparing any expensive fish or meat. The technical precision a chef uses when slicing vegetables, fish or meat and then putting them on the plate is the essence of what we do. I encourage cooks to approach every day with a sense of curiosity and to push themselves to think critically about the food they work with.

There are so many variables in the food, so there's no way that I can ask them to replicate a recipe that's on a piece of paper.

I ask them to communicate the changes that they see, taste the food or the dish with attention, and think about the whole operation. The goals for my cooks at Gramercy Tavern are to think critically about food, to communicate their observations, and to leave their station better than they found it.

Gramercy Tavern's kitchen is modeled after a European-style organization. It has a central stove, a beautiful, large, powerful piece of fire that combines heavy sections where pots and pans are cooking and large surfaces that are very warm but not at cooking temperatures where hot food is plated. Cooks face each other so that they can see and hear each other and communicate. Fish dishes that are prepared on one side of the stove are cooked and timed perfectly to be done at the same time as the meat dishes and cold dishes. They are facing the one chef who is orchestrating it all—that is what defines the French kitchen and Gramercy Tavern's kitchen.

You can't imagine how many people come our way and ask whether they can work or study in my kitchen.

Now more than ever, chefs are coming out of a variety of culinary schools in the U.S. The schools are sophisticated and have improved at professional as well as technical levels in preparing people of all ages to work as cooks. We deal with probably five culinary schools on a regular basis in New York City and another five culinary schools around the country. The average age of New York cooking school graduates is much older than European or Asian counterparts. We have cooks right out of culinary school with little to no experience, as well as those who have worked in restaurants for many years.

Regarding male versus female cooks, I'd say on average about 20 percent to 25 percent are women, but when it comes to hiring, whether a candidate is male or female is not a consideration. I see a growing number of women in the restaurant industry and a growing number of female chefs who are reaching the highest level—not just as owners of businesses who are in charge of their own kitchens, but those who are reaching the point where they are nationally recognized. I see that as an encouraging trend.

On a management level, over the last few years I have made it my goal to communicate the restaurant's numbers to the managers in our monthly meetings and have them take a more active role in making business decisions. I had never done that in the past. Now when we talk about labor costs and food costs, they understand the actions that we take in the restaurant and contribute advice. They are responsible for making decisions on certain aspects of how we run the restaurant.

Tools

Knives are the primary tools chefs use to express what they want to accomplish with the ingredients.

In the past, most chefs in the U.S. and Europe used German or French knives. However, today if you peek into kitchens throughout the industry, you will find that most chefs use western-style Japanese knives or a traditional Japanese knife. German and French knives are still visible in the kitchen, but every top chef I know owns at least one Japanese knife. Japanese knives are certainly my favorite.

The Japanese knife-making tradition is one of the most specific in the world in terms of each knife's function. By understanding different kinds of Japanese knives and knowing how to use them, we are able to be more precise and more delicate. We use one knife for filleting fish and breaking bones, another for portioning fish, and another for making precision cuts for vegetables. It's not just for novelty or for great looks that the fish roaster at Gramercy Tavern uses a deba for certain boning tasks and a hybrid Japanese western knife for cutting pickles. Today using Japanese knives has become part of the fabric of the cooking at Gramercy Tavern. Thanks to The Gohan Society's knife demonstrations, we are benefitting from a deeper understanding of the history of Japanese knives, as well as how they are made, maintained, and sharpened.

We also use other tools in our kitchen that are inspired by Japanese chefs. For example, we have two special Japanese cutting boards that are set out during service, and two cutting boards that are set out during prep time for performing very specific jobs. Formerly, we used spoons and spatulas to create and plate food in delicate ways. Now we are learning how to prepare and plate food using long metal chopsticks. I have always admired the precision of Japanese chefs when they plate their dishes, and I know that it takes much practice.

Not many non-Japanese chefs know how to do it, but we are learning and have taken some important steps forward.

Serving the First Lady, Michelle Obama, was one of the most moving moments in my career.

Not long after the 2008 presidential election, First Lady Michelle Obama came to Gramercy Tavern for lunch. She wanted something very specific, something that was carefully handled, not too heavy, vibrant and alive, and with ingredients that revealed their origins. I had a chance to speak with her a few times during lunch. She wasn't there to hear the history of every food on the plate, but she expressed an interest in and a commitment to sharing with people how exciting it is to serve those kinds of foods. I couldn't have felt more proud that someone like her chose to eat at my restaurant.

A Day in the Life

No job in the kitchen is beyond the responsibility of the chef.

There is not a day that goes by that I don't think about my experiences at Bistro Shima in Tokyo's Roppongi district. I learned all the fundamentals that help me do my job well today. I was made to understand that learning every task—no matter how humble—is essential. Even the Friday night cleaning regime of standing in the grease pit in the middle of the kitchen taught me a lesson. It was a rude awakening but it has kept me grounded ever since.

Leaving the restaurant late on Friday nights, I faced an hour-and-a-half commute on a crowded train to Koshigaya because I did not have the money to live in Tokyo. Usually there were no empty seats. All the way home, I asked myself, "Are you serious about this job?" I guess I was, because I did that for an entire year.

What I learned from that experience is that there is no job in the kitchen beyond the responsibility of the chef. At any moment in the day, I know how my cooks and staff are feeling and what's happening in the restaurant. I understand the operation from every angle. Recently I recognized that for the sake of a better restaurant and for the team, I had to learn to delegate many jobs but not retreat too far from any one of them. But the truth is, I don't miss cleaning the grease pit.

THREE

DAVID BOULEY

Owner/Chef, Bouley, New York City

David Bouley was born and raised near Storrs, Connecticut. From an early age he was strongly influenced by life on his grandparents' farm, drawing upon their French heritage that instilled a love of the land, an appreciation for fresh products, care in preparation, and the inspiration to cook and enjoy healthful meals.

Chef David studied at the Sorbonne and worked with some of Europe's most acclaimed chefs. He returned to New York City, working at Le Cirque, Le Périgord, and La Côte Basque. In 1985, he became chef of Montrachet restaurant and in 1987, he opened his own restaurant, Bouley. He earned a four-star review from *The New York Times* and the James Beard Foundation awards for Best Restaurant and Best Chef.

In 2011, David Bouley opened Brushstroke, a Japanese restaurant owned in collaboration with Yoshiki Tsuji, President of the TSUJI Culinary Institute based in Osaka. The restaurant adheres to the traditions of kaiseki dining and includes Ichimura, an eight-seat sushi bar. His latest project is Bouley Botanical, an event space, learning center, and commissary kitchen.

Influences

As a youngster, I thought, "Cooking is something I want to know more about," and I connected to it.

Whenever I was seven years old, I tried to pick a peach on my grandmother's farm in Connecticut. The branch bent down a little bit when I pulled on it, but the peach stayed put. My mother said, "Let's try that one over there." She put my hand around a plump peach hanging nearby. I gently lifted it up and let it down. Voilà! It fell into my hand. She said, "This is the peach to eat. The other one is not ripe yet."

Growing up in a French environment on a farm in Connecticut, I ate extremely well. My mother and grandmother were wonderful cooks. My grandmother raised rabbits, pheasants, ducks, and a few hundred chickens, and she had many acres of fruit trees and grapes. We'd all go out and pick dandelions and other wild greens for salad. They made everything from scratch, so I learned a lot about cooking. Then I started making dishes for my friends. The next thing I knew, I fell in love with cooking. Good cooking can come from within a chef, or it can be inspired by Mother Nature. But one or the other can ignite an entire career of cooking from just one or two experiences.

I'm a student of 1970s cooking and nouvelle cuisine.

I never went to cooking school. As a young cook, I worked for and learned from some of Europe's greatest chefs, including Roger Vergé, Paul Bocuse, Joël Robuchon, Gaston Lenôtre, and Frédy Girardet. Back in New York, I worked at Le Cirque, Le Périgord, La Côte Basque, Montrachet, and Roger Vergé's restaurant in San Francisco.

In the late 1960s and early 1970s, I saw American and French chefs going back and forth from America and France to Japan. I also saw Japanese chefs go to France to learn French cooking, then go back to Japan and cook French food. But when these American and French chefs came back from Japan, they just changed the vegetables a little bit, and they made tasting menus. They didn't really know how to use Japanese ingredients in their cuisine. When I worked at L'Atelier Saint-Germain de Joël Robuchon in Paris, Joël Robuchon was the first person I met who used soy sauce. He combined soy sauce with butter, ginger and lemon juice.

When I opened Bouley Restaurant in 1987, its menu was based on the seasons, French cooking techniques, and a close relationship with all of the ingredients. That is what I learned from my grandmother and from the chefs I worked for—a natural approach. Bouley was one of the first New York City restaurants to be so closely connected to the ingredients. I went to the farmers' markets to buy ingredients and products for the restaurant. I spent time with the farmers on Sundays and went to their farms.

My relationship with the farmers and the ingredients was similar to that of a Japanese chef. For example, a Japanese chef who worked with a farmer might say, "Maybe cut more branches off so I can have a stronger taste here." One farmer I worked closely with was Rick Bishop. Together, we brought artisanal ingredients like the fingerling potato to Bouley and to the farmers' markets.

I didn't have time to think about anything except jumping out of bed, running to work, going home, and passing out. That was my life.

Bouley was the number one restaurant in New York City for six years. From around 1994 to 1996, we had the first restaurant in a Zagat Guide to achieve a food rating of 29 out of a possible 30.

During that time, I was trying to make sure everybody was happy. I didn't have time to think about anything except jumping out of bed, running to work, going home, and passing out. That was my life. I was stressed out. Then, in 1996, the landlord took back my lease, so I decided to close the restaurant.

At that point I was very curious about what else I could do with my life. I was so tired and so burned out that I almost took off my chef's jacket and did something else. Then I got an offer to cook for the royal family in Bangkok because the Queen of Thailand had eaten twice at Bouley. "Of course," I said, "okay." After telling another customer about my plans to travel to Asia, he said to me, "You don't have a restaurant, so now you have time. Come to Japan a few weeks early and we will teach you Japanese cooking." The customer's name was Mr. Yoshiki Tsuji, owner of the TSUJI Culinary Institute in Osaka.

If we want to learn, we have to ask questions.

When I was in Japan, Mr. Tsuji took me to many different Japanese restaurants. At the time, I didn't know that the way I spoke about what I was eating helped Mr. Tsuji decide which restaurant to take me to next. I didn't realize that I was in training until one night when I met with Mr. Tsuji's colleague, Mr. Hata, for dinner, along with several other Japanese chefs who were attending the TSUJI Culinary Institute.

As we ate, I asked Mr. Hata, "Is there vinegar in this?"

Mr. Hata said, "No."

I asked him two more times, "Is there vinegar in this?"

Mr. Hata said, "No, no."

Ten minutes later he finally said, "You're right."

Then I asked, "Mr. Hata, is this young ginger or mature ginger? I think it's young ginger."

Mr. Hata said, "No." Ten minutes later he said, "You're right."

When I saw Mr. Tsuji the next day, he told me, "Mr. Hata said you passed your test." Mr. Hata told him, "I remember only one chef in my whole life who asked as many questions as Mr. Bouley. His name was Paul Bocuse." Paul Bocuse is the father of nouvelle cuisine and was named the Chef of the Century by The Culinary Institute of America. As a result of this visit, I started to understand the Japanese palate. I realized that if I wanted to learn, I had to ask questions.

Cuisine

We make a dish that is a "handshake" between a French chef and a Japanese chef.

It's only now that chefs are starting to understand how to incorporate Japanese techniques and ingredients from Japan into their cuisine without losing their identity. In 2008, I opened the new Bouley. The menu is modern French with Asian influences. This is an example of how we combine two cultures and create a new one. We do a flan here with crabmeat. This dish is a "handshake" between a French chef and a Japanese chef. We have the porcini—wild edible brown mushrooms—and flan. The flan is similar to *chawanmushi*, which is a Japanese egg custard that dates back to the fifteenth century. We purée the porcini and add crabmeat and dashi, but not just dashi. We put a lot of flavors and spices into the broth of the dashi, French style. Then I stick it with *kuzu*. And, of course, we finish it with black truffles.

For authentic Japanese cooking we need artisanal ingredients, produced by artisans, in the hands of artisanal chefs.

In 2001, Mr. Tsuji and I decided to collaborate on Brushstroke, a Japanese restaurant in New York City devoted to kaiseki. Why didn't kaiseki chefs leave Japan to cook in other places? It's because they didn't have artisanal ingredients. That's why Mr. Tsuji and I put a lot of preparation into finding artisanal ingredients for Brushstroke. We met in Kyoto and went to the auction market for special Kyoto vegetables. We spent one entire week with experts from the Department of Agriculture learning about Kyoto vegetables. They taught us all about the evolution of the vegetables there, the soil, and everything else. To have artisanal Japanese ingredients for Brushstroke, we brought seeds from Kyoto so we could grow Osaka and Kyoto eggplants, five kinds of Japanese root vegetables, and other artisanal products on my small farm and on Rick Bishop's farm in upstate New York.

Mr. Tsuji and I also hired a research team of five agricultural experts led by a famous Japanese professor to travel from British Colombia, Canada to San Diego, California looking for a year-round source of Japanese vegetables. The team spent an entire year visiting the many Asian markets and farms up and down the West Coast, researching and tasting vegetables. So in 2011, after nearly 10 years of research and planning, we opened Brushstroke in New York City with Chef Isao Yamada as the kaiseki master. We wanted Brushstroke to be about Japan's culinary traditions, its integrity, focus, pride, and its artisanal ingredients.

Trust your senses and they will not lie to you.

When my grandmother baked, she could be in the backyard but would know exactly when to go into the kitchen to take the apple pie out of the oven—and it was always perfect. That's because she smelled the sweetness; she smelled the crust; she smelled the caramel. For her it wasn't a calculation. She had no alarm, no timer. She used her senses. But in professional cooking we're five, 10, 20 steps ahead. The intellectual side of our brain takes time to organize 10 steps so that we can bring the food out. If we have to think each time about one thing, we're never going to get anything out. But our hands are moved by our senses.

Every so often I'll teach a cooking class. One class was with a Spanish chef, and the dish was paella. After I finished talking, I asked everyone in the class to come up to the stove and listen to the paella cooking over an open flame. I took my microphone so everyone could hear the crackling. It was getting crispy. If there was too much humidity at that time, the bubbles would have sounded different. If the heat was too high, it would burn, and we would hear that, too. So cooking by our senses tells our hands what to do. Our motivation is through our senses. This is something that we don't want to take for granted when we go into the kitchen. But most chefs don't say, "Well, today I'm going to really pay attention to my senses." If they did, they'd be better cooks.

When you cook a dish that you're worried about, I suggest that you rely more on your senses. If you've prepared it before, your senses will remember what was right and what was wrong, and this will be the guidance that you need. Your senses can tell you everything you need to know. Stop thinking, because that's going to distract you. Allow the senses to recall what they are supposed to do. Even if you have never made this dish before, you probably have used certain ingredients before. For example, onions. What do they smell like when they are cooking and getting sweet? Remember that. What do they smell like when they are still full of water? They smell bitter; they smell acidy. Trust your senses, and they will not lie to you.

Ingredients

Taste the bouillon first. That's the sign of a good chef.

Every time I open the lid of a bowl, I smell the top, because that's where the fat goes, and that's where the aroma is. When I see fish, dumplings, another dish, and a soup on the table, and the chef first goes right to the fish, I think, "Oh, it's too bad that you don't know. Always taste the bouillon, because this is what you influenced." The other tastes are a natural byproduct of the ingredient. We can influence the flavor of a piece of fish but not as much as we can influence the bouillon. That's our signature on the dish.

It's important to understand what is unique about an ingredient or product. I don't want to steal what Mother Nature put into it. And an ingredient is not always the same, so I can't depend on a calculation in a recipe to prepare it. Take cooking rice, for example. As rice ages, it dries out, so I need to cook it in more water. Where does the recipe tell me that? It doesn't. I look at the packaging date on the box because it tells me how old the rice is. As the rice gets older and drier, I add more water.

Kuzu is a great ingredient. It's a thickening agent that doesn't dilute or overpower taste.

Kuzu is one product that can be integrated into cooking without causing the other ingredients to lose their identity. There are so many different applications of kuzu. At Bouley, we use kuzu everywhere. It is a stable thickening agent; it thickens clear. It has no taste. We can use it in pastry. We can make noodles out of it. And we also use kuzu powder. We put sweetbreads or fish in the powder and then we sauté it. It makes an amazing crust. Nothing makes a crust like kuzu. We can also use it in place of roux. Roux is flour and butter. Instead of roux, I use kuzu to thicken any kind of sauce. It has a textural finish that is cleaner and better than cornstarch and arrowroot for thickening. We're making so many things with it. Now, we're even making a kuzu-bread.

In French cooking, when we use a thickening agent like cornstarch, we have to cook it out, which means that we simmer it for a while. In effect, we're removing the starch. If the sauce thickens very quickly, it probably has too much cornstarch in it. The more we heat it, the thicker and more rubbery it gets. Kuzu, on the other hand, is more stable than cornstarch and potato starches. Once kuzu thickens a sauce, the texture doesn't change. Kuzu will thicken liquids like tomato water, but it won't dilute it or overpower the taste.

I learned from Japanese chefs how to kill fish.

Most fish caught commercially in America are thrown live into a box, where they suffocate and die. When the fish lands in the box, its fins are pushed into its stomach. The acid and enzymes from the stomach seep into the fish's flesh or into the other fish around it. That's why a lot of our fish, when we lay them out for preparation, have many problems. All those blemishes and the ruined flesh are due to trauma because the fish wasn't killed the proper way.

I learned from Japanese chefs how to kill fish. They put a knife straight into its spinal cord near the base of its head and kill the fish instantly. But during a charter fishing trip off the coast of Cape Cod, I learned an even more effective way to sustain the fish's freshness after it is killed. Mr. Kondo of the Japanese Imperial Fisheries Institute taught me the way to do it. After someone on the boat caught a striped bass, Mr. Kondo killed it, but it was still flopping around like the severed legs of a dissected frog in a high school biology class. Mr. Kondo then told the boat captain that he wanted to put the fish in a tub of seawater. When I asked why, he explained that after he kills the fish the proper way, he puts it in the water. The oxygen in the water goes into each incision and pumps the muscle. The muscle still reacts to the oxygen, so the flesh is cleaning itself in the water. He allows the fish to sit for a minimum of two hours in the water after he kills it. This process actually keeps the flesh fresher longer. That's why I paid Cape Cod fishermen 15 cents more a pound to kill the fish on the boat for me in 1993 and 1994.

There is a little-known Japanese technique for giving sushi its crunch.

In our restaurant after the chef kills a fish, he lets it sit in water for a minimum of two hours and then puts the fish on a wood board and throws salt all over it. The water in the fish's flesh will start to seep out because salt extracts moisture. In five, 10, 15, or 20 minutes, there will be a little puddle of water, depending on how fatty the fish is and how long the salt stays on it. Next, the chef rinses the fish quickly in water or in water with a little bit of vinegar. Now he has detoxed the fish further and has improved its texture. The salt creates the crunch that we like in sushi. Without the salt, the flesh would be soft and mealy. That little bit of salt creates the crunch.

Japanese chefs expand and go vertically and deeply into ingredients, whereas in the western world, we expand outward, horizontally.

Not long ago, our incredible sushi chef at Brushstroke taught me one of the finer points about sushi and sashimi. Our sous chef served us some bluefin tuna that looked like the one I had just bought the day before, but he said, "This fish is six days old. Taste it."

It was amazing, because the color level was the same as the one I had just bought, but the sushi chef had put it through a special drying process: a day in a paper towel; a certain amount of air but not too much air; a little bit of vinegar with a brush; a little salt water; and then a rinse. This pulled the water out of the cells of the fish, raising the level of glucose. I didn't know that in sushi, drying the fish builds in more flavor. But this isn't the case with sashimi.

I sometimes wonder: How much more can I learn about food? I feel as if I've at least got my master's degree in cooking. At one time I even thought I had reached the Ph.D. level. But when I discover things I don't know, like preparing fish Japanese-style, I feel as if I have gone back to the third grade—again. I am always amazed to learn how the Japanese chefs take a product to a higher level.

A Day in the Life

I have been through the grinder many times, but one of my most tortured experiences as a chef didn't have to do with actual cooking.

I was asked to cook for the king and queen and royal family of Thailand—about three hundred people in Bangkok. And, of course, I had to bring a gift and present it to the king and queen. No big deal, or so I thought.

I arrived in Bangkok three-and-a-half weeks before the royal dinner because I was helping to open a new restaurant in the Plaza Athénée. So for the three-and-a-half weeks prior to the royal family's dinner, I ran the restaurant at Plaza Athénée every night. One night we prepared a banquet for the Red Cross, and the king and queen were there. There must have been 50 billion flowers everywhere. The king and queen walked from the street under a canopy of flowers, and then up a long staircase in the hotel to the banquet room. They were treated like gods.

After that, the thought of giving the king and queen my gift made me a lot more nervous. Then someone from the palace made matters worse when he told me, "The king and queen will be seated on an elevated platform because no one can stand taller than the king and queen. When it's your time to give them your gift, stand up and walk up the steps to the platform. When you are at the top step, get down on your knees right away. Then walk on your knees the last four or five feet to where they are seated and hand them your gift. They will have a gift for you, too."

"Oh, my God," I cried. "Do I have to wear my long French apron?"

"Oh yes. You have to wear a long French apron, everything." They insisted that I wear the apron and my chef's uniform because of all the photographs. They said, "Don't worry. You can do it."

How was I going to walk on my knees in a long French apron? I figured out that I needed to move my knees a little at a time, so I practiced for five nights in my hotel room. Every day that week I ran the kitchen upstairs in the restaurant and cooked for banquets. And every night I had nightmares that I fell flat on my face, that my apron ripped off, that I couldn't walk on my knees to the king and queen. I got more and more nervous! How was I going to do this? I practiced, practiced, practiced. I put my apron on and moved on my knees. And every night I didn't sleep, and I got more and more tired.

Finally the night came, and I wasn't thinking about the food or anything else. Then it was time for me to go out there and deliver my gift to the king and queen. There were people everywhere. Ambassadors from all the countries in Asia, including Cambodia, Vietnam, and the Philippines. Even Vice President Dan Quayle was there, representing the United States. The king and queen sat on an elevated platform. I thought, "Oh, my God, first I've got to get up there, then onto my knees!" I walked up the stairs. Just as I was on the top step and ready to kneel, everybody stood up—including the king and queen! So, I just walked over to them and gave them my gift—an exquisite handmade glass apple from a famous artist in upstate New York.

After the dinner, I went back to the hotel and got drunk. I finally got to relax. I was so exhausted that I passed out and slept for 12 hours. That was probably one of the most stressful situations I've ever been in, and it had nothing to do with cooking the food, but everything to do with presentation.

FOUR

WYLIE DUFRESNE

Owner/Chef, Alder, New York City
Founder/Chef, wd~50, New York City

Wylie Dufresne was born in 1970 in Providence, Rhode Island and moved to New York in 1977. In 1992, he earned a B.A. in philosophy at Colby College in Maine. After college, Wylie Dufresne enrolled at The French Culinary Institute (now the International Culinary Center) in New York, and then worked in various Jean-Georges Vongerichten's restaurants from 1994 until 1999. In 1999, he became the chef at 71 Clinton Fresh Food.

Chef Wylie opened wd~50 in 2003. His restaurant received one Michelin star in 2006 and again in 2007. In 2008, Frank Bruni of *The New York Times* awarded wd~50 three stars.

Wylie Dufresne has been nominated for multiple James Beard Awards, including Best Chef New York City for seven consecutive years, winning the award in 2013. Alder, Wylie's second restaurant, opened in Manhattan's East Village in March 2013. A Lower East Side landmark for modernist cooking and one of the most influential restaurants in the world, wd~50 closed at the end of 2014.

Influences

> *Everything I liked about sports I found in the professional kitchen.*

I was originally drawn to cooking because of the physical aspect. I saw cooking as a team sport, and I liked playing sports. I remember the visceral reaction of going to work in my first real kitchen, Al Forno in Providence, Rhode Island. There was a chef—the coach—and the players—the cooks. We'd come to work in the morning and prep—that was like practice. The service was like game time—everybody was working toward a common goal. It's hot. It's frenetic. There's a lot of energy. You make mistakes, but you go on. Much like sports, there's an opportunity for redemption in the kitchen. It's physical. It's demanding. It's grueling. Everything that I liked about playing sports I found in the professional kitchen.

As a young person, I was drawn to many aspects of eastern and Japanese philosophy and culture. Although I found it very interesting and studied philosophy in college, after working summer jobs in restaurants between my junior and senior year in college, I knew that I wanted to try being a chef. So, after I graduated from college, I attended The French Culinary Institute.

Career Path

> *I immersed myself in French cuisine, in French culture, and I learned the techniques.*

After graduating from the FCI, I went to work for Jean-Georges Vongerichten in 1994, whose influences are derived from many cultures, one of which is certainly the Japanese culture. When I started working for Jean-Georges, he had two restaurants: Vong and Jean-Georges. On Monday, Wednesday, and Friday, he was at Jean-Georges, and on Tuesday, Thursday, and Saturday, he was at Vong. So three days a week I had Jean-Georges all day, all the time—and it was great. I got to learn a lot from him, and because he had a smaller staff back then, it was easier to really get at the "essence of Jean-Georges." He was very generous with whatever information he had. If I had a question, he would answer it. If I wanted to know how to do something, he would show me.

Eventually I became the sous chef at Jean-Georges, and in 1998 I was hired as chef de cuisine at Prime in The Bellagio, Las Vegas, another of Jean-Georges' restaurants. I very much enjoyed working for Jean-Georges, and I continued to learn a lot from him. If you know where and how to look, you can see a lot of Jean-Georges in Wylie Dufresne. I'm proud and pleased it's there. I stayed with Jean-Georges because I was constantly learning.

After working for nearly six years with Jean-Georges, it was time for me to go out on my own.

In 2000, I was hired as the chef at 71 Clinton Fresh Food on New York City's Lower East Side. It was my first chef's job, and I could do whatever I wanted. For me, technique is one of the most interesting things about cooking, so Japanese cooking techniques appealed to me. While I love to eat, the actual act of preparing the meal is most interesting to me. That interest led me right to dashi. And when I opened wd~50, my interest in all things Japanese increased.

Once I had put my toe in the pool of the Japanese kitchen, it was very addictive, and I became more interested in Japanese ingredients and tools, such as Japanese knives.

One of the things that intrigued me the most was the patience of the Japanese. In Japan, I saw that patience firsthand. Chefs there study for years to be a sushi chef, and for years all they do is make rice. The chef at the restaurant Masato in New York City told me that for three years all he did was make rice. But when you eat a piece of his sushi, you can see how those three years paid off. That level of patience is common in Japan. If you ask a Japanese chef what he does, he'll say, "I make rice. For three years now, I've just made rice."

You couldn't find any chef in America who would do that. American chefs are impatient. They want to be a celebrity overnight, but they need to realize that it takes time and it takes patience. So I tell them, "Don't be in such a hurry to get there." Patience is a mentality, a discipline, a rigor, a commitment. It's dedication. And that's impressive. I don't think that we Americans make those types of commitments quite as readily. As I got to know the Japanese culture and understand it, I've wanted to know more and understand more.

Ingredients

Any chef worth his or her weight is curious about or interested in seeing food's starting point, because as chefs, we're the endpoint.

I think that the source of the ingredients is always important. Maybe there are cooks who don't care, but I find it fascinating—whether I go to a farm and see what happens when the duck gets slaughtered, or watch the seaweed pulled out of the water and harvested, or talk to the farmer who pulls the vegetables out of the ground. I find all of those relationships very interesting, but it's more than that. I think that from a food safety perspective, we ought to be interested in where ingredients come from and what processes they go through. Chefs are responsible for other people's safety. I'm feeding thousands of people a year. I should feed them responsibly.

Knowing an ingredient's source also helps a chef understand how to process it. It's very inspiring to see ingredients in their raw state and to then imagine what to do with them or to see them go through several layers of handling. It gives me ideas about how to handle the product. There are many generations of chefs who have worked very hard to establish relationships with farmers and with craftsmen. I think that I would be doing a disservice to all those who have come before me if I suddenly ignored that.

I like seaweed, or *kombu*, because its flavor is not super strong. Even though it lives in the ocean, it doesn't taste like a mouthful of seawater. It has a very mild ocean flavor, and I like incorporating that into my dishes. When I was in Japan, I saw old-fashioned artisans shape seaweed by hand. Other people use machines. Seeing the different ways that the seaweed was handled and the different ways that it was processed was very interesting to me.

The challenge of making Japanese-inspired dishes in America is finding the ingredients. For me, it's about finding the best ingredients, but that can sometimes be difficult. For example, we can source good kombu and bonito flakes, but I have a hard time getting *kuro* edamame. The regular edamame that you eat at every Japanese restaurant is good, but kuro edamame is a higher level of soybean that tastes almost like corn, peanuts, or a little bit of both. The outer skin is black, but an emerald green bean inside shines through. When you pop the soybean out of its skin and eat it, it's so delicious and flavorful that you'll never want to go back to the other edamame.

Cuisine

I'm extremely interested in Japanese ingredients and Japanese cooking technique, but I'm not a Japanese-trained chef and I'm not trying to make Japanese food.

One New Year's Eve we had a customer rent our restaurant for the entire night, and we were working on a dish for his meal. We wanted to make dashi because the main course was going to be fish, but I don't like French-style fish stock. I have over a thousand cookbooks, including lots of Japanese cookbooks in both Japanese and in English. The instructions were pretty simple, so we tried making dashi, and I loved it! I'm sure it wasn't a very good version, but it was still delicious, and I've been working on it ever since.

Whereas Japanese chefs add bonito flakes to their kombu stock and then take them out after 10, 20, maybe 30 seconds, I leave mine in for almost 10 minutes. We've had a lot of Japanese people tell us that our dashi was too strong and they sent it back. They'll say, "This is not right." In many ways, the beauty of Japanese food is that it's very soft, very gentle. My dashi, on the other hand, has a little bit more punch; it's a little stronger. I don't know whether it's right or wrong, but it's different. Dashi is properly made if the temperature isn't too hot and it doesn't pull any of the bitter notes out of the kombu.

I'm not a Japanese-trained chef and I'm not trying to make Japanese food. I will make miso soup my way, but if you don't like it the way it tastes, it's not a problem. You tried it, we move on, and we get you something else. But when a customer says, "This isn't made right," or "This is poorly made, poorly executed," I have a problem and may take issue with the customer. You may not like the way something tastes, but it will be hard for you to come to my restaurant and criticize the way it's prepared.

I love using Japanese ingredients, but I don't try to use them in traditional Japanese ways.

Being a chef in New York City means I can use ingredients from anywhere. I can use ingredients from Japan, or I can use a technique from Japan, I can add spices from Mexico and vegetables from India, but I'm still cooking an American food. For example, we make our own udon. We wanted to learn how to make udon, so we did some research. We saw that Japanese chefs walked on and stomped on the dough made from *udonko*, a high-gluten flour. But the closest we could find here was bread flour. So we tried different amounts of water and flour to make the dough and put it in two bags. Every day we stomped on it in the restaurant, like they did a thousand years ago. Then we let it rest before we rolled it out.

We wanted to flavor the dough, which is very un-Japanese. We decided we liked the combination of grapefruit and pine needles, so first we made a clear dashi with clarified grapefruit juice. We wanted to do a wd~50 version of a big bowl of udon noodles in the broth with vegetables and seafood—seared scallops, fish, steamed Chinese broccoli, and a raw radish. So where does the pine come in? We take pine oil and put it in the dough, so when you eat the noodle it tastes like Christmas. It's served in a big, round bowl like one you would get at a ramen house. It doesn't look any different, but you would never find anybody else who would put those flavors together.

Our udon at wd~50 is a Japanese dish in inspiration, in its appearance, in its ingredients, and even in its technique. No Japanese chef would make a dish like that, but it's true to several aspects of Japanese cooking—the rigor, the discipline, the technique, the ingredients, the respect, and the patience. These aspects all come together in a way that shows what we do at wd~50. We take certain familiar ingredients and present them in an unfamiliar way, or we take unfamiliar ingredients and present them in a very familiar way. This notion happens over and over and over again in the restaurant. It's about paring down, paring down, paring down. It's not necessarily about modernizing.

It's my view that American chefs don't have a truly traditional cuisine to follow because this country is not old enough to have a unique cuisine. Think of any dish that is considered American, and I can tell you the country it's from. With the exception of barbecue and the sauces and dry rubs—those are uniquely American—our cuisine comes from people who immigrated here. So I'm not turning my back on any cuisine by using the techniques and the ingredients in the way that I do. On the other hand, I think most cultures—particularly those in Asia—strive to hold on to their culinary past. From a food standpoint, that is something that American chefs don't have to do.

Training

I want cooks to come here and exercise their brain a little bit. I want them to think while they're here.

For me, training is about education. I want to create an environment where my cooks and I can continue to learn. The way we cook is deeply rooted in the desire on my part to educate myself and the people who work with me. One of the things that I tell my cooks when they take a job at wd~50 is, "You're going to be responsible. Make sure that all the ingredients are prepared for certain dishes and that you have all these ingredients at your stations. The other thing you have to do is contribute ideas. You have to put stuff out on the table. I can get anybody to cut vegetables. Anybody can do that."

Historically, the kitchen is not a place where anyone brings an opinion, but at wd~50, I want opinions. Anybody can give me an idea or be an inspiration for an idea, whether they're wait staff, busser, person at the door, or the dishwasher. I'm open to anything that we can do to improve something or to make something new. I want to create a forum and an opportunity for people to put ideas on the table. In the kitchen, that translates to, "Okay, guys, what have you got for us to work on today?"

For example, striped bass season is about to start, so I might say, "Let's think about a dish with striped bass." Or, "I went to dinner last night and I heard two guys having a conversation. One guy said to the other, 'Wouldn't it be cool if you could deep fry mayonnaise?' What do you guys think? How does that sound? Where do we go with that? What form does it take?" I don't say, "How can we make that dish?" But it's a jumping-off point, sort of like a shotgun spray—wide open.

Inspiration for a dish can come any time, so you need to be ready.

We give our customers a complimentary amuse-bouche—a small appetizer. Twice a week I choose a cook whose job it is to come up with those new little dishes. I try to teach my cooks to be open to inspiration. I tell them, "You need to be ready, because inspiration for a dish can come at any time. Whether you have a pad and a paper on you at all times, a good memory, a voice recorder, or an arm you can write it on, be ready. Even the way the light hits a building can inspire you to put the food on the plate, but you need to be open and ready to think about something in a different way." I am constantly going around to different stations and saying, "All right. You've got a week to come up with a new idea—not a new dish but an idea that we can build a dish out of."

At wd~50, we are more than a decade into this social experiment, and I believe it's working. We have a kitchen environment where people can really learn, so I hire those people who want to be part of this way of cooking. I have more college-educated cooks than the average kitchen, but that's not a rule. It just happens to be that those are the people who fit in. It's a demanding environment, they work long hours here, and they must use their free time for more learning, experimentation, and discovery on their own. I don't necessarily feel bad about that. As a result, they are getting a deeper, richer experience. They aren't being told, "Just shut up and do it like this because this is how we have been doing it for months and it works."

When cooks finish their time here, and someone asks them, "What was it like working at wd~50?" all I really want them to say is, "It made me think." When I asked an instructor in cooking school how long to work for somebody, he said, "As long as you're still learning, I don't see why you need to leave." I have cooks who come and go, and I tell them, "There are certain things you haven't done, haven't experienced yet. But if you need to go, then go. I wish you the best."

Tools

If you hold a Japanese knife in your hand, you can feel if it's right for you.

I bought a small Japanese knife when I worked for Jean-Georges, but I put it away because I had ruined so many knives by sharpening them the wrong way. When I was at 71 Clinton Fresh Food, one of my cooks had a couple of Japanese knives and loved them. So I pulled that knife out, used it, and loved it. Then a customer gave me a deba knife as a thank-you gift. When I used it, my cook said, "You know, that's a right-handed knife. You're left-handed." So I returned to the store where he had bought it and I said, "I need to get a left-handed knife." From that point on I was hooked on left-handed Japanese knives.

If you hold a Japanese knife in your hand, you can feel if it's right for you. A lot of people in the last couple of years have asked chefs why they like Japanese knives so much. For a lot of us it's so obvious. They are extremely sharp, and each type of knife has a particular purpose. Watching a Japanese chef in a sushi restaurant slice fish with a traditional Yanagi knife is fascinating. Plus, the level of care and workmanship that goes into making Japanese knives is unequaled anywhere. For example, when I was in Sakai City, Japan, I was mesmerized as I watched Mr. Ikeda, a blacksmith, hammer hot metal into an incredible chef's knife. I was profoundly moved when he said, "We want to make you this knife."

A Day in the Life

Two of the most famous chefs in the world stood in the middle of my restaurant and talked to each other.

In 2004, I got a call from The Fat Duck, a three-star Michelin restaurant outside of London. "Chef Heston Blumenthal is visiting New York in three weeks, and he wants to eat at your restaurant," a staffer informed me. At that time, The Fat Duck was considered by some to be one of the top restaurants in the world, so this was a big deal. We like cooking for everybody, but we get a particular thrill out of cooking for our own, and when a top chef like Heston comes to our restaurant, it puts everybody on pins and needles. Then, four days before Heston's visit, a member of Ferran Adrià's staff called and said he wanted to eat at the restaurant on the same day! Ferran Adrià is one of the most creative chefs today. At the time, he worked at the three-star Michelin restaurant elBulli in Catalonia, Spain. Both of these chefs are very, very influential. So this was like a papal visit—squared. These were two of the most famous chefs in the world. They were the top of the top.

So it was really a big deal that they were both coming to wd~50—and on the same day! Should we tell them? Do they become one table? What's going to happen? My head was about to explode. I wasn't ready for this caliber of person in a single form, let alone two. But more importantly, what were we going to make? We sat down and talked. What were some of our best dishes? What dishes were clever and creative? What would make them pay attention to us? We needed to cook something that somehow would leave a bit of an impression. We decided that we would cook the same menu for both of them.

Ferran came with his people, and they began eating. I don't know how else to say it—he was like the Pope. He was somebody very serious, very heavy duty, but someone who we were so excited to cook for, and yet terrified at the same time. So we cooked, and he and his group ate. After a short time, he stepped into the kitchen, said hello and met everybody. Then he went back to the table, sat down and ate again, and all the while he and his people constantly looked into the kitchen and took notes—while we had heart attacks.

About an hour and a half into the meal, Heston and his group arrived. When he came into the kitchen to say hello, I said, "One of your friends is here." He turned around and saw Ferran, who immediately stood up. They greeted each other, and now the two most famous chefs in the world stood in the middle of the restaurant and talked to each other. This was surreal. All the staff in the kitchen freaked out. Since there was a pause, I thought we'd better gather ourselves and go on. Ferran had finished his meal, but Heston had just started his. Even so, they continued to talk. Much, much later they both went on their way.

Afterwards—maybe around 2 a.m.—I took everyone out to a bar to celebrate. It had been one of the most draining experiences ever.

These chefs have the ears and eyes of everybody, so I needed them to say something positive about their experience at wd~50.

It was a success. We all got a lot out of it, and the world didn't come to an end. Afterwards, Ferran invited me to spend a week in his kitchen and work with him, and he sent one of his guys to work in our kitchen. Subsequently, a friendship grew out of it. I already knew Heston, and I continue to have a good relationship with him. That day was one of the best at wd~50, but also one of the most terrifying.

FIVE

BEN FLATT

Owner/Chef, Flatt's by the Sea, Noto, Japan

Benjamin Maxwell Flatt started cooking at an early age in his father's restaurant in the country town of Sofala in New South Wales, Australia. After attending school Ben Flatt moved to Sydney where he worked in the food and restaurant industry, predominantly as an Italian chef. After meeting his wife Chikako, they moved to Japan's Noto Peninsula in the mid-1990s and worked with her parents in their highly acclaimed guesthouse, Sannami. It was there that Chef Ben learned traditional Japanese knife techniques, Noto fermentation and pickling, and the preparation of Noto seasonal cuisine. Ben and Chikako Flatt have operated Flatt's by the Sea guesthouse for almost 20 years, offering Noto traditional cuisine and handmade ingredients served in modern Italian cuisine.

Career Path

I was brought up in Australia in a cooking family and started working in kitchens when I was about 13 years old.

My parents had a restaurant called Flatt's Café in a small country town of about 80 people. The town was far away from anywhere, so we had to grow our own or buy all of the ingredients for the restaurant from local farmers. My parents kept a lot of livestock, such as goats, pigs, chicken, ducks, geese, and pigeons, that at some time of the year became part of the menu. I learned from an early age to work with fresh, local ingredients. It was a great place to learn about food, local farm-fresh ingredients, and the preparation of livestock. People would drive 200 to 300 kilometers from Sydney just to eat in my parents' restaurant. My mother and father made people happy with their great food and the wonderful stories my father told and still tells to this day.

That was the start of my cooking career. After high school, I moved to Sydney to get a taste of the Sydney food scene and to try my hand as a chef in the "Big Smoke." That's when I went out for Japanese food for the first time with a friend. We went to one of those places where we sat at a table and the Japanese chef cooked Japanese food in front of us, teppanyaki style. He did amazing tricks, like dancing with his knives, throwing salt-shakers around, and flipping cut vegetables at some of the customers who then caught them in their mouths. I think it's an Australian style of Japanese food that doesn't exist anywhere else. It was quite amusing and really intriguing, because the chef had to be a showman as well as a good cook.

From the age of seventeen on, I worked in restaurants all over Sydney and learned new cooking techniques. I developed an interest in Italian food, so I went into Italian cuisine. My favorite position was second chef's assistant to the head chef, because that position was where I really got to work with food and to help create the head chef's food and dishes. Finally, I became the head chef of an Italian restaurant in the center of Sydney. That was the last job I had in Australia. I didn't know then that I would soon meet my future wife, Chikako, and end up living in Japan.

Training

My in-laws taught me traditional Noto cooking techniques.

In 1995, Chikako and I moved to the western side of Japan to the Noto Peninsula on the Sea of Japan, where she was raised and where her parents ran a traditional Japanese guesthouse. Their guesthouse had a reputation as one of the top guesthouses in Japan in terms of food. Once I landed in Japan and tasted the local cuisine from Noto, I fell in love with it.

We lived with Chikako's parents, and I worked in the kitchen of their inn. My in-laws taught me traditional knife skills and Noto cooking techniques, including how to make sashimi and other Japanese dishes, and how to pickle organic and seasonal mountain vegetables. Chikako's father did most of the sashimi and preparation of the fish. So when I learned how to prepare fish, I was taught by my father-in-law. If I was doing any other type of food preparation, I learned from my mother-in-law. Both Chikako's mother and father learned cooking techniques from their parents—techniques that were handed down from generation to generation. They always said, "We do it the same way that it has always been done in Noto."

Chikako's mother was one of 10 women in Japan who was honored with an award from the Japanese government for teaching Japanese food preparation to the next generation. In the kitchen, she did most of the pickling and cooking. She had a seasonal calendar plan for what to pickle and when, from fish to mountain vegetables. She had over 100 different types of pickles in her "pickle room," as well as homemade miso, ishiri, and semi-dry fish. When I saw her drying fish outside on the line for a day and a half, I asked her what kept it from going off. She said, "I leave it in salt water overnight before drying." A simple answer, but important if you want to successfully make semi-dry fish.

Living and working with Chikako's parents was a great opportunity to see firsthand the background of real Japanese food. That's when my whole ideology—my ideas of cooking—completely changed. From that point on, my cooking philosophy was extremely influenced by Japanese cuisine and the local fresh ingredients of Noto.

Cuisine

The biggest challenge is understanding people's tastes, and making sure that the dish has harmony.

In 1997, after Chikako's parents moved into their new guesthouse, we took over the old guesthouse, added a bakery and café, and changed the name to Flatt's by the Sea. The building is still a traditional Japanese guesthouse, but our lunch and dinner course menus are now "Noto-Italian." Our unique cuisine is based on Noto's philosophy of natural seasonal flavors enhanced by Italian cooking techniques, but with fresh local traditional ingredients served in the traditional surroundings of a Japanese inn. Even to this day, Chikako's mother comes to our café, and we sit down and talk about what's happening this season and what ingredients are available. I've been living here for many years, but there's always something new to learn, something that I've missed or some new skill that I've got to study. That makes me more and more interested in Noto food culture and gives me more ideas for new dishes.

Cuisine from the Noto Peninsula hasn't been influenced much by big cities like Tokyo or Osaka. Those cities have swapped their ingredients throughout history. Because Noto is a peninsula, for many years the only way to get here was by boat. As a result, Noto has kept a lot of its unique and interesting aspects, including pickling and cooking techniques.

I don't see my cooking as a blending of Italian and Japanese cuisines. It's still Italian food, but I'm using what's available in this area, such as vegetables from our farm and fish from the local Noto fishermen. The ingredients come into my kitchen as raw products, and I then turn them into pickles, sashimi, or other dishes using many of the techniques I learned from my in-laws.

Once I learned traditional Noto cooking techniques, adapting them to my style of Italian cooking wasn't that difficult. They inspire me to make more new dishes, like the summer dish of flying fish with blue cheese from the sea.

Flying fish has a nice texture for summer sashimi, so I prepare it by cleaning and cutting the fish into sashimi-sized pieces. About three months before, I prepare a traditional pickled fish called *hinazushi*, which is rice and fish that have been pickled for three months, which results in a flavor like blue cheese. That's why it is called "blue cheese from the sea."

I take the rice from the pickling process—not the fish itself—and add it to the flying fish sashimi. Next, I deep-fry the wings from the flying fish. Then in a cocktail glass I put a little bit of hinazushi and the flying fish. Next, to give it balance, I take a sansho leaf—it has a beautiful fragrance, not like the dried ground sansho berries which are quite peppery—and I blend it with just a touch of virgin olive oil and a little bit of sugar to make a very, very light oil dressing with the flavor and aroma of the herb. Finally, to finish it off, I put the fried flying fish wings on the top of the glass and have this amazing summer dish!

Ideas for dishes like this one come from knowing the origins of the ingredients and their flavors, how they are traditionally used, and when they are available. Then I taste. I believe one thing chefs need to do more is to taste and try different ingredients, foods, and cuisines. This improves a chef's palate-vocabulary. The more types of foods and cuisines a chef tries, the better his food-vocabulary becomes. When chefs understand how herbs work and how ingredients blend together, they can create amazing dishes.

The first time I tried a traditional Japanese breakfast, I was amazed at all of the different flavors and how stimulating they were to my palate. The gentle sweetness, bitterness, hot, sour, and deep umami flavors warmed my body, and I experienced the deep and subtle flavors of all the ingredients. Every mouthful made me wonder how I had lived for so long without knowing about this food. And it gave me a new understanding of the food, setting the stage for my journey into taste and the evolution of my cuisine.

At Flatt's by the Sea, we make everything from scratch. In Noto, fresh seafood from the Sea of Japan inspires me.

The Sea of Japan off the Noto Peninsula boasts the best and freshest seafood and fish in all of Japan. That's why so many Japanese travel from all over the country to Noto, especially to eat the winter fish and crabs! One thing I've found about the crab from this area is that the meat is very sweet, tender, and beautiful, and there is a lot of meat inside every crab. Because I don't want to waste any of the crab, I use other parts of it, too. For example, I crack the head open and extract the liquid—what they call the *kani miso*—and then I bake it into a paste. Traditionally, the paste is eaten with rice or as a side dish for saké, but I use it to make a crab miso cream sauce for pasta. Then I take all of the meat from the crab and put it on top of the pasta and dress it with the crab head and claws around the sides of the dish. The flavor of the crab miso is much stronger than the flavor of the meat, so it tastes like you've just eaten 20 crabs. It's simply amazing! The flavor is intense and very powerful, but it's delicate at the same time.

Ingredients

I preserve the original texture and color of the flesh so that when guests eat it in one of my dishes, they can taste the pure flavor of the fish as well as the flavors of the other ingredients.

I was excited when I first picked up Japanese ingredients, and I knew I had a lot to learn about how to use them. But as I became familiar with them, I saw the similarities between Japanese cuisine and the Italian dishes that I'd been cooking, so the ingredients became easier to use. We've had many guests who have had a lot of contact with Japanese food, but when they visit us, they like to try my Italian food, which employs traditional local ingredients. When they eat it, they say, "Wow, that is so unbelievable. I did not know you could do that with traditional Noto ingredients!"

The first thing I do in the morning is ring the person who buys fish for us from the local fish market. After he tells me what's available, I order only what fish I need for our guests' meals that day. It's an auction market, and since all of the fish are sold by 7:30 a.m., I have to make a decision straight away, but I don't clean or scale the fish until I'm ready to prepare it, usually later that morning. From about 7 to 8 a.m., we prepare breakfast for the customers who have stayed overnight at the inn. Our breakfast is a traditional Noto Japanese guesthouse breakfast—seven dishes, including pickles, some semi-dry fish of the season, fresh daily picked vegetables boiled lightly with *katsuobushi*, squid in a light Japanese-style vinegar sauce, miso soup made with fresh fish bones, tofu, and locally grown rice.

At about 10 a.m., after the customers leave, I start preparations for lunch by cleaning and scaling the fish I bought that morning. The Noto technique that I now use for cutting up fish is completely different from the way it's done in Australia and many other European countries—it's a lot gentler on the meat of the fish. As a result, I preserve the original texture and color of the flesh so that when guests eat it in one of my dishes, they can taste the pure flavor of the fish as well as the flavors of the other ingredients.

If I'm also doing a mountain vegetable and herb pasta, I'll pick the vegetables from a nearby local river or the mountain behind our house. Lunch usually ends at about 3 p.m. We have a break, and depending on the time of the year, I'll go out to cut wood for the fireplace or go up to the farm. If it's yuzu season, I'll pick yuzu.

Then onto the dinner menu, where the guests can choose a five-, six-, or seven-seafood course meal based on the four seasons of fish in Japan. The winter fish are kingfish, monkfish, crab, cod, and other parts of the cod, like shirako, which is cod sperm. The first time I ever tried it, I realized that it had the same texture as crumbed, fried lamb's brains. The texture is very milky and creamy. The Japanese usually eat shirako in a clear soup or in vinegar, but I deep-fry it. When you bite into it, it has a creamy flavor. Our customers love it!

In European cooking, we use the intestines and organs from cows, sheep and pigs, and nobody really thinks twice. But once you start talking about fish intestines and organs, foreigners in Japan always become uneasy. They say, "I can't eat that part of the fish!" One of the funniest things that I ever saw was when my two kids were sitting at the table arguing about who was going to get to eat the eye of the fish. I couldn't believe that!

Ishiri brings out the umami of any flavor in any type of food.

This year we made about 400 liters of ishiri squid sauce. *Ishiri* sauce looks like soy sauce, but it is called "squid soy," or "squid sauce." It's made from squid guts that have been salted and fermented in big vats for two years. Ishiri has a distinctive flavor and brings out the umami in food. For example, when I put it into a dish like potato soup, it brings out the ishiri flavor and also increases the umami flavor of the potato.

There are different ways to make ishiri. Here's how we do it. After letting the salt and squid guts ferment for two years, we drain the liquid off, throw out the paste that's left in the bottom of the bucket, rinse the bucket, and start another batch with new squid guts and new salt. Many other people who make ishiri pour off the liquid and then add water to the squid and salt paste that's left in the bottom of the bucket to start another batch. We don't do it that way, because it doesn't give as good a product the second time. Adding water to anything waters it down slightly, and it doesn't taste exactly the same. It also develops quite a pungent odor.

After two years of simmering in the bucket, there's pretty much nothing but taste. The juice that comes out of the bucket is basically black liquid. There are no guts or anything in there by that stage, but we boil it once and skim off any of the impurities.

We do a few dishes that are made with just squid guts. We pickle the squid and eat it—guts and all—for breakfast. It tastes fantastic! And when the squid is salted and dried, then we grill it with rice, miso soup, and pickles. I also create another interesting dish with squid. I put three or four rings of squid, some mushrooms, salt, and two or three finely chopped vegetables into an empty scallop shell. I cover the mixture with water and ishiri and then heat it until it boils using a little steel container that holds a candle to heat the bottom of the shell. These are all traditional dishes from the Noto Peninsula.

Whenever I go down to Australia, we have a lot of barbecues. Everybody there uses typical marinades with garlic and herbs. But I make an Australian barbecue with an ishiri marinade twist. I marinate chicken breasts or thighs in straight ishiri and garlic, but only for about half an hour or so. The marinade goes right into the meat and flavors it. I throw it onto the barbecue and cook it, skin down, so the skin gets nice and crispy, and then I turn it. The ishiri makes the texture of the chicken really soft and really moist. The ishiri brings out the umami flavor from the meat of chicken. It's so delicious!

Ishiri brings out the umami of any flavor in any type of food. That's one of the interesting things about Japanese food. I use some ingredients to bring out a deeper flavor that's always been there, but I have to encourage it to come out—from the back of the food. That's something we don't usually do in European cooking. We don't use any ingredients other than salt to bring out flavor. We don't understand the technique of using something like umami. As a European-trained chef, this is something that I had to learn. Ishiri is one of those ingredients, but there are others that also bring out that back flavor. The Noto region is also very famous for its seaweed. We use seaweed to make a *dashi* broth that is one of the umami tastes and becomes the base of many Japanese dishes, such as soup, dipping sauce and *nimono*, which is a stewed or simmered dish.

I use suzu salt in pretty much all the foods I cook.

The sea salt from the Noto region has a sweet ending, instead of the salty or bitter finish that makes you want to drink a glass of water straight away. The salt from here doesn't have that flavor. Instead, you first have a salty flavor and then you get a sweet finish. It's called "suzu salt" because Suzu is the name of the area in Noto where the salt is made. When I'm talking about sweet, it's not sugar-sweet. On the tongue suzu salt has that salty zing, but the aftertaste doesn't keep getting saltier. It changes the flavor. It's still salt, and it's still salty, but it melts in your mouth. I use suzu salt in pretty much all of the food that I cook. I even put it into water to cook pasta and in the bread that we bake. It adds a completely different dimension to those foods.

There's another salt from Noto we use for pickling. It is saltier because it has to last throughout the many years of pickling to bring out the flavors. This salt has quite a strong flavor. I use this salt when I make pickled plum, pickled daikon and *funazushi*, which is a fermented sushi. This year we made a lot of pickled fish roe and *konka iwashi*, which is sardine pickled in rice husk. When rice is cleaned, the fine brown powder from it is called "rice husk." To pickle the fish, I first clean the fish and then layer them in the bottom of the bucket. Next, I cover the fish with the rice husk, salt, and chilies. Then I just keep putting in layers of fish and layers of rice husk, salt, and chilies all the way up to the top of the bucket. Then I put a heavy weight on top of that bucket and leave it to pickle—for two years!

A batch of pickled fish weighs about 20 kilos, or about 45 pounds. I have to check it every so often, take water off the top and also make sure the fish hasn't gone off, but otherwise I just leave it. We can actually eat it after a year, but it's better after two. Traditionally, we usually eat pickled fish with breakfast or with rice. I only cut a little bit because it's quite strong. The finished product is basically Japanese anchovies, but there's no oil involved. It tastes a bit like anchovies but has a lot more depth in flavor. I also use it in several pasta dishes.

Tools

It doesn't matter how much you try, you just can't properly cut fish without using a Japanese knife.

In my kitchen, my knives are my most important tools. I started off with traditional French knives, but since I moved to Japan, most of my knives now are Japanese knives. I use a *yanagi* knife for cutting sashimi and fish. It's the traditional slicer that is only sharpened on one side. I use one small knife just for cutting and peeling potatoes and other vegetables. It's this lovely little 5-centimeter (a little less than 2 inches) rounded but quite wide knife. It's just insane how easy it is to peel vegetables with it.

Most Japanese knives are made for specific jobs, whereas in European kitchens, the basic knife is usually one size, except for small paring knives. I have four knives that I use for different jobs in the kitchen. For example, in addition to my yanagi, I also use a deba, which is a heavy, short, fat knife. I use it for cutting through bone, cutting through fish, gutting fish, and scaling fish. I also use a 20-centimeter, or nearly 8-inch, double-edged, western-style Japanese knife that is as sharp as a razor blade. I also use the *usuba*, which is a traditional vegetable knife.

When I worked in Australia, I mostly used a multi-purpose French knife, a paring knife, and maybe a boning knife. Japanese knives are completely different, so I had to learn some new cutting techniques. My father-in-law taught me the techniques for using the sashimi knife. I also had to learn to use different knives for different tasks and get used to their different sizes.

I have learned one thing about knives. No matter what kind of knife you have, you need to learn the proper technique for using it and sharpening it, and that can be a challenge. But I think that if you've learned proper knife techniques with French or German knives, you can learn how to use a Japanese knife without much difficulty.

A Day in the Life

I remember one day that was among the most challenging in my career.

Once I turned up in a kitchen in Sydney where the head chef, the second chef and all the other chefs had quit. The only person left standing in the kitchen was the kitchen hand. He had no idea of the menu or anything else, since his job was to wash dishes, cut up and clean lettuce, and do other prep work. I had 90 minutes before service and a menu that was five pages long because the last chef there was a complete lunatic. The manager and I had to go through all the fridges to see what was there. He told me what was being used for what dishes and how the dishes looked. Then I had to get somebody to go out and pick up whatever was missing from the menu. Next I needed to get the actual menu up and running so that when the first customer of the 70 people who were booked for lunch walked through the door, that customer was going to get food that was at the restaurant's usual standard. It was terrifying. Extremely good training—but totally terrifying!

Here's my advice to people who want to become chefs. Drop out of whatever you're doing for a year and work as a temp chef for one of those temp chef companies. When they send you to a job, you could end up in a sandwich shop making sandwiches or cooking in a Chinese takeaway. You could be doing any kind of cuisine in any type of situation. So, you have to adapt, walk into that kitchen, look around, figure out which ingredients and tools are available and which aren't, see what's on the menu, understand what the menu is, and start cooking. You can't say, "I don't know how to do that."

❖

SIX

EDDY LEROUX

Head Chef de Cuisine, Restaurant Daniel, New York City

Eddy Leroux began his formal culinary training at age 14, was a finalist in the national competition for best French apprentice at age 18, and landed a job in Paris' Michelin three-star restaurant, Lucas Carton, under chef Alain Senderens at the age of 23. After a five-year tenure with Senderens, and a short stint as Chef de Cuisine of the renowned Le Normandie at the Mandarin Oriental Hotel, in Bangkok, Eddy Leroux spent four years as Chef de Cuisine under Laurent Gras at the Waldorf Astoria's legendary Peacock Alley in New York City. In 2002, he joined Daniel as Executive Sous Chef, and in June 2005, was promoted to Chef de Cuisine.

Influences

My aunt inspired me to want to become a chef, and I started experimenting with dishes in the kitchen at home.

I grew up in Northern France. My family lived in the North of France in a border town close to Brussels. My mother cooked for the family, but it was my aunt who was really passionate about food. She gave me a first edition of *The Escoffier Cookbook: A Guide to the Fine Art of Cookery*. Every Christmas my grandfather rented a communal room, and we made Christmas dinner with all of my 40 or so cousins, uncles, and aunts. My aunt was always the one in charge of the meal and the cooking. I spent each Christmas Eve watching her in the kitchen, making mocha cakes, melting chocolate for pastries, making foie gras, or whatever kind of dish she was creating. My aunt inspired me to want to become a chef, and I started experimenting with dishes in the kitchen at home.

My background and tastes were formed by growing up in France and by the great local fresh ingredients we ate every day at home. But I also lived in a border town, where I had many classmates who came from other countries and cultures. My friends always brought interesting and exotic foods for lunch, and I was insatiably curious to taste whatever they had. Since then, I've never looked back.

Career Path

When I left a restaurant, there was no way I would have the recipe. I had to write it down myself in my own book.

Between the ages of 16 and 20, I attended a culinary school as part of my high school education. In my program, I went to school for two weeks, then spent anywhere from two weeks to two months in a restaurant, and then went back to school for another two weeks or two months, and so on. The basic program lasted two years. Once I passed the exam, I went on to study for another two years to earn a culinary baccalaureate. I not only learned how to cook, but also how to manage a culinary business.

In France during the 1970s and 1980s, the recipes in restaurants were like the sacred book. Everything was guarded. When I left a restaurant, there was no way I would have the recipe. I had to write it down myself in my own book. When I started cooking, I always had paper and a pen to write down my ideas and how the chef de partie—the station chef or line cook in charge of a particular area of production—made the dish. Training in France was based on observation. We never had any manuals that said, "Here are the recipes of Lucas Carton."

When I started at Lucas Carton, for example, I had to bring my book and watch my chef de partie prepare a dish—once, twice, three times, and then ask him, "Can I do it?" Then I made it the way I saw him doing it while he watched me and corrected me. But he never gave me the recipe.

I worked in two different palaces close to Monaco and one in Annecy, L'Impérial Palace. At that time, in the 1970s and into the 1980s, there were many chefs from Japan working and studying in France. When I was at L'Impérial Palace, I worked with a Japanese Chef de Partie named Fujo. I was devoted to this chef. Of course, loyalty and a strong work ethic were essential. Working closely with this Japanese chef had a profound impact on me. Fujo worked by the book and was disciplined about the process, the technique, the recipe, and the taste.

My military service lasted one year, during which time I cooked for President François Mitterrand and for one of his cabinet ministers.

The big thing I had to learn was how to create complete menus. I mostly prepared family style dishes and cuisine bourgeoise, but sometimes I created special meals for a cabinet head or a foreign delegation.

Chef Alain Senderens always brought interesting Japanese ingredients and cooking techniques back to France for his chefs to try out.

After completing my military service in 1994, I spent the next five years working for Chef Alain Senderens at Lucas Carton in Paris. I worked my way up to sous chef by the age of 25. The restaurant was owned by a Japanese restaurant group, and Mr. Senderens made many trips to Japan to give French cooking demonstrations. He always brought interesting Japanese cooking techniques and ingredients like wasabi, mirin, and bonito flakes back to France for his chefs to try out. At that time, he served two famous small dishes, or amuse-bouches, at the restaurant, which were heavily influenced by Japanese cuisine. One was a cassolette of salmon with shiso and leeks, and the other was marinated chicken wings with soy sauce.

Then Chef Senderens got a three-year contract in Bangkok at Le Normandie at the Mandarin Oriental Hotel. The first chef he sent stayed there for only one year, so I moved from Paris to Bangkok to finish the contract. At my age, to have an experience cooking abroad was a great opportunity. The Thai chefs were precise and disciplined but also fun to work with. And I learned a lot about how Thai cuisine balanced three or four fundamental tastes in each dish: sour, sweet, salty, and sometimes bitter. The staff at the Mandarin Oriental had trained with some of the best chefs, including Joël Robuchon, Jean-Claude Vrinat, owner of Taillevent, Jean-Georges Vongerichten, and others.

Little by little, I experienced Japanese food in New York.

After I returned to Paris, the Mandarin Oriental Hotel in Bangkok called me and offered me a position as the head chef at Le Normandie. I was ready to go back to Bangkok when I got a call from the headhunter in Paris who had placed Laurent Gras at Alain Ducasse's Peacock Alley at the Waldorf Astoria Hotel in New York City. He asked me to help Laurent as the Chef de Cuisine. I didn't really want to go to the U.S., as I was really excited about my time in Asia, but eventually I was persuaded by Laurent.

After Peacock Alley closed in 2001, I stayed on with the Waldorf as their chef for the banquet department. Then, in 2002, after helping at a city Meals-on-Wheels dinner hosted by Daniel Boulud, he casually asked me, "What are you doing?" and invited me to meet with him the next day. He offered me a contract as Executive Sous Chef at Daniel. In June 2005, I was promoted to Chef de Cuisine.

I fell in love with New York and its great diversity of cultures and fabulous food. And I began to learn about Japanese cuisine. The first time I had real Japanese food was in 1999 or 2000 in New York City at Sushi Hatsu, now Sushi Seki. The Japanese chef-owner cooked for me while I sat at the counter and watched. He brought many wonderful dishes. I could see his skill in preparing the fish. His cutting was precise, and he was respectful about the rules of touching and cutting the fish. Most chefs here don't do it like that. He was immaculate, too, and calculated. Just to watch the way he cut a piece of blue fin tuna was amazing. The thing that I liked the best was the way he torched a piece of salmon in the skin while it was on the grill.

There are similarities between French chefs and Japanese chefs— their craftsmanship, the way they perform their work, their respect and care for the ingredients, their mentality. That's why some ingredients interplay between both cuisines. It's like a melody. It's about harmony. Sometimes I'll go to the market or have dinner in an ethnic restaurant where a certain spice or ingredient will make me think: "What if I tried this back at Restaurant Daniel?" Influences are everywhere. That's why New York is the entire world in one town.

Cuisine

When I conceive of a dish, I first write down my ideas. Then I do very basic drawings of the plate. I set up where I want to put things.

Our goal at Daniel is to improve. Everybody contributes: "I think something needs to be added—a spice or some other ingredients." We share our ideas, and then we reinvent. That's the way we progress. At Daniel, I focus on everything with fish. Other chefs handle appetizers and the other stations. We change the menu not four but five times a year. Five times because we have a special menu for Indian summer, the transition between the end of the summer and fall. We also have a market menu that varies every week, so we create dishes on a daily basis. We experiment with a dish and then maybe put it on the menu as a special during the week. Most of the time these dishes are very good to start with, but it is through the discussion and debate process that they usually become fantastic.

I don't try to copy Japanese cuisine, but on the seasonal menu I have many dishes that include Japanese ingredients and influences, such as rosette of scallop with hatcho black miso or black cod rubbed with a mixture of bonito flakes, seaweed, and sesame seeds. When I conceive of a dish, I first write down my ideas. Then I do very basic drawings of the plate and I set up where I want to put things. I use symbols to show "This will be here, this here," and so on. I like the Japanese sense of aesthetics. There is a kind of overall simplicity in the dishes, with a delicate balance of diverse flavors and textures presented against a seasonal backdrop. Restaurant Daniel dishes are all about seasonal flavors.

Ingredients

I think about the products and ingredients and ways I can maintain their integrity.

My goal is to focus on one ingredient or product and to try to bring out the essence of that ingredient in a multidimensional way. For example, I'll use a particular ingredient cooked in one dish and also use the same ingredient raw as garnish or even like a pickle! I think about ways I can maintain the integrity and the texture of products and ingredients when I cook with them, without changing the flavor or adding additional flavors. I want to balance the flavors and textures and, most of all, create a dish that tastes good to people of different cultures and ages. That's the most difficult challenge for a chef, because people have very individual tastes and preferences.

For a chef, the difficult part in constructing a dish is to find harmony in every step. You cannot have something too strong with something too mild. What you need to do is to construct the taste to move like a crescendo.

When I visited Japan, I wanted to see what ingredients and foods might work with my dishes back in New York. Ishiri sauce, for example, can taste strong, but I'll use just a few drops so that it absorbs into the other ingredients to bring out the back flavor. I want a mellow taste. I don't want anything to shock or turn people off. I really like *shichimi togarashi*, a popular Japanese seven-flavor spice mixture, too. It looks like espelette pepper, which we have in the southwest of France near the Spanish border. It's mild and fragrant but slightly spicy—something that's going to give a little kick but not kill your mouth with a burning flavor. I season the Kobe beef with togarashi and sansho pepper. I love sansho pepper!

I also use some Japanese cooking techniques. I cook Kobe beef on a chunk of Himalayan rock salt in the oven. That's called "ishiyaki," which is a traditional Japanese type of grilling where dishes are cooked on heated stones. As the salt degrades in the oven, it absorbs into the meat, so I don't need to season it afterwards. I also make a saké béarnaise with wild shiso to go with Kobe beef and serve it with a *soubric* of spinach, which is like a spinach flan.

I like to use rice vinegar for cooking or in vinaigrette, because it's much sweeter than any other type of vinegar. I mix white wine vinegar from France and rice vinegar from Japan. The white wine vinegar is very high in acidity, but the rice vinegar has acidity and sweetness, so the mixture has a sweet and acid taste in your mouth.

Regarding ingredients, my greatest influence from Japan came from my trip to Ishikawa Prefecture.

I have always appreciated high quality, local fresh ingredients, but in Ishikawa, everything was sourced from within the area and was perfectly in season. Since then, I have tried to source many ingredients for Daniel from local farmers and suppliers in our region. I am fortunate that there are many fine small suppliers around New York.

This led me to meet Tama Matsuoka Wong and collaborate with her on a cookbook, *Foraged Flavor*, about local wild plants and their great taste. I appreciate the ancient Japanese cultural tradition of nanakusa, harvesting the seven edible wild herbs of spring, and sansai, foraging for wild vegetables. I was delighted to find that many of these same plants grow wild in the New York area. One of my favorite wild plants is the *tara no me*, also known as "king of wild vegetables."

I remember the first time that Tama brought me some from the wild. They looked like strange, thorny sticks with the bud only at the end. Everyone in the kitchen loved touching this plant and eating it. Of course, I changed and adapted the traditional Japanese ways of preparing these ingredients to my style of cooking. I find that the deeper I go in exploring these foods, the more interesting they become. It satisfies my curiosity and at the same time keeps me humble, because there are always new things to learn.

Training

Training in France was based on closely working together and observation. We never had manuals with recipes.

Restaurant Daniel has internship and externship programs with The Culinary Institute of America and the Institute of Culinary Education. Before candidates do a six-month internship, they do a one-day externship so that we can see their cooking and cutting techniques. We also give them a variety of kitchen tasks and ask them to prepare basic dishes like an omelet or some tourné vegetables or even a dish of their choice. When they spend the day with us, they see how tough the service is and how long the workdays are, so they are not in for any surprises. We don't want a new intern to say, "Oh, my God. What am I doing here?" At least the students know the working environment here before they make a commitment to us.

On the floor, everybody is intense and busy trying to make the service better, so you cannot ask your sous chef, "How do I do that?" Although I wasn't trained this way, we often give a new chef the basic recipe: "First do 300 grams of carrots. Then do this, and next do that."

I think that giving new chefs the recipe can prevent them from being creative and original, which are traits they need at Daniel. We have to be flexible and able to adapt. For example, if the customer asks for something not on the menu, we should be able to execute it without asking any questions. The chef should be able to do what the customer wants, since we have a lot of regulars at Daniel. Some even call in the morning and say, "I would like to have duck à la presse or côte de boeuf." We never say no. The customer is king. Within the limits of what's possible and available, we have to make it happen. We can have 40 to 50 people every night who are repeat customers.

Many new chefs hold a misconception. They believe that after four years of culinary school, they are going to be the sous chef in a restaurant and run the show. It's not like that. They need to start at the bottom and then achieve all the way. Depending on their personality and skill, it can take them a certain number of years. But to be a chef, they really need passion and skills. They won't be a chef or a sous chef in a restaurant just because they have a degree. Becoming a chef is a process, and cooking is an artisanal craft. Young chefs need to observe masters who give them the tools and the incentive to progress. Observation is the most important skill a new chef needs to have.

Tools

It was Laurent Gras who told me about professional Japanese chef knives—he had a wonderful collection.

My first knives were Swiss and German knives, but they were difficult to keep sharp. Plus, after only one or two years, the blades of my knives looked like a roller coaster, so I had to buy new ones. I saw a wave of Japanese chef knives hit France in the 1980s. Global was the most popular brand of knives with French chefs at that time. But when I talked to Japanese chefs about Global knives in France, they just laughed. It was Laurent Gras who told me about professional Japanese chef knives—he had a wonderful collection. I couldn't afford the Japanese knives he used, so I started with a line of Misono. I was really happy with them. I still have them, and they are still perfectly flat and sharp. Now I also have a Masamoto knife, too.

With knives, it's also a matter of the weight. Some of them are, of course, heavier than others, so you need to change your technique a little bit—not radically, but you need to get a feeling for your knife. You have to be at ease and confident enough to close your eyes and do a nice béarnaise without thinking. It takes time. And you have to pay attention to correctly sharpen your Japanese knife using the proper technique. It takes training and practice, but it's not that difficult. I'm happy that I made the switch. Japanese knives—their durability, their precision—they are the number-one chef knife in the world.

A Day in the Life

We have some customers who come every week.

We have one customer who always comes on Thursday morning. He loves cooking, so he spends four hours with us performing mise-en-place. He also observes how we do our specials, so that when he and his wife or a friend come to dinner, he can explain how it's prepared. He's the only customer who comes to the kitchen in the morning and spends some time with us. When we celebrated his 10-year anniversary of coming to Daniel every Thursday, we gave him his own Daniel chef jacket.

❖

SEVEN

NOBU MATSUHISA

Chef/Restaurateur, Operates Nobu Restaurants
and Hotels Worldwide

Nobuyuki Matsuhisa was born in Saitama, Japan. After graduating from high school, he worked at the restaurant Matsuei in Shinjuku, Tokyo for seven years. In 1973 at the age of 24, Nobu was invited by a Peruvian customer to Lima, Peru where they opened Matsuei Sushi. It was difficult for Nobu to find many of the Japanese ingredients he needed so he had to improvise, and, as a result, developed his unique style of cuisine, which incorporated Peruvian ingredients into Japanese dishes.

After leaving the restaurant in Lima and working in a Japanese restaurant in Buenos Aries, Nobu moved to Alaska and opened his own restaurant. Sadly, a few months after the restaurant opened it was destroyed in a fire. In 1979, on the advice of a friend, Nobu moved to Los Angeles to start again, working at Japanese restaurants Mitsuwa and Oshou. In 1987, almost ten years after the Alaskan fire, he opened his own restaurant Matsuhisa in Beverly Hills. In 1993, he partnered with Robert De Niro and opened Nobu New York to critical acclaim. Today, Nobu has 30 restaurants and six hotels located throughout the United States and in 14 countries.

Influences

I fell in love with the atmosphere and smell the moment that I stepped into my first sushi restaurant.

My father owned a lumber yard in Saitama, Japan, and our family members helped out. I was the youngest of four boys. I was almost eight when my father was killed in a traffic accident. I recall that sad day of his wake even now. I felt so lonely after everyone left. My mother, grandmother, and brothers huddled in silence. We had absolutely no idea of what to do, but we survived. From then on, whenever I looked at my father's photo albums, I spent most of the time gazing at a photo of him taken when he was working in Palau, Micronesia. I told myself, "Surely I will go someplace like my father did when I grow up." That's when my dream of working in a foreign country was born.

When I was still a youngster, one of my brothers took me to a particular sushi restaurant that was near where we lived in Saitama. At that time, this restaurant was a popular place where business people and government officials entertained important guests. The moment that I stepped into the restaurant and heard the rattling sound when the sliding door opened, I fell in love with the atmosphere and smell of cooked rice and fish. I knew right then and there that I wanted to become a sushi chef.

When I was in high school I was a bit of a juvenile delinquent, so I had to live under the custody of a guardian, whom I reported to once a week. I had no interest in going into the family business, but instead wanted to travel—like my father—to a faraway place like Palau. However, instead of traveling after high school, I went to work for Matsuei, a sushi restaurant in the Shinjuku Ni-chōme District, a popular area in Tokyo filled with restaurants and bars. I was energized when the master—the executive chef—and other staff at Matsuei welcomed customers with a loud "Irasshaimase!" as they entered the restaurant and sat down. But when my friends with paying jobs stopped by the restaurant, I was embarrassed because I was still under the care of a guardian, so I vowed to take my job and living situation more seriously.

My master told me, "Learn by watching."

During the first three years that I worked at Matsuei, I mostly delivered sushi and washed dishes. I was not allowed to touch the ingredients. Finally, the master gave me the job of going to the Tsukiji fish market early each morning with him to buy fish. After carrying a heavy basket of fish back to the restaurant, my daily routine was to remove their scales and gut them. I did nothing but that for months.

Little by little, I learned other kitchen tasks like stuffing fried bean curd pockets and making maki. After a while, I made the sushi for delivery. The two days a month that I had off, I trained to make rice. I concentrated solely on my work until I was 22 years old. That was the only thing I could do.

On the days that the restaurant was closed, I went to well-respected sushi restaurants and sat at a table—not at the counter—and observed the sushi chefs, staff, and customers while I ate. Once in a while someone would ask me, "Are you a sushi chef?" I'll never forget how happy that question made me. I eventually bought my own Japanese knives and learned to sharpen the blades—one of the most important things every chef needs to learn.

In my third year working at Matsuei, I was given the responsibilities of a sushi chef. My first day behind the sushi bar, I was so nervous that my knees shook. But a customer encouraged me, "Just make sushi!" That's when I learned the importance of standing up and performing to the best of my abilities as a chef when an opportunity presented itself.

Youthful energy is not only 1 + 1 = 2, but it can become 100! That is my mathematics of life.

In 1973 I was 24 years old and still working at Matsuei. I had pretty much forgotten about going abroad when one day a regular customer of Japanese-Peruvian descent suggested that we open a Japanese restaurant in Lima, Peru. His suggestion immediately made me think of the old photograph of my late father in Palau and rekindled my early desire to visit and work in an exotic foreign country. I thought that perhaps Peru was such a place.

I consulted with my master at Matsuei about opening a Japanese restaurant in Peru, but he was not encouraging. Also, my family—especially my mother—was strongly opposed to the idea of me immigrating to a new county. She was worried that because South America was so far away, she would never see me again. While I struggled with whether or not to leave my current restaurant job, I met my future wife. I thought about how happy I was and wondered if I should take on such a new challenge. But my new business partner convinced my master that this was a great opportunity. When my master did me the honor of allowing me to use Matsuei Sushi as the name of our restaurant in Lima, I felt very proud, because this placed his seal of approval on my skill as a sushi chef.

I was also fortunate to have a wife who was my ally. With her support, I was unafraid to pursue my lifelong passion of working abroad because we took on this challenge together. I also received a lot of support from my new business partner. This was my first experience overseas, and although I felt homesick, my wife and partner were steadfast and assuring. After much work, the restaurant in Lima finally opened.

Ingredients

Finding alternative ingredients for my dishes made every day a challenge.

Because Lima, Peru faces the Pacific Ocean, I was able to procure an abundance of fish. I was also able to obtain many local vegetables and fruits but few traditional Japanese ingredients. Also, the local rice was an issue, because after it was cooked, it wasn't sticky like Japanese rice. When a Japanese restaurant becomes known for its rice, the Japanese customers pour in. So I found ways to achieve more Japanese flavors, even without using Japanese ingredients. I tried mixing the local rice with mochi rice. When rice vinegar wasn't available, I bought soy sauce and acetic acid, combined kombu and salt, and then diluted it. I was worried about using acetic acid, so I also tried using wine. Finding alternative ingredients for my dishes made every day a challenge. It was difficult, but I made the effort and achieved many of the Japanese flavors I wanted, and I came up with many ways to use local fish and vegetables.

Cuisine

I have given customers a sense of Japanese traditional aesthetics while broadening their idea of what constitutes Japanese cuisine.

When I was in Peru, it was wonderful to come up with sauces and dishes that made me feel like I was in Japan. One of the best condiments I came up with in Peru was a kind of *gari*, which is a sweet, thinly sliced young ginger that has been marinated in a solution of sugar and vinegar. I made my mixture by marinating Portuguese ginger, called "chium" or "hedychium," first in salt, then in vinegar, and then flavoring it with vinegar, sugar, and salt. In place of fresh Japanese wasabi, I used powdered wasabi, added horseradish, and then local hot pepper. Coming up with mixtures like these offered me the pleasure of making new discoveries. It was wonderful to come up with sauces and dishes that made me feel like I was in Japan.

When a dish comes back to the kitchen because of a customer complaint, it is a difficult moment for any chef.

One day a dish of thinly sliced flounder sashimi was returned to the kitchen with the comment, "This is inedible because it is too fishy." I thought, "What can I do to correct this?" There was a Chinese restaurant in Lima that served excellent food, and I particularly liked the steamed whole fish with hot oil poured over it just before serving. This Chinese dish inspired me, so I tried drizzling my sliced raw flounder with hot olive oil. It tasted great! The customers were pleased that the fishiness of my original dish was gone, and they enjoyed the new dish. That's how I created the "new-style sashimi" drizzled with olive oil.

After working at Matsuei Sushi in Lima for three years, my partner and I couldn't agree on how to run our business, so I decided it was time to move on. In the end, exploring the use of local ingredients to recreate Japanese cuisine in Peru taught me that the ultimate reward was my customers' satisfaction with the meal. Extending this lesson to my other restaurants, I think the reason that my dishes have been so well received in the U.S. and around the world is that I have given customers a sense of Japanese traditional aesthetics while broadening their idea of what constitutes Japanese cuisine.

Training

> *For chefs to develop to a professional level, it is crucial that someone with experience is there for them as a guide and supporter.*

From my first job at Matsuei right up until today, my work as a chef and restaurateur is a culmination of my training and experience. I feel it is my duty to teach what I know to young chefs who want to grow. Mentors are critical. For chefs to develop to a professional level, it is crucial that someone with experience is there for them as a guide and supporter. Travel is also an important part of training, because it allows a chef to learn about other food cultures and to form relationships with chefs from around the world.

Chefs must also learn how to communicate with their coworkers in the kitchen and with suppliers, many of whom speak different languages. For example, when I had the restaurant in Lima, I took Spanish lessons so that I could buy fish and other ingredients every morning at the market and converse with the other workers in the restaurant. Twenty-five years later, Spanish is still useful communicating with many of the staff at the restaurant in L.A.

I impress upon chefs at all levels the need to develop a philosophy that is hospitality-based so that their customers always enjoy themselves. My ultimate goal as a chef is for my customers to say, "Your food tastes wonderful!" And I want my cuisine to be seen as the creation of a committed culinary professional.

I tell culinary students that to become an accomplished chef, they cannot take the easy way out or use shortcuts. Professional results in the kitchen do not come quickly. Being completely immersed in cooking because they want to create delicious dishes can be a lifelong journey, and there will be many exciting discoveries along the way. If you choose to do this kind of work, I want you to smile and be happy by making lots of tasty dishes. This is what motivates me, and what I continue to strive for in my life as a chef.

> *When I think about my career, many hard times flash through my mind.*

After running the restaurant in Lima for three years and working as a sushi chef in Buenos Aries for a year, I found myself up against the wall. I gave up on working as a chef abroad and went back to Japan. I was alone, without a friend. I was ashamed to return to Japan in defeat after making such a big to-do about working abroad. But I decided to pursue my dream one more time. In 1976 at the age of 27, I mustered all my courage and moved to Anchorage, Alaska to open another restaurant. Because of my setback in Peru, I saw this as my last chance, so I wanted to succeed no matter what. After working to build the restaurant for nearly two months straight without a break, I opened it in the fall. Fortunately, the number of customers quickly grew, and I was finally able to take a break—but not for long.

A Day in the Life

> *The night of November 23, 1977 is one I'll never forget.*

It was my first day off after working 50 days straight. I was having a drink at a friend's home in Anchorage and celebrating Thanksgiving when a frantic phone call came from my partner. "Nobu, you must come to the restaurant right now. There's a fire!" At first I was dazed, but in such a small town I could hear the sirens of the fire engines. I raced to the restaurant and got as close as I could. It was dark except for the smoke, cinders, and flames that filled the winter sky. I couldn't feel the cold of the snowy night or the intense heat of the fire as I watched my restaurant go up in flames.

Less than two months after I had opened the restaurant, it was gone. My only thoughts were, "I have debts. This is the end of my life." I felt numb for days. I couldn't eat. I even considered suicide. But with my family at my side and with time on my hands, I thought how best to live each day. I heard the laughter of my children, and soon the process of healing began. I said to myself, "I am alive. I was given this task by God and must carry it out." With a new perspective on this terrible event, another opportunity presented itself. A chef friend called me from Los Angeles and told me to come there.

So in 1979, I borrowed $500 from a JAL pilot friend, bought an airplane ticket, and with only $25 in my pocket, I went to work in a restaurant in Los Angeles. In 1987, I opened Matsuhisa, Beverly Hills and then Nobu New York in 1994. I spent two weeks in the New York restaurant developing the dishes, training the chefs, cooks, and other staff, and explaining my philosophy to them. By the time Nobu London opened in 1997, the colleagues who had trained and grown in New York were able to do their part. From that point on, many more restaurants opened, one right after the other. The best advice I can give to young people is to never give up.

In hindsight, the fire at my restaurant in Alaska was a turning point in my life, and getting through it gave me the impetus to go forward. I learned that I was stronger than I thought. I learned that it is better to take a big risk than to just have an easy life. From that lesson comes my advice to young chefs: Concentrate on your goal of being a chef, and take the chance to live your passion and achieve your dreams.

❖

Photo Credit: Sam Polcer

EIGHT

DAVID MYERS

Chef/Restaurateur, Founder of
David Myers Group

From David Myers' early kitchen experience with Charlie Trotter to his years with French Chef Daniel Boulud, he has been recognized for his culinary talent and artistry. His awards include the Michelin star for his L.A. restaurant, Sona, *Food & Wine*'s Best New Chef (2003), Angeleno's Chef of the Year (2004), and GQ's Men of Style (2008). The James Beard Foundation nominated him for 2004 Rising Star Chef of the Year and Best Chef Pacific (2008) awards.

In 2007, he opened Comme Ça, a classic French brasserie in Los Angeles, and in 2010, he expanded the concept to The Cosmopolitan Hotel in Las Vegas. David Myers opened Pizzeria Ortica in Costa Mesa in 2009. In 2010, he expanded his restaurant group internationally, focusing first on his much-loved Japan. Sola by David Myers is a high-end patisserie located in Mitsukoshi Ginza, Tokyo, and Isetan Shinjuku, Tokyo. David Myers Cafe, a California-inspired restaurant featuring Japanese ingredients, also opened in Mitsukoshi Ginza, Tokyo. In 2013, he opened Hinoki & the Bird in Los Angeles.

Influences

I'll never forget that first experience eating sushi, because it was filled with excitement and a little bit of fear when eating raw fish.

My first real interest in Japan came about in 1997 when I was working at Charlie Trotter's in Chicago. This young Japanese cook came from France to work there as well, and when he walked in, I was very intrigued, because he had just one bag, not five, wore a jean jacket, and immediately started working. The way he worked was fast and smooth, and his cooking style was very simple. I thought, "Wow, maybe this is just the Japanese way. Very simple, very minimal." We quickly became very good friends and started working together. I learned a great deal from him through the way that he cooked and prepped food. He had only one knife, a simple French knife. When I asked why, he said, "I have one knife and it's terrible. But I only need one." So it was that mindset—that *bushido* "way of the warrior" sense—that I have now come to know. That chef was Nori Sugie. We became great friends and still are friends to this day.

That was the start of my interest in Japanese culture and cooking. I'd never even had Japanese food before I met Nori. He took me out for my very first sushi experience in 1997. It was scary, exhilarating and exciting all at once. Oh, I loved it! We drank hot saké, ate sushi, and then, for another first, I had *fugu* skin! My first time eating sushi was definitely crazy, but I loved it. I especially loved the various textures of the food.

Looking back on it, it pales in comparison to sushi I've encountered in Japan since that first experience. I went from having a salad of fugu skin to now regularly eating the *shirako,* or liver of wild fugu, or the hormones of sea cucumber inside a little egg custard called "chawanmushi." My palate has completely evolved over the years. But I'll never forget that first experience eating sushi, because it was filled with excitement and a little bit of fear when eating raw fish.

The Japanese care so deeply, and they have such emotion about their food.

I started buying books on Japanese cooking, and I realized that I wanted to delve deeper into a simpler lifestyle—very much like a monk—where I could focus on one thing and eat and live very simply. For monks it's obviously about religion, but for me it was about cooking. During my time at Charlie Trotter's and at Restaurant Daniel in New York City, I tried to pare down everything in my life.

When I dine in Japan, I'm usually very quiet. Even if I'm talking to someone, I speak in a low voice unless I'm in a yakitori restaurant where it's fun and loud. I love the food. I love the service. I love the culture and the aesthetics. To me, aesthetics are very important in food. You can admire the beauty of the seasons because they are represented in the dishes and the overall meal. The Japanese care so deeply, and they have such emotion about their food.

Career Path

I could have opened a restaurant when I was 22 or 24 instead of 28, when I opened up Sona, but I needed time to mature and develop my leadership skills.

My training has been predominantly French, and it is based on the great techniques of chefs like Charlie Trotter, Gerard Boyer, and

Daniel Boulud. But my training was also influenced by these chefs' interest in Japanese style—its minimalism, the quiet nature of the Japanese people—and in Japanese ingredients. I think French chefs get great inspiration from the Japanese.

Before I was with Les Crayères in France, I went to Lake Pierre because Nori told me that the chef was Japanese and was phenomenal with fish. Nori thought I could learn from him even though he was very tough. And he was very tough.

For one month I stood there every day with this chef. I cleaned his knives and did whatever he needed, as well as my own job. One day he finally started teaching me. We would eat lunch in five minutes while the rest of the guys went outside for an hour and relaxed. We'd go back to the kitchen immediately, and he would make his stocks so that I could learn how he did that. He made me taste everything we cooked, and through working together, we found our groove and improved. It was great. We weren't friends, mind you, but I think he respected me for wanting to learn from him.

I could have opened a restaurant when I was 22 or 24 instead of 28, when I opened up Sona, but I needed time to mature and develop my leadership skills. I'm glad I did what I did, but chefs don't have to take that path. They don't have to work at five great restaurants. What chefs need to do is to go out and see the world—to go out and taste. A chef's palate is the most important thing. Chefs need to see and understand great food in order to realize great food. I don't go out and work at different kitchens anymore. Instead I go out and eat.

Ingredients

If you want to find Japanese ingredients here in the U.S., go directly to Chinese or Japanese markets.

One of the things I'm doing, ingredient-wise, is bringing in more unique ingredients from Japan. We also have California and Japanese ingredients grown here by Japanese farmers using classic farming techniques. We then blend the ingredients together to create a different style of cooking. It's not fusion, but rather a blend of incredible, impeccable California ingredients mixed with Japanese approaches and the development of dishes. We have a close relationship with our purveyors and our growers, which is what I see in Japan. We're out there meeting with the fish guys and the vegetable people every day. When we opened Sona, I was at the fish market every morning for the first three years. I tried to use small farms and food companies that had the best ingredients and products. That was our mission, so we sought out those vendors when we looked for product. My advice is that if you want to find Japanese ingredients here in the U.S., go directly to Chinese or Japanese markets.

When it comes to ingredients and products, you must have to be tireless about asking questions and seeking out something better.

Dive in and learn about all of the unique ingredients that are available. At the market, you can find different seaweeds, kinds of tofu, and many other Asian ingredients or products. Just study them, buy them, and see what works best. That's what I've done. I've tried every salt and rice from my local Japanese market in search of the next great one. The owners always say, "You again?" I'm a pain in the butt, because I ask, "What other kinds of rice do you have?" I've already gone through your 17 varieties, but I always want to try a different one. The key to getting unusual ingredients is an insatiable curiosity. I'm the type of guy who's never satisfied, so I'm always trying to find something better or figure out how to make it better, which is why I'm forever the wanderer when I go to Japan.

Cuisine

I see experimentation as a big part of the process of what I do.

I experiment with ingredients and styles of cooking, but by no means do I call it "fusion." I absorb techniques and find a way to work with them. A lot of chefs today are using circulators, sous-vide cooking and other ways or tools—some old and rediscovered and some new—to prepare their dishes. These are just techniques, and it's a matter of incorporating them into your arsenal of cooking and your style. I'm leading a group that focuses on a natural, holistic style, which is more like what's happening in Japan.

People have asked me if my desire to keep trying harder sometimes conflicts with my focus on simple food. The fact is that they're constantly in conflict with each other, so I don't try to balance the two. I just do it. For example, I cooked dinner on a Saturday night for some very, very serious eaters, some who were chefs. I said to them, "Gentlemen, I've been traveling a lot in Japan, so what I'm going to cook for you tonight is based on my travels. I think I'm going to cook a temple-inspired meal. Like a little bundle of energy—very quiet, very focused. It will be an extremely intense use of the ingredients. I'm just going to let the ingredients explode."

And that's exactly what I did. The food had Japanese ingredients and had a Japanese feeling, but it wasn't Japanese in style—it was my style. There was no preset menu, and I'd never done the dishes before. But that's the way I cook. It's spontaneous, like I'm riding on some sort of wave. That's when life is good, because everything else goes away and all I see and feel is the dish. If I like the dish, I'll probably put it on our tasting menu for the week or serve it à la carte. But I wouldn't cook it again—I let the team cook it. That's what we do.

From day one, cooking for me has been about creativity. It is also about working with great people and giving them the opportunity to excel and showcase their skills. We're willing to take risks in cooking and try stuff that other chefs probably wouldn't. When you're young, you're trying to find something—searching. I saw this really cool sign at a boutique store in Tokyo called Batsu. The sign said, "We are young and we can't help but to create." It was very, very inspiring, very cool, and so radical and edgy. I appreciated that.

Nori Sugie's dish had only four ingredients, but it was perfection.

While I was working at Charlie Trotter's in Chicago, I invited a bunch of cooks over to the house for dinner. My friend and coworker Nori Sugie and I were cooking. He was going to make a course, and I was going to make a course. So we went to Whole Foods in Chicago to shop. When we got to Whole Foods, we split up, and when we met up at the register, my cart was full. Nori had maybe four ingredients. I said, "Nori-san, what are you cooking?" He looked at my cart and said, "Are you opening a restaurant?" So he bought his four ingredients, and I bought 50 or so ingredients that I needed. I was going to make risotto and something else.

I cooked risotto and another dish. Nori cooked soup and a duck for us. Nori Sugie's dish had only four ingredients, but it was perfection. It was the greatest duck course I've ever had. He created this phenomenal course with duck, shallots, eggplant and wasabi—that was it. Everything was cooked in the same pan. It was all very simple, a very minimalist style of cooking and plating.

I learned a lot that day and realized that there I was with 50 ingredients, doing this really in-depth, lavish, crazy risotto, which was good but complicated. Nori created the best dish of the night with just four ingredients. That night I saw the difference between the western and the eastern mindset.

Training

Treat people as if they can operate on the highest level, and they'll rise to your expectations.

There are natural leaders, and there are others who learn to be good managers. In either case, to successfully run a restaurant, you have to put the team first, and you have to do what's best for the business as well. You have to be very humble but also very tough. Treat people as if they can operate on the highest level, and they'll then rise to your expectations. You can't change your standards no matter what, and you can never let up, not even for a second.

When you're the leader, you're not a friend, but you can be a teammate or a partner. You can develop friendships through this process, but you're still leading the team, hopefully to success. To go in and yell and to lead by fear is easy, but weak. The test of being a good leader is to inspire your team to follow you into hell. And if they will, not blindly, but because they truly believe in you, then you've done your job. And if they waver at the slightest bit of difficulty or if they stab you in the back, then you haven't done your job.

We can teach people how to cook, but we can't teach them how to have the inner drive to be the best.

My number one goal at Sona was to deliver the ultimate dining experience, and my second goal was to create great, great chefs and amazing people. Anyone who worked at Sona went through an involved training process with us. When someone came on board, we got really, really serious. First we worked like crazy on the teambuilding, and then we moved on to developing their technique.

From there, we broke them down and then helped them build their way back up. We sent them to different farmers' markets to pick the vegetables and then had them write reports on certain ingredients.

These folks are then thrown into crazy, unique learning situations, where they meet and study with very different people and then contribute to the overall discussion. At Sona, we were hands-on. We took a very holistic, very in-depth approach to training, instead of just showing new chefs how to do a job and then having them go home at the end of the day. If we were going to teach a chef about fish, we'd throw them into a tank with the sharks. I'm serious about that—the shark were in a cage, of course.

We certainly had cultural diversity at Sona. I had Japanese, Chinese, Korean, Swiss, French, German, Indian, and, of course, Spanish employees. It was great to be able to work with all of these people. And at Sona, I also had a phenomenal chef and a great pastry chef. But the whole team made the restaurant what it was.

> *I think the key to my business success is that I hired good people, phenomenal leaders, and learned from the best mentors.*

My investors are focused on the business side—they're levelheaded and I'm not. I'm very emotional and caught up in my business. They're much more likely to take a stand-back-and-see approach. For example, they want me to use my energy where it really works—where it makes them the most amount of money—but they also encourage me to put my energy into what I love the most. That's the money-side of the business, and I don't really care so much about that. Well, I do care about it, simply because I need to pay my staff, and I want to be paid, too. So I've learned to focus on what I'm good at doing, focus on what makes money, focus on what people love, and also take risks and be creative.

My business partners and advisors give me the support and the ability to take those risks, but they ask, "Should we really do this?" or "Should we really go to Japan?" I say to them "Go do it; get global, go to Hong Kong, or wherever." I think the key to my business success is that I have hired good people, phenomenal leaders, and learned from the best mentors. I'm open to their advice, and they know that I'm not quite sure about many aspects of running a business.

Tools

I realized I had terrible knives, and I desperately wanted to buy Japanese knives.

The chef I worked with at Lake Pierre had Japanese knives, and so did a chef I knew from Osaka. Their knives were perfectly sharp, and they knew how to sharpen them. All I had was a crappy western-style knife. After I was done working in the kitchen for the chef, I'd go home and practice sharpening for hours—and I mean hours—so that my blade got to looking like a half-moon. One night I wore my skin off on the whetstone. The next day I had to peel four cases of garlic and the garlic oils got into my raw fingers—I was in tears. But I went home and practiced my knife sharpening even more. I grabbed the Band-Aids and just kept trying. I realized I had terrible knives, and I desperately wanted to buy Japanese knives. I tried to find them in Paris, but to no avail. In the end, the chef at Lake Pierre ordered two knives and a sharpening stone for me from Japan.

Once I got to New York City, I bought a chef knife for $500, which was an incredible amount of money for me at the time. I was about 23 years old, but I needed the Japanese knives. I loved them, so I bought them. But I had a really hard time sharpening them because of the angle of the one edge, particularly the *honesuki* and the poultry-butchering knife, called a "garasuki." I didn't want to screw up my knives, so I used them and they got dull. I tried to sharpen them, but they still weren't right, and I got so frustrated. I've since learned how to sharpen them.

Today, Japanese knives are the only knives I use, and they are the only knives that the other chefs in my kitchens use. This is not by my choice—it's just what they prefer—and it makes all the difference in the world. And from an aesthetic point of view, I love the look and feel of these knives. I love Japanese knives; they are all I use now.

A Day in the Life

"Do I stay home every night and cry or go out and celebrate?"

I want diners to look back and say they had a great time eating in my restaurant, that they felt inspiration—even aspiration—and that they were taken care of. I want them to say how great it was because my restaurant is a special occasion kind of a restaurant. For example, we had a guest one evening who told me that she had advanced breast cancer. She told me that she asked herself, "Do I stay home every night and cry or go out and celebrate?" She came to Sona that night for dinner instead of staying home and crying. That touched me deeply. Some months later, she came back to the restaurant and told me that her cancer was in remission and she came back to Sona to celebrate. She was stronger than ever. When we've touched someone like her, it makes it all worthwhile.

❖

NINE

NILS NORÉN

Vice President of Restaurant Operations
for the Marcus Samuelsson Group
Past Executive Chef, Aquavit, New York City

Nils Norén was born in Stockholm, Sweden. After attending culinary school, Nils worked in several of Stockholm's top restaurants. He was Executive Chef at Restaurant Riche, Chef de Cuisine at Restaurant KB, and served as the coordinator of cooking classes at Restaurant Akademin.

In 1998, Nils Norén was hired as Chef de Cuisine at Restaurant Aquavit in New York City. He worked closely with Chef Marcus Samuelsson before being promoted to Aquavit's Executive Chef in 2003. Nils Norén left Aquavit in 2006 to become the Vice President of Culinary Arts for The French Culinary Institute's culinary, pastry, bread, and Italian food departments. In 2011, he left the FCI to become the Vice President of Restaurant Operations for the Marcus Samuelsson Group.

Influences

At 19, I was playing percussion in a reggae band when I woke up one morning and thought, "I've got to do something. I want to cook."

When I was seven or eight years old, a school friend and I made a cookie recipe. I was so fascinated that I could take flour—something that doesn't taste very good by itself—add sugar and a couple of eggs, mix it, roll it, cut it, bake it, and out comes something delicious. Then, when I was 12 or 13, my dad took me to London, where we went to jazz clubs and his favorite Italian restaurant to eat spaghetti carbonara. This was the best thing I had ever tasted! When we came back to Sweden, I looked in every cookbook I could find for recipes for spaghetti carbonara so I could replicate them, find the one I liked best, and then perfect it.

At 19, I was playing percussion in a reggae band when I woke up one morning and thought, "I've got to do something. I want to cook." I went to an unemployment office that same day, and two days later I was auditing a cooking class. A week later I started cooking school. That was how it started, and I've never looked back. I think that from that time on, I've never worked less than 12 hours a day in the kitchen. I stayed at the school as much as I could, and I was there as early as possible. When I had an internship, I worked double shifts every single day because I felt I had to do this. Cooking became a passion right away, but to this day, I have no idea why I woke up that morning and decided I really wanted to be a cook.

Career Path

I got my first restaurant job after I graduated from culinary school at the age of 20 and went to work for one of the few one-star Michelin restaurants in Sweden. I started working in pastry, but they soon promoted me to sous chef. Less than a year later, I started cooking professionally; I was sous chef for a one-star restaurant! That was really scary, but I had worked hard, and it paid off. For the next eight years, I worked at a lot of different restaurants in Sweden. The first restaurant was French, and then I cooked in all kinds of places, from Asian to classic Swedish. I was executive chef for the first restaurant to receive the star from Michelin for cooking Swedish food.

There are a lot of similarities between Japanese food and Swedish food. I think that is part of why I find it so appealing.

I first had Japanese food with a good friend and coworker who had worked in the first Swedish restaurant to serve sushi. On our days off, we went to his house and made sushi. It wasn't perfect and probably not the best, but we'd make these huge platters of sushi, maki, sashimi, miso soup—the whole thing. I loved it! I'm sure someone from Japan would say that it was horrible, but for me, not knowing the standard, I thought it was great. It certainly left me longing to know more about Japanese food. So I bought my first Japanese cookbook, and soon after that, I was hooked!

There are a lot of similarities between Japanese food and Swedish food. I think that is part of why I find it so appealing. In Sweden, we have so much herring, gravlax, and other types of cured or raw fish. The textures and flavors are familiar to us. In terms of flavor, Japanese food has a little bit of sweetness to it, and Swedish food does, too. Also, the taste of Japanese food, like Swedish food, is very clean. In Sweden, there were a couple of stores near us where we could buy

Japanese ingredients, and I think I was in that store at least three times a week. I was always trying to persuade those stores to get more and better-quality ingredients.

> Marcus said, "Nils, I need a sous chef. I don't want anyone else. I want you."

When I visited New York for the first time, I went with a friend of mine to Aquavit because we wanted to see what it was all about. At that time Marcus Samuelsson was working there as a cook, and over the next two weeks I got to know him before I went back to Sweden. When Aquavit's executive chef unexpectedly died, the owners asked Marcus if he wanted to be executive chef. That's when he called me and said, "Nils, I need a sous chef. I don't want anyone else—I want you." Aquavit was a one-star restaurant when I came to work there in June 1995. In September 1995, we got our three-star review from Ruth Reichl, the food critic for *The New York Times*, so we tripled the number of stars in no time.

Cuisine

When I worked at Aquavit, we actually served Swedish cuisine in two ways. The cafe was more casual but a lot more traditional. For fine dining, we needed to adapt the menu, because even though we could find a few Swedish ingredients, we couldn't find everything. Even if I wanted to be super-traditional, I couldn't.

> When I create a dish, I get a shape in my head. I start to work from the shape and then think about the flavors.

Because there are similarities between Japanese and Swedish food, we used the ingredients, ideas, and techniques from both, and I think there's room for both. If it's good food, it's good food. If it's well executed, well thought out, all the textures are good, and if it tastes good, then it's a good dish. Sometimes when I create a dish, I get a shape in my head. I start to work from the shape and then think about the flavors. It might sound odd, but I work a lot with shapes. My food is highly designed for several reasons. Because I like shapes, I always work that way, and I also think about how the food should be eaten. Flavor is the most important part of the dish, but it has to make sense. You need to arrange everything the way that it's meant to be eaten. So that's how I work out a new dish.

For example, I had an interesting cooking project at American architect Philip Johnson's Glass House in New Canaan, Connecticut. The house was designed in the 1940s and is now a museum, but when Philip Johnson was alive, he had the longest-running salon in America, with the greatest minds in architecture, art, and design talking about important issues and new ideas. In 2008, the museum decided to bring back the salon with a moderator and ten guests to talk about various topics, and they asked me to cook the food. One of the topics at the salon was "simplicity."

I thought about simplicity in food and asked myself, "What's the simplest shape you can make?" It's a circle! So I based the whole menu and every dish around a circle. For example, I made a tomato salad based on circles. There was a slice of tomato sitting on a round crouton, which sat on top of a small circle of goat cheese, next to pureed spinach and basil. I repeated this on the plate in one row of circles. Setting limitations for myself—like saying that every single element of this dish is going to be round—made this project more interesting. It forced me to think differently than I normally do.

I prepared another meal where I created the dishes around colors. Every single dish had one color—white, yellow, red, or green. If I say every component in a dish has to be yellow, then I can't think about it in a normal way. I have to think in a different way, which means that I end up creating some interesting dishes. But I still keep in mind that food should be eaten and enjoyed, and it should not be complicated.

> *Whether you pay $3 for a sandwich or $200 for the chef's tasting menu, it doesn't matter. It's the whole experience, from the front of the house to the back of the house, that's important.*

Another important way the Japanese mindset has influenced my cuisine is the relationship between the prepared dish and the whole dining experience. Everything sets a tone, and all of the elements of dining are important and connected as one—including walking up the stairs to the restaurant, opening the door, being greeted by the hostess, and being seated. The tableware, the flowers on the table, and the plated food are all part of the experience, too. A successful chef must focus not only on what goes on in the kitchen, but also in the front of the house, because at the end of the meal, what the guest leaves with is part of the experience. If even one thing doesn't live up to the guest's expectations, then the meal is not going to be as good as it could or should have been.

I think many chefs are not trained to see the dining experience as a whole and don't understand the importance of working with the front of the house. If the front of the house doesn't deliver the food the way you want it, then the service won't be as good as you want it to be either—and you want it to be good, because you want to perform at the highest level, whether you're cooking simple or complicated food.

For example, even when I serve a cheese sandwich, I want to be sure I serve the best cheese sandwich in the best way possible. If I serve it over the counter with a paper napkin, I want to make sure the paper napkin is the right size for the sandwich and that it's handed to you so you'll have a good eating experience. It doesn't matter whether you pay $3 for a sandwich or $200 for the chef's tasting menu. It's the whole experience, from the front of the house to the back of the house, that's important.

Traditionally, the relationship between the front of the house and the back of the house has always been difficult, because it's often an "us-against-them" mentality. A lot of the difficulty, especially here in New York, occurs because the front of the house makes more money. They get the tips—the back of the house doesn't. On the other hand, many cooks come into the business because food is their passion, whereas a lot of the waiters and waitresses are just there to make some money until they can get a music gig or an acting job. They may not care as much about the product.

There are ways around this problem, and that's where management comes in. As the chef, if you start at the top and make it clear how you want things to work by setting standards and expectations, then it's going to trickle down through the organization. If you're a chef who is serious about having a successful restaurant, then you must make sure that the front of the house and the back of the house work together. There's no other way.

Ingredients

I really like Japanese apple vinegar. It's so bright and flavorful. It's fantastic!

There are a lot of good, high-quality Japanese ingredients used in American restaurants these days, and many chefs take them for granted. For example, if I say to a chef, "Use mirin or miso or soy in the dish," they will most likely respond, "Oh, okay," and not give it a second thought, because many of these Japanese ingredients are part of the restaurant's pantry. The chefs will use them in their dishes, but the dishes have nothing to do with authentic Japanese food.

When a non-Japanese chef uses a Japanese ingredient, it triggers other chefs to try it, too. At first, only a few chefs may use a particular ingredient, and then many other chefs start using it, too. But it all starts with one or two chefs. I think that most professional chefs really respect the tradition and quality of Japanese ingredients. The quality of ingredients means a lot to me, and I think that's something that every chef can appreciate.

There's a good reason why Japanese-inspired food is so popular. The ingredients are simply delicious! I love kombu, miso, and mirin, but one of my favorite ingredients from Japan is apple vinegar. It's so bright and flavorful. It's fantastic! Let's say I want to make a dish with fluke. What can I find that'll add a little bit of sweetness to brighten it up? I really want to use this Japanese vinegar, so I'll try it and make adjustments to make it work. *Katsuobushi* is great, too. It's dried *bonito*, or tuna, fish flakes used to make dashi stock. That's what I start with. Then there's the Japanese fish sauce, *ishiri*. When you smell it and eat it, it's like opening a can of Spam. It has the smell of canned meat and is definitely umami. I've used it in a few dishes. If you find a Japanese ingredient you like and it's a good product, you'll be able to find a way to work it into your food, one way or the other.

> *The only reason I use new techniques and different ingredients is so that I can make better products for my guests.*

Nearly every style of cooking in every single country has been influenced by ingredients from other places and cuisines. In Swedish food we use a lot of spices, such as cinnamon, cardamom, and ginger, because we were one of the first countries in the world to start trading with the Far East and Asia. Someone who doesn't know that might say that we're engaged in "fusion cooking," but we've been using these spices for hundreds of years.

I don't like the label "fusion cooking" because it implies something negative, but the reality is that most chefs today are influenced by other cuisines. It's the same as when people say "molecular gastronomy." It sounds disgusting, but it doesn't really describe what it is. I think labels like these tend to give a negative impression of chefs that they don't deserve. The only reason I use new techniques and different ingredients is so that I can make better products for my guests, and I believe that should be every chef's goal.

Training

You can make the best onion soup, but if your station is a mess, it doesn't really matter. You will not succeed.

I think one of the most important skills that a chef needs is organizing a station. If you cannot be organized, both physically and time wise, it's not going to work. When I was the Vice President of Culinary and Pastry Arts at The French Culinary Institute, we put a lot of emphasis on organization, teamwork, and time management. The average age of the students there was about 26. Some came in with experience, and some had none. The students didn't expect that they needed to know very much about these three things, but in time they learned that each one is an important part of cooking.

Students think that creativity is the most important part of being a chef, but it's actually not. They will eventually have a chance to be creative, but they won't get that opportunity right away. Good chefs need the right mindset. They need to be curious, look at everything, and taste and read as much as possible.

One thing I always tell new chefs is, "By deciding that you want to make culinary arts your career, you will never taste food the same way, ever again." This is good in one way, and not so good in other ways. For example, before entering a cooking school program, if you're at a restaurant, you can say that a meal was good or bad and just walk away. But if you are a chef, you can't do that anymore. Instead, you need to ask questions. If the meal was good, why was it good? What was the flavor? Was the balance good? Or if it wasn't good, what was it that fell short, and how could it be done better? You have to think critically, because you'll learn from that as well.

During my time at the FCI, we had several famous guest Japanese chefs demonstrate various authentic Japanese cooking techniques. To prepare for these special events, the students read ahead of time about the specific Japanese ingredients, products, and cooking techniques to be used in the demonstrations. The more background they had, the more they learned from the demonstrations. Plus, they had a greater appreciation for the chefs' skills and for Japanese cuisine.

I also made it clear to the students that when they started out in this profession, they were not going to be chefs when they left, but they would have the tools to become great chefs. The FCI emphasized classic learning because chefs must learn the basics, but the school also took the position that chef training needed to be progressive and include newer cooking techniques that may not be standards of the industry, at least not yet.

One of the more important resources in any kitchen is the person you work next to.

When I was a chef at Aquavit, I wanted anyone who interviewed for a job to have basic skills, absolutely, but after that, attitude was most important. I usually interviewed people twice. If I got a good feeling from the person and I thought he or she had the right attitude, then I could teach him or her exactly what to do and how to do it. I don't think you can train adults to have the right attitude—they either have it or they don't. I always told new chefs, "One of the more important resources in any kitchen is the person you work next to. In my kitchen, there are people from around the world—Japan, Peru, Brazil. They have grown up with different foods and know different things about foods. That's why you should talk. Learn from each other. I've learned so much from all of them."

The trend toward modern Japanese cuisine and western-style, Japanese-inspired menus provides opportunities for chefs who know techniques for preparing raw and cooked fish and using soy, miso, mirin, and other Japanese ingredients.

Ten or 15 years ago, Japanese restaurants could get kitchen staff from Japan. Today it's more difficult and expensive. As the trend toward Japanese-related cuisine continues, many chefs and restaurateurs will find it easier, faster, and less expensive to hire domestically trained chefs with Japanese cooking skills who speak English rather than bring traditionally trained Japanese chefs from Japan with limited English-language skills.

Another trend directly relates to the popularity of Japanese cuisine and the Japanese mindset regarding ingredients. Today, we care much more about our ingredients than we did even 10 years ago. Many customers are willing to pay extra for the highest quality ingredients. As chefs and consumers, we care more about what's in our food products. For the longest time, especially in this country, the goal was to make food that was cheaper and lasted longer. That was the most important goal. If the taste wasn't so good, it didn't matter that much. We had lost the connection between where food is grown and how it ends up in its final form. Now, we have reversed that trend. We're going back to caring about where and how ingredients are grown, and we want the end result to taste good. I think, to some degree, we have the trend in Japanese cuisine to thank for that.

A Day in the Life

Chefs must deal with unexpected things quickly and efficiently.

When I was starting out as a chef, I didn't sleep at night. I'd wake up because I forgot to order this or that or I didn't put something on my list. I can't tell you how many sleepless nights I had. But those sleepless nights also helped me to be organized and to write everything down. Eventually, something disastrous is going to happen in the kitchen, whether it's the grease tipping over just before service or something else. If something happens, you can't just say, "Oh, this is terrible, what do I do?" Yes, it's terrible, but it's not going to go away, so you've got to act on it right away. You can't say, "If things aren't exactly right, I can't work!"

At the old Aquavit location, we had a small fire that damaged our exhaust fan. So the next day at lunch, the kitchen was really hot because the exhaust fan wasn't working. I was standing next to the window expediting, and the dining room was full. Then, smack in the middle of service—it couldn't have been busier—the kitchen was at least 100 degrees. Of course, hot air rises, so the sprinkler went off. Cold, dirty water was spraying all over the lines, all over the already plated dishes, all over everything in the kitchen, and all of the food was swimming in dirty water!

What did we do? We had the kitchen upstairs, but that wasn't going to be enough. So we got all the cassette burners going and moved everything we could upstairs. We actually managed to get the food out! By dinner service, we had the sprinkler fixed, but the exhaust fan was still down. We had to take turns standing on an upside-down milk crate with a bucket of ice water held over our heads to cool down the sensor so the sprinkler wouldn't go off again. All of these unexpected things happened, but we still got every dish out for lunch, we made it through dinner service, and the next day, everything was fixed and back to normal.

Another time that I had to make the best of a bad situation was in 2000, when I did an event in Mozambique. I was cooking for the King and Queen of Sweden and about 2,000 guests. The hotel was beautiful, built in the 1920s and located right next to the ocean. But when my team and I walked into the kitchen, there was the dirtiest kitchen I'd ever seen! We had to cook for the King and Queen of Sweden and all of those people, so the food had to be good! There was no way I could say, "I can't do it."

I asked the people at the hotel, "Okay, give us another room." So we took another room and cleaned the whole place up and tried to do what we could. But we had another unexpected, even bigger problem. We had all sorts of food products sent in from Sweden for the dinner, but unfortunately, someone forgot to put the perishables in the fridge, so we had to throw a lot of it out and find substitutes.

Four of us worked four days straight without any rest. So what would have been the alternative? I couldn't just run out and go back to Sweden. They expected to have food. Could it have been better? Yes, but at least we had a place that was reasonably clean where we could cook. We had someone drive into South Africa, pick up some salmon, and bring it back so we could make gravlax and other Swedish dishes for all of the guests. With a lot of extra work and juggling, the dinner was a success! I learned a tremendous amount from these experiences, and now I never worry. That doesn't mean that I'm not quality driven. I absolutely am. But if something happens, I say, "Ok, don't worry, we'll figure it out. There's always a way around it."

❖

TEN

BEN POLLINGER

Executive Chef Ben Pollinger leads New York City's Oceana with a distinctive style of cooking that artfully blends the finest seafood with the best ingredients from a global pantry. His creations express a dedication to seasonal products and classic technique with a vast array of flavor profiles. In addition to maintaining Oceana's Michelin star–rating since 2006, Ben Pollinger has received many outstanding reviews including a three-star review from former *New York Times* critic Frank Bruni. He was named a rising star chef by *Esquire* and he has appeared on programs such as *Today*, *The Martha Stewart Show*, and *ABC News'* "Chef's Table." He has also been featured in *Food & Wine, Bon Appétit,* and other food publications.

Ben Pollinger donates his time to various charitable organizations including City Harvest, The New York Harbor School, Autism Speaks, and the James Beard Foundation. He also serves on the Program Advisory Committee at the International Culinary Center and is an advisor to the Alaska Seafood Marketing Institute.

Influences

Every chef I worked for influenced me to different degrees. Some places were good for what they offered, and some were not. But I learned something wherever I was.

I cooked for five years before I went to cooking school. And not all of the places I worked were excellent restaurants like Oceana. I had been exposed to so many kitchens and restaurants by the time I got to cooking school that I didn't really need to worry so much about the basics. However, I was a clean slate going into it. Because I already had a decent set of basic skills, I was able to focus more on the bigger picture. I wasn't struggling with the basic knife work, so I had more time to focus on technique. And I did.

Chef Christian Delouvrier was a huge influence on me, particularly in terms of my precision. When I began cooking with him, my cooking skills were more mechanical. I could move around in the kitchen quickly. I could multi-task and focus, but I had never been called upon to do precise work. At Christian's restaurant, Les Célébrités, the goal was not about volume, and the level of precision was excruciating.

We're talking about fine, fine knife work. Vegetables had to be cut and prepared in a certain precise way. Meats had to be cooked and prepared to his exact specifications. Sauces were made to a particular consistency and taste. The dishes were small but had a high degree of sophistication and were always consistent.

There's an old term in the kitchen called "production cuts," which means that the cuts can be a little sloppy. Christian was the first guy to take that concept away from me.

The challenge was to balance precision with speed. Les Célébrités was a busy restaurant with relatively few cooks and grueling shift work, with long hours in a hot kitchen. I had to learn how to push myself and stay mentally focused while cooking.

I worked with Christian twice in my career. First, I worked at the restaurant Les Célébrités, where he cooked contemporary modern French food, and then at Lespinasse, which returned to a more classical-style restaurant with a rustic touch.

I have seen two different styles in his evolution as a chef, but in both it was all about precision. From him I learned about rustic French county cooking, reflective of the southwest of France from where he came, as well as modern French cooking.

I also had the good fortune to work at La Côte Basque under Jean-Jacques Rachou. La Côte Basque was a classical French restaurant, one of the last of what has become a dying breed. There are only a handful of restaurants in that style still open, so I feel fortunate that I had that experience to work there when it was in its prime and had a major influence on the dining industry.

My next big influence was Alain Ducasse, at his restaurant Louis XV in Monte Carlo. At Louis XV, I learned a tremendous amount about the cuisine of the Riviera, southern France, and northern Italy. That region of the Mediterranean has greatly shaped my cooking. It is in tune with Japanese concepts of purity of flavor and simplicity. The focus is more on ingredients and less on sauces that weigh food down or mask the flavor. There is less reliance on dairy products and a greater focus on vegetables and seafood—a healthier balance of foods. The preparations and approach are philosophically similar to Japanese cuisine.

Next I went to work with Floyd Cardoz at Tabla, a restaurant in New York City owned by the Union Square Hospitality Group that prepared New Indian Cuisine. From Floyd, I learned about influences that were based on a particular region. When I cooked with him, there was a need to learn the origins of ingredients. I remember one humbling experience. There was a spice that I had found in a spice market, and it wasn't necessarily Indian. Floyd asked, "What can you tell me about this spice?" I said, "Not really much, other than how it tastes." Then he pushed me to know more. "But what can you tell me about it? Where did it come from?" Now I don't use any ingredient without understanding its context, because that knowledge helps me make a better dish.

At Tabla, I was able to experiment with my own food, even though I was working under Floyd's umbrella. I accepted that, much like an artist's apprentice in a master's studio, I was working in Floyd's style, but I still had the opportunity to come up with my own dishes. I wanted customers to sit there at the end of their meal, and if they happened to have one of my dishes say, "Floyd is a great chef and that was a great dish!" That was the goal, and accepting that meant I was on the right track as a chef.

Career

Leadership and management are two different things.

I got an awakening at Union Square Cafe in terms of understanding how the goals of the restaurant and the kitchen related to my personal goals and the goals of the executive chef. I learned the value of relationships between people, how to manage others, how to delegate and hold people accountable, and also how to instill trust in me. At that time, the Executive Chef, Michael Romano, was the driving culinary force. From him, I learned that leadership and management, which are often used interchangeably, are really two different things. Management is more task-oriented. Leading people is another story. One of the important things I learned about leadership is the need to inspire other people. Can you inspire them to want to do the job? Can you inspire them to create their own level of expectations?

In my case, Michael inspired me by giving me an opportunity to manage and lead his kitchen. This was a great responsibility. This was my first executive position, and I made plenty of mistakes, but Michael showed me an extraordinary level of patience, understanding, kindness, compassion, and tolerance. He had been through many of the same things that I went through, so he was able to say, "Okay, but now we want to do something a little different. Here is how we grow." He taught me through example.

I learned about hospitality as it related to taking care of those who worked for me. I learned to inspire others to do their jobs to a level of excellence while balancing support, respect, and accountability. Michael treated everyone who worked for him with a level of personal respect that most other chefs did not and still don't extend. It took me time to grasp this concept, including the ability to work with the restaurant owners and management and in an executive capacity with the supporting team.

I also learned a lot about food from Michael. He taught me a lot about technical aspects that I use to this day. I don't think I ever really expressed to him the degree to which he influenced me. He left a lasting impression. I'm a better cook, for sure, but I know that I am also a better leader. Michael Romano is a very inspiring and passionate chef.

Breaking out as a chef in a high caliber restaurant was a huge challenge.

I worked for 16 years in a lot of kitchens, so it was a long time before I became an executive chef. I had many job offers as a chef in small, casual restaurants. They were good businesses, but that wasn't what I wanted to do. I wanted to break out and become a chef in a restaurant of a particular caliber. My years of practice, training, and teaching allowed me to do that at Oceana.

Taking over Oceana as Executive Chef was the greatest professional challenge I've ever had. For several months, I had to write out everything for the cooks and staff. I had some people who were with me, but no one knew me or knew my work. It took time to build up that knowledge, so I had to be there every morning. It took time to teach the staff how I wanted things checked in, how to make the preparations and make the sauces, how to do the ordering. I had to be there at night to tell them how to close down the place and clean the kitchen. I had to be there in the middle of the process, too.

Oceana always had a global, seasonally driven menu with Asian and Mediterranean influences. So it was very natural for me to come in and do that style of cooking, although I made my own menu. I was comfortable creating complex dishes at Oceana. I felt as a chef that I had reached my goal of managing and cooking at a first-class restaurant.

Another challenge came two-and-a-half years later, when we moved the restaurant's location and changed its concept. Oceana went from being a very formal restaurant with 100 seats to an upscale, yet approachable, restaurant and bar that was double in size.

In the old Oceana, the kitchen was small, and I was in the center so that I could see everything going out. Dishes were brought to me before they went to guests. I had that kind of control.

In the new, larger environment, I physically couldn't be everywhere at the same time. As a result, I had to have more trust in my team. It required more skill in developing a team in the kitchen. I needed to spend more time and attention training and therefore had to trust the executive sous chefs, the sous chefs, and the cooks. The transition from closing the old Oceana to opening the new Oceana in midtown Manhattan took only three weeks.

Our lunch clientele are business people, and on the weekends people from the suburbs come for special occasions. As a chef I have my own style, and there is a place on the menu for my creative influence, but there also needs to be a place on the menu that gives the guests what they want or expect. I realize, fully accept, and am at peace with that fact. Not everyone comes to the restaurant viewing the chef or the food as the focal point. It might be the location, the nice decor, pleasant ambiance, or the great service that draws them here. It could be any number of things that the restaurant is as a whole, but it's not only about the chef and the food.

Ingredients

One of the hallmarks of Japanese cuisine is its focus on the simplicity of the main ingredient—directing it, seasoning it, or garnishing it with one other element that has complexity.

I see the evolution of Japanese restaurants as a reflection of the way people can eat every day. At a time when upscale western restaurants have become focused on the indulgent aspect of eating, Japanese cuisine has given western chefs a reality check. Asian influence, in terms of food and cooking, is derived from the true flavors of ingredients and translates these into modern restaurant cuisine. This philosophy from Japanese cuisine affects my cooking and the way that I express my cuisine on the plate.

The prominence of Japanese ingredients is growing, because they are more available and are frequently highlighted on food shows, in newspapers, and in food magazines. For example, one of my favorite

Japanese ingredients, the herb *shiso*, no longer simply comes in a plastic package with 10 leaves tied together with a rubber band. That was a good product, but now there are local farmers in the New York metropolitan area who grow two, three, and four different varieties of shiso.

> *Twenty years ago, when I used Japanese ingredients, I had soy sauce, wasabi, rice, and raw fish. That was about it.*

Now the number of other Japanese ingredients has increased many times over. In 2010, when I cooked a special dinner at Oceana for The Gohan Society, I used many ingredients and products from the Ishikawa Prefecture in Japan. The ingredients were soy products, wheat products, rice products, and barley products. I used roasted barley in the husk to make barley tea and added *amazake*—a sweet rice saké with no alcohol—to some other ingredients when I poached fish.

We were not trying to arbitrarily combine ingredients that didn't necessarily make sense together as a dish. Rather, we were focusing on them in different combinations. The miso became two different sauces on a plate. One miso sauce on the plate was in a little bit larger quantity, more like a traditional western sauce. The other miso sauce was an accent. It had a saltier taste and a stronger flavor.

Cuisine

> *I want to avoid palate fatigue.*

Some dishes are great, but after three, four, or five bites, they need different elements to wake up the palate and keep it stimulated. For example, if one part of the dish focuses on an acidic ingredient, then I might include a sweet ingredient to lower the acidity. Or if I have a mellow sauce that loses its novelty after a couple of bites, I include an intense ingredient. This sharpens the palate again and refreshes it. The challenge is not to replicate the flavors. It's okay to include the same ingredient prepared in a different way or in a different course.

When coming up with a new dish, I might explain to my sous chefs what I am looking for, what I am thinking about, and tell them, "I'll work on this part—you try the other part." Sometimes I delegate different parts of the dish and then bring it all together to see the results. That's one way I experiment. Sometimes I might do it all by myself. Once I get some results, I experiment some more. Then I will cook the dish with my sous chefs present. I'll teach them, tell them what I am doing, and talk out the process and the key points. Sometimes I include the cooks at that point, but usually it's just the kitchen management. Then I'll have one of my sous chefs or the executive sous chef cook the dish so I can tell him or her when they've got it right. Next, we teach the cooks how to do it. At all points, we all are ensuring and guaranteeing the caliber and quality of the food going out.

Training

I want to hire cooks who aspire to be chefs.

When I interview a cook, I'm looking for someone who wants to develop from the ground up and grow in this profession. I want people who have goals that are similar to mine or to those I had at that point in my career. Ideally, I want someone who is passionate about cooking and who wants to be a chef. The people who become better cooks down the road often have more questions about style and philosophy, about the process of cooking and what we do here. I'm not impressed if the person's first questions are, "What are the hours? What's the pay?" I admit those are valid questions, but working in this style of restaurant is a vocation, not a job. People don't go into it for the pay. I'm sorry, but the pay is lousy and the hours stink. I want to hire people who, when we are in the thick of it, will extend themselves.

I hire people who care about more than food—they want to take care of other people. That's why I impress upon my sous chefs a sense of responsibility to the people who choose to work with us. If people are willing to work long hours for me at low pay with a lot of uncertainty, it's because they like what I do with food and they feel that I can make them better cooks. That's one of my goals—I make all my cooks better cooks.

Tools

One of the most transformative experiences for me in my cooking career was learning the proper way to sharpen a knife.

I first learned about Japanese knives when I worked for Christian Delouvrier. There was a dish that called for finely diced bell peppers. I had my knife and was going at it, but the cuts were too big and uneven, and because my knife wasn't sharp enough, I was crushing the peppers and making them mushy. I just couldn't get it right. Then one of the sous chefs told me that even if my knife was sharp, it wasn't going to do the job properly. It wasn't a good knife.

The sous chef told me, "Your western-style knife wasn't made for fine cutting. You need to go out and buy a Japanese knife." He told me that a Japanese knife was not going to be cheap and that I needed to invest the money because it was a valuable tool—something I would have for my entire career. The chef explained that Japanese knives are made in a manner that allows chefs to do fine work.

I eventually bought several Japanese knives, all of which have influenced the way I cook. They allow for finer, more precise work and make smaller and cleaner cuts than a European-style knife. With Japanese knives, I can also do fine cutting work with herbs, ginger, garlic, and other ingredients that are the supporting elements of a dish. Instead of mashing them on a cutting board, which causes them to lose the juices, I can cut them precisely so they remain dry. When the juice hasn't been beaten out of them and the herbs are cut cleanly through the cell structure, they release more flavor into the dish.

Japanese knives are also the best knives for cutting fish, because the same principle that applies to cutting herbs applies to cutting fish. The first time I heard that, I said, "Come on!" However, now I better understand the physical nature of fish—the skeleton, muscles, and fat structure. I know that if I cut the fish incorrectly, I will bruise the flesh and destroy some of its flavor.

Another great thing about Japanese knives is how long they stay sharp, and that is due to the hardness of their steel, how they are made, and how they are sharpened. I was trained in the French and German method of knife sharpening using an oil stone, but I never felt my knives were sharp enough. I never felt I accomplished it the right way using that method. Once I met Mr. Chiharu Sugai at Korin Japanese Trading and saw his knife-sharpening video, *The Chef's Edge*, all of that changed. I watched his traditional method of sharpening Japanese knives again and again, and he also came to our restaurant and gave all of our chefs a knife-sharpening demonstration. One of the most transformative experiences for me in my cooking career was learning the proper way to sharpen a knife.

A Day in the Life

When I took over the old Oceana from the previous chef, most of the staff of 25 had left.

There were two sous chefs, six cooks, and me at Oceana. For several months, I'd worked from 7 a.m. to midnight six days a week. I'd get home at about 1 a.m., shower, go to bed, wake up at 5:30 a.m., dress, and go back to work. Even though everyone was pretty tired, I agreed to teach a cooking class for 20 of our customers at the restaurant on a Saturday morning in December.

After working another late Friday night, we came in the next morning before 7 a.m. to set up the cooking class, taught the class and served lunch, and finished at about 2 p.m. The people loved the class and the lunch, but we were going into dinner service two hours behind—plus it was a record night with 220 reservations! This meant a full two turns of the restaurant, so we had to do the whole thing at least twice and then some.

Then, in the middle of service, we had a big problem with one of the cooks not performing to the best of his ability. His sous chef told him, "This isn't right! That isn't right!" The third time this happened, the cook finally threw his hands down, took off his apron, and said, "I'm done. I can't do this. I'm not going to work here and take this anymore," and he walked out.

Since there was nothing else I could do, I walked up behind the line and started cooking. I said, "It'll be fine. Let's do it. We don't need this guy." This had been an 18-hour day and a 106-hour week. We were already beat going into this dinner service, and we were two hours behind. At the same time, this challenge had a positive outcome for me and my team. It built a stronger bond and a sense of unity among the team members. We were able to pull it off. Coming from behind and getting ready for dinner was a confidence booster. So that cook walking out on us turned into a good thing. The whole experience helped me earn my staff's trust and respect, which I had been doing gradually over two months. And it earned them my loyalty, respect, and gratitude. We didn't realize it, but at the end of service we had set the restaurant's record, and we got through it. It was a perfect night.

Photo credit: Nigel Parry

ELEVEN

ERIC RIPERT

Eric Ripert was born in Antibes, France and grew up in Andorra, a small country located in the eastern Pyrenees bordered by Spain and France. After attending culinary school in Perpignan, he moved to Paris and cooked at legendary La Tour D'Argent before taking a position at the Michelin three-starred Jamin. After fulfilling his military service, Eric Ripert returned to Jamin under Joël Robuchon to serve as Chef Poissonier, or Fish Cook.

In 1989, after working under Jean-Louis Palladin as Sous Chef at Jean Louis at the Watergate Hotel in Washington, D.C. Eric Ripert moved to New York in 1991, where Maguy and Gilbert Le Coze recruited him as Chef for Le Bernardin. In 1995, at just 29 years of age, Eric Ripert earned a four-star rating from *The New York Times.* Since then, Le Bernardin has maintained its superior status and has received universal critical acclaim for its food and service.

Eric Ripert is a frequent media guest, TV host, and the author of three award-winning cookbooks. He is president of the Jean-Louis Palladin Foundation and Chair of City Harvest's Food Council.

Influences

My first interaction with the Japanese culture was not only on the food level, but also with the service, the tableware, and the way Japanese cuisine differed from French cooking.

My first contact with Japanese cuisine was in 1984 at the first Japanese restaurant in Paris. I didn't know what sushi was. I went there because I'd heard about it, and I was curious. But I made a mistake. I thought wasabi was something sweet. The color looked so inoffensive that I ate a lot of it in one bite. Whew! That was my first contact with Japanese food! Although I was not accustomed to eating raw fish, I was fascinated by how they were preparing the rice and fish. And that incident with wasabi really made me curious about Japanese food. I also went to a yakitori restaurant in Paris. Although I couldn't see the staff grilling the yakitori, I knew they were doing it the traditional Japanese way. It felt as if this food was from another planet. I'd never seen anything like it.

The chef I worked for, Joël Robuchon, was a fanatic about Japanese food and culture. At that time in Paris, he was the first chef to go to Japan and immerse himself in the culture. And he was the first chef to bring Japanese influences into French cooking. Nobody before him had ever done that. So my first interaction with the Japanese culture was not only on the food level, but also with the service, the tableware, and the way Japanese cuisine differed from French cooking.

So while the French create sauce to hide the smell and to complement the fish, the Japanese do the opposite.

When I came to the U.S. in 1990, David Bouley took me to a Japanese restaurant, and explained the food to me, and taught me how to eat sushi and drink saké. Slowly, I developed a passion for sushi, and slowly, I absorbed it and began integrating Japanese ingredients into our cooking here at Le Bernardin. No one in the world has the reverence for fish and the knowledge about its preparation like the Japanese. Of course, the French cook fish well. However, the French invented sauce for fish a long time ago, when there was no ice or refrigeration, to hide its bad smell. So while the French create sauce to hide the smell and to complement the fish, the Japanese do the opposite. Their fish is so fresh and so beautiful that they hardly do anything to it. They find the perfect cut and add the perfect little touch that's going to elevate the fish to the next level.

Coming from a different background and discovering this philosophy has become very addictive. The more I know—and I know a little—the more I want to know. When I went to Masayoshi Takayama's restaurant in Los Angeles for the first time, it was a revelation. That guy is good! I finally went to Japan in November 2007. I ate in a lot of places where Mr. Robuchon sent me. "Go there! Go there! Go there!" I didn't even know the names of the places he referred me to because I couldn't read them. No one spoke English, and they didn't tell me the name of the restaurant. At one place there was a guy just doing tempura. And another was just doing sushi. I went to some places where they were creating food a little like the way Masa does by using tasting menus with interesting influences.

The only Japanese chef's name I remember is Jiro, because it sounded French to me. I was very impressed with his restaurant because the 78-year-old master, Chef Jiro Ono, said, "You come at 12:35 p.m., not 12:30 p.m., not 12:45 p.m., but 12:35 p.m. The rice is cooked for 12:35 p.m." When he gives it to you, you eat it immediately. The rice goes into your mouth and melts—it's extraordinary! Then you eat 20 pieces of sushi in 20 minutes—it's perfection. I was there the day they told Chef Ono that he had received three Michelin stars. He just said, "Thank you. Eat your sushi." I'm sure he was celebrating, but he had a very silent way of doing so. He wasn't jumping up and down on his table or shaking his knives. But I knew he was happy, because he smiled.

Cuisine

When I look back and compare my cuisine today with what it was 15 years ago as it relates to Japanese food, I can see how my approach to cooking has evolved, no question.

I have a better understanding of cooking and a better sense of harmony because of my experiences with Japanese cuisine. But when I traveled to Japan, I experienced an avalanche of influence. I'm still digesting what I learned there. There is so much to learn. One Japanese chef studies tempura for 15 years. Another one is a sushi master, and another does just rice for 10 years. You can imagine their level of mastery! So for me, when I go to Japan and I see everything so quickly, it's hard to digest. It's like when you eat a beautiful chocolate cake—you have to pace yourself.

Japanese cooking is highly ritualistic. Everything is sacred, and there are certain traditional ways of doing things. This is similar to French cooking in some respects. But Japanese chefs don't have the ego, and they don't promote themselves like western chefs. It's not about money—it's not about glory. It's about the craft, the respect for the culture, for life, the seasons, and the connection. So sharing all this is fantastic.

I have also been exposed to cooked Japanese food, and it is very different from the raw fish in sushi restaurants. All of that experience is channeled here to Le Bernardin. Now I sometimes restrain myself, because I discover that 90 percent of the menu has a Japanese influence. Then we have to go back to French cuisine—at least a little bit! I love the idea of the exchange of culture, because it's going to create a generation of chefs who will benefit from the best of my culture as well as the best of Japanese culture. You can imagine what it's going to be in the future—it's going to be genius! I want to see the next generation. Chefs cooking today are the pioneers for the next generation of chefs, and what we will have built is a solid bridge upon which they can create even better cuisine.

> *It would be totally crazy to be in New York City and cook like a chef in the middle of Brittany. It would mean that we are not open to what we see around us.*

Of course, there will always be traditional French cuisine, and there will always be traditional Japanese cuisine. For example, imagine you are a chef who has never been exposed to the outside world—and I'm thinking France now. If you live in the heart of Brittany and you don't have exposure to other cultures, what you do is a very traditional French cooking from Brittany, because you're inspired by your world—your neighbor, the next village, and the fishermen. So as artists, chefs are inspired by what surrounds them.

However, you cannot stop the future. And you cannot stop the fact that artists are going to be inspired by what they see and what they experience. People who are exposed to other cultures, especially in a city like New York, experience exactly the same artistic process as chefs in Brittany. We chefs are inspired by what we see and what we taste. Our cooking is fusion because cooking this way is logical and normal for us, and because we're seeing things that inspire us. It would be totally crazy to be in New York City and cook like a chef in the middle of Brittany. It would mean that we are not open to what we see around us. It's a lost battle to think that traditional is going to stay traditional. Chefs coming here are going to see something inspiring, and they're going to want to integrate that inspiration into their cooking. So the future is fusion, no doubt.

But fusion can go too far. It's our responsibility to mentor and to educate the younger chefs to be creative without being disrespectful of tradition. And it's our role to help them understand other food cultures. If we do that, we won't see excess, but if we bring food cultures together without any guidance, we're going to see some dreadful combinations.

The French and the Japanese have strong food cultures and are respectful of their traditions, so it's very hard for them to be creative like the American chefs.

There are no boundaries here in the U.S., so we are open to anything and everything. Sometimes it's great and sometimes it's not, but in the end, I think it's positive.

Now the French are slowly looking at what the Spaniards are doing, and they're saying "Oh my God, it's great what they're doing!" It took the French 20 years! They're slow, but when they get something, with all of their culture, they're going to do something fantastic. That's progress! It's the same for the Japanese cooking culture. I think chefs in both cultures need to be shocked a little bit.

I think that Japanese food is going to be even more influential here than in the past. I think we're going to see more and more influence here and more of our ingredients over there, too. Already the French are exporting fois gras and truffles to Japan. Today, you go into a restaurant like Jiro, and they use black truffles for sushi. You go to Masa, and he uses everything. He's one of the greatest masters, and he's using white truffles from Italy, black truffles from France, fois gras—it's already fusion. The French like the Japanese a lot. The cultures are very similar—but I think the French are more grumpy.

Ingredients

Today, French chefs use many ingredients from Japan, but it wasn't always like that.

I remember cooking in France in the 1980s. If you talked about ginger, you were the "anti-Christ" of cooking! People would look at you and whisper, "That guy doesn't know anything. He's stupid!" In fact, at that time most chefs in France didn't even know what ginger was. They had no clue! Maybe one chef said something bad about ginger because he didn't know how to use it, and then every chef in France was anti-ginger. And anyone who used ginger—that guy was a clown! But no more!

As far as other Japanese ingredients go, *yuzu* goes well with French food, especially fish. This ingredient is so magical. We have never had anything like it in France. Of course, we had regular lemons, but even 15 years ago a lime was considered exotic. Today, I use yuzu a lot. And miso! I love miso, and we use it here at Le Bernardin in many different ways. Sometimes it's subtle and sometimes it's more prominent. For instance, we have a mahi mahi recipe with mushroom broth. We mix miso, mirin, and yuzu to make a thin paste that is the consistency of sauce. We put the mahi mahi and paste in the middle of the plate. Then we pour the broth on top, and the paste dissolves into the broth. Some guests may not necessarily know what miso tastes like, but I think they enjoy the broth mixed together with the sauce, because we sell it a lot.

I think one of the challenges that western chefs have when using Japanese ingredients is that we don't have the right guidance.

Sometimes, we go shopping at the Japanese grocery stores and we buy things. Sometimes, a distributor sends us ingredients or products, but a distributor may not necessarily know enough about a product to help us use it. Then we just experiment with it. When we find an ingredient that we love, we look at it, taste it, play with it, and we then try to integrate it and use it in many different ways. But we don't have anyone who comes into the restaurant and says, "In my city in Japan, we prepare it like this and that." That would be a big help.

For instance, in one dish we used white soy sauce from Japan, and it was good. A day later, the soy sauce didn't taste as good. The next day, it became darker and changed in flavor and lost its freshness. It was the same recipe and the same soy sauce. What we didn't know was that white soy sauce oxidizes in the bottle. It would have been helpful if the rep or someone who uses this soy sauce had told me, "Watch out for this." Instead, it took us six months to figure it out. We kept wondering, "Why isn't it the same?" I'd like a shortcut to know exactly what's supposed to be done with particular Japanese ingredients and products. Of course, we can find out on our own, but it can take months of effort to understand them.

Training

When I left school, I was very proud of my certificate, but when I went into the restaurant kitchen, it was a cultural shock to find out that I was basically incompetent.

A lot of new chefs fresh out of culinary school who work in restaurants at the entry level are surprised or probably disappointed because they think they will be the next Thomas Keller. Instead, they're peeling carrots and turnips—and they still struggle to do that right! I see this a lot, but it usually doesn't take chefs long to realize that basically what the school gave them is a passport to enter a restaurant.

When I hire a cook to work at Le Bernardin, I want a person who is passionate, has good knife skills, is clean, and has a good attitude. Being a team player is important, too. A cook has to work as part of a team. For many, there's a struggle at first and an adjustment period. Then most of them understand the situation, start learning, and begin moving up. But their expectation of becoming instantly famous and making money right out of culinary school is something that really scares me. Even students graduating from the "Harvards" of the culinary world are going to get a restaurant job at the entry level, because they are really apprentices who need to spend many more years learning their trade.

When it comes to on-the-job training at Le Bernardin, we have a big team and what amounts to a mentoring program, where we have many stations around the stove and many different tasks. The first and most important task is to become a saucier, and then a sous chef. But the sous chef's job is more like a management position. It's not necessarily a cooking role, although sous chefs do cook. The saucier is the highest position, and it takes about three to four years to get there. A chef has to stay with us for at least three years or there is no hope of learning the sauce.

The sauce is the most esoteric and magical work that you can do in our kitchen, because you cannot measure flavor.

There's no such thing as "metrics of flavors" or a recipe to "add three inches of that flavor." You cannot weigh it, because you don't have "ounces of flavor." There's no way of measuring flavor—someone has to teach you or mentor you. I think it's very exciting for us to share that with the cooks. And the cooks know that the learning process of becoming an associate is something very special. That's the excitement of becoming an associate, and for us it's a way of keeping them on board and really mentoring them on good practices.

Everyone has a different palate and a different level of sensitivity. Although some chefs have better and more sensitive palates than others, chefs need to be trained in tasting. As a chef, you have to be exposed to different flavors and different products to create references in your mind. Then when you cook and you say, "I'll put in garlic," your mind will taste garlic exactly like a painter who imagines a color and says, "I'm going to use that red." By storing a library of flavors in your mind, you can use those different flavors to create something harmonious, which is the final dish. And for that, you have to be trained and taught by someone who has also been taught, because you just can't out of the blue invent a dish like that.

Sure, you can be lucky and one day make a great sauce, but tomorrow it'll be a bad sauce, and you'll have no idea why. It's very important for restaurants to have consistency. You want to be good today, and you want to be good tomorrow, and in one month, with the same product. You can't say to clients, "Sorry guys, today I was lousy, but yesterday I was a genius!"

The biggest problem I see in restaurant kitchens I've visited around the world is that the cooks are too busy to taste the food.

So how do we train chefs to be consistent with flavor? By tasting. Too often they do everything but taste the food! So here at Le Bernardin, we have boxes of biodegradable plastic spoons, and the chefs, including myself, constantly taste the food. And I mean constantly. We taste the food all the time. I learned that from my mentor, Joël Robuchon, who always insisted, "Taste the food! Taste the food! Taste the food!" We make sure everyone tastes.

There's something else about flavors and taste that chefs need to know. Let's suppose you are cooking some broth—and broth is very delicate. Water doesn't catch flavor in the same way that fats catch flavor. Oil, animal fat, and butter retain flavor. Flavor in water is much more volatile, and it's very different. For example, when you make tea at home, it has a certain flavor when it's first made. An hour later, it has another flavor. The tea you make in the morning—will you drink it at night? Probably not.

Sauce is the same. Broth is the same. They evolve. If the tea evolves in a cup or in a pot, just imagine how garlic and spices evolve. When you have acidity, it basically eats everything—destroys everything. But if you add it to your recipe at the last moment, it elevates the flavor. Spices—some of them evolve and expand, and some die. Garlic, depending on how you use it, sometimes brings out sweetness or sometimes the pungent flavors. If nobody tells you these things, it will take you 30 years to figure them out. That's why it's so important to teach new chefs and cooks about flavors, because they don't know if the sage in the broth is going to expand or die. Only the guy who's been trained knows.

If a dish looks beautiful and is cooked beautifully but has one little detail wrong—like the salt—the dish is dead.

Timing is essential, too. Sometimes you want to have everything infusing for a long time—like a meat stew. If you serve it right away, it's not the same today as it will be tomorrow, and the day after it may be fantastic, and sometimes three days later, it's even better. But some cooking has to be done at the last second because if you let flavors develop together, you kill everything. But if you don't taste your food and you don't know what you're serving, then whatever you've done is meaningless. If a dish looks beautiful and is cooked beautifully but has one little detail wrong—like the salt—the dish is dead. No salt, it's bland. Too much salt, it's disgusting. So every detail, every aspect of the cooking, is linked together.

This is how we train our new chefs. It is a process, and nothing can replace time. Nobody learns in an instant. It takes a lot of practice, a lot of repetition, and it's a long process. This is the key to achieving the level of cuisine we want. There's no doubt about it—it takes time.

There is one more thing that is important in training new chefs. We cannot have someone in the kitchen who does not speak English. It's too hard to manage. For example, one time we hired a lady from Korea who was fantastic and sweet. She said, "Yes" to everything, but she didn't do anything right. We would say, "Can you do that?" She said, "Yes." We asked, "Do you understand?" She said, "Yes," and then she did it completely the opposite! This makes it very difficult for us. Cooks don't have to be experts in English, but they need to understand and be able to communicate with others in the kitchen.

I would love to learn the Japanese way of making dashi and cutting fish.

Chefs have a lot to learn from one another. I would like a Japanese chef to teach me how to make dashi. I have my own way of making dashi. Mine is much stronger, with much more intense flavors, because I think now with an American chef's mind—flavors and contrasts. Contrast to me, most of the time, elevates the main product. The biggest example of this is the use of lemon juice. It cuts the richness and gives an illusion of lightness to the fatty ingredients. That's the contrast. I notice in Japan that dashi is extremely light, and the flavors are very subtle. I love it, but I don't know how to make it harmonious so that the flavors are not spiky. I think I do a good job, and I think what we do is right for the fish, but again, I would love to learn the Japanese way of making dashi.

I also want to learn more about cutting fish. First of all, it's essential in a restaurant like Le Bernardin. And Japanese chefs are masters at cutting fish because they know the right thickness for that fish. If it's cut too thin, you lose the crunch, or if it's too thick, it's mushy in your mouth. That's very important. And we can learn that from Japanese chefs.

When you talk to good cooks, you will find in Japan that you have good cooks and bad cooks, just as you find in France, in Italy, in Spain, and in America—worldwide. The bad cooks are the bad cooks—they don't know. But the good cooks create harmony. They understand their craft, and they understand their flavors and how to balance them. These principles are universal.

Tools

> *To me, cooking starts with the two most essential kitchen tools: the knife and fire or heat.*

To cook, you have to learn how to domesticate fire, and then you have to learn good knife skills. There is no cooking without knives—period—because the knives give you the precision that you need to create delicacy and harmony in dishes. If I said to you, "I'm going to use ginger," and I cut my ginger very precisely, then I'm going to be able to add exactly the amount of ginger flavor that I want to my broths. If I don't know how to cut the ginger, I'm going to add something chunky, something big, and it's going to totally change the dynamic of the broth. Or if I cut vegetables too thin, I can't taste them. If they're too big, they're gross. So knives are at the core of cooking—I cannot cook without a good knife.

My relationship with my Japanese knives is an extension of how I approach cooking, my customers, and everything else in the restaurant—they're all connected.

The following is an analogy between cars and Japanese knives. Let's compare driving a Ford Taurus with driving a Ferrari. The Taurus is easy—you just put it in your garage at the end of the day. A Ferrari always needs little things here and there, but the pleasure of having a Ferrari is obviously another experience. Japanese knives, for me, are Ferraris. I don't know any chef who doesn't have a sentimental relationship with his or her Japanese knives. But you must give those knives constant attention. For example, you need to sharpen them in the proper way, or you can ruin the edge. Also, you're not going to dump your Japanese knife in the water and wash it quickly. That could break or scratch the handle or blade, and you don't want the blade to be scratched—you want it to be perfect.

A Japanese knife is a beautiful but very demanding object. What I've learned about Japanese knives is that you have relationships with them, and they are temperamental and demanding because of the quality of the steel. And two things—the knife and fire—are the two most essential tools for cooking. If you haven't mastered both of these, then go make sandwiches at Wendy's.

A Day in the Life

One of the worst days of my life was my first day entering a professional kitchen—it was La Tour d'Argent in Paris—and realizing that basically I was a loser at cooking.

I was 17. First the chef said, "Cut some shallots," and I cut myself in 10 seconds! So then he said, "Okay, go do Hollandaise sauce. I need 32 yolks." So I start in on it, and then I told the chef that the stove was too hot. He asked, "Are you crazy?" And then I fixed too many egg yolks and it wasn't strong enough, so he said, "Okay, go pick chervil." And I said, "What's chervil?" Then he just shook his head and said, "Where are you from? How did you end up here?"

That day I couldn't use my knives because I didn't have knife skills. I couldn't do carrot julienne. Basically, I was useless. And I realized I was useless, and I really thought I was going to be fired. That was a horrific feeling. La Tour d'Argent in the 1980s was still a very prestigious and classic restaurant and an institution in France. So I didn't want to lose that opportunity, but at the same time, I did not have the level of skill necessary for working there.

How did I survive? I worked hard. I had to learn. There was no choice. I put in very long days, but not only that, I didn't have many days off. And the kitchen—it was a very, very hot kitchen. So physically, it was very difficult to be a cook in that kitchen. But when you're 17, 18, 19, or 20, you recover.

Dominique Bouchet was the chef of La Tour d'Argent, and he's the one who kept me on board, so I'm thankful to him. After about 19 months, the biggest gift he gave me after training me was to send me to Joël Robuchon.

❖

TWELVE

TONI ROBERTSON

Executive Chef, Mandarin Oriental Hotel Group, Singapore

A graduate of the renowned Cooking and Hospitality Institute of Chicago, Executive Chef Toni Robertson has prepared her exquisite cuisine in some of the world's finest hotels, including The Ritz-Carlton Chicago, Four Seasons Beverly Hills, and as Executive Chef at the Palace of the Lost City Hotel in South Africa. Toni became the first female Executive Chef of a luxury hotel in Southeast Asia at the Pan Pacific Hotel in Singapore. She joined the Mandarin Oriental, New York team in 2005 and moved to the Mandarin Oriental, Singapore in 2014.

Toni Robertson was the first female chef to be inducted into the Singapore chapter of the Chaine des Rotisseurs, the world's oldest international culinary organization. She is certified as a sommelier from the Court of Master Sommeliers and was welcomed into the Order Mondial under the direction of Master Sommelier George Milliotes.

154 · TONI ROBERTSON

Influences

Food was always my passion.

My fondest memories from Burma, where I was born, are walking to the local market with my grandmother every morning to buy the ingredients for the day's meals. Even as a little girl, I was enthralled with the hustle and bustle and the sounds and smells of this gathering place as we went about our daily ritual. It was there that I first learned how to appreciate food and how to select the best ingredients. It was in the market that I think my passion was born. By Burmese standards, we were well off. We were of Chinese descent, and my father was a successful businessman who wanted all of his kids to be educated professionals—preferably doctors. But school was never my strong point, so I always seemed to find my way into the kitchen, usually to hide out.

Our family cook would put me to work. "If you're going to hide in here, peel some garlic. Chop some of this. Stir this pot." She gave me simple tasks to do, and I started to learn about cooking from the ground up. But in Asia, being a cook was not like it was in America or Europe. It was not a particularly desirable position and usually meant that you would work as a servant for others, so the idea of being a chef never really entered my mind. There were no famous chefs in Burma to idolize. But I knew that I loved food and cooking.

In 1979 as a teenager, I immigrated to the United States amidst the political turmoil in my country. My parents were still in Burma, so I first stayed with my oldest sister Peggy, a doctor, in Hawaii, where I learned English by watching soap operas on TV. We moved to Chicago a year later, where I was able to complete my high school education. Peggy had a great passion for cooking, and I think if she had not gone into medicine, she would have been a great chef. She and her husband, Patrick, also a doctor, took vacations around the world to faraway places like Paris, where they would eat and drink at the great restaurants. Peggy even went to cooking classes. I learned my first real dishes from my sister. I think the first thing I ever baked on my own was rum baba. I was underage and already into the rum! Then I made a soufflé. Imagine making a soufflé and being so excited when it actually turned out perfect! I was addicted.

Although food was my passion, cooking as a profession was still not a realistic option for me at that time. I had another stop to make along the way. After graduating from high school, I joined the U.S. Air Force and became an emergency room medic. With a family full of doctors, it wasn't such a stretch for me to gravitate toward medicine. I loved the Air Force because it opened up so many opportunities for me. In fact, I served seven years on active duty and another five years in the Air National Guard. I often say that the experience I gained in running an emergency room, working in that "controlled chaos," was perfect training for preparing me to work in the kitchen. I was fortunate enough to be stationed early in my career in a little town in Germany called Spangdahlem in the Eifel mountains, where the borders of Belgium, France, and Luxembourg come together.

Every weekend that I could get away, my mission was to find somewhere new to eat. It was normal on a Friday for my friends and me to hop on the train and head down to Paris. We didn't have a lot of money, so we would go to a little bistro or a sidewalk cafe, watch the world go by, and share items on the menu. I thought I was eating in the dining room at the Ritz! Instead, I was sitting outside at the Café de la Paix, dreaming that I was sitting in the same chair that Ernest Hemingway sat in, sipping espresso, and eating baguettes and cheese. That was my introduction to the culinary world.

Living in Europe also gave me the opportunity to try cooking the foods that I ate on my dining excursions. We always had single friends over to the house for dinners when I experimented with new dishes, and on holidays I cooked feasts and invited service people who didn't have family close by. I had the best Christmas parties at my house! I learned recipes from cookbooks or magazines like *Gourmet*, *Food & Wine* or *Good Housekeeping*. I also worked the overnight shift at the U.S. Air Force Emergency Room, and we used to do potluck dinners with themes. I always made a main dish. For example, if it was Mexican night, I would make the meat dish, and everyone else brought taco shells, lettuce, or tomatoes. If you came to our emergency room at 2 a.m., patients, nurses, doctors, the ambulance drivers, even the security and local police were there eating those potluck dinners. It was a big buffet for all of us, and it was fun.

Career Path

I was lucky to be hired at the Ritz-Carlton Chicago as the "salad girl."

There came a time when I had to follow my passion for cooking or decide to stay in the military. It really was not that difficult a choice. I had to give it a shot. I knew I wanted to realize my dream and cook for a living, so I left the service, moved back to Chicago, and enrolled in the culinary program at the Cooking and Hospitality Institute of Chicago to learn the basics. Today, CHIC has grown into a premier culinary training academy in the Chicago area, teaching hundreds of students, but at the time I attended, we had only five students in my class. I was fortunate enough to receive one-on-one training, which I think was instrumental to my early development. After I graduated, I was lucky to be hired at the Ritz-Carlton Chicago as the "salad girl." I started in the basement and washed lettuce all day long for the entire hotel—all three outlets and banquets. I literally worked my way up from the bottom!

My first interview at the Ritz-Carlton was with Chef Fernand Gutierrez, who was a legend in the Chicago area. He was a typical Frenchman—large, loud, and, for me, very intimidating. But Fernand was also a chef who was ahead of his time. In a day and age when kitchens were the exclusive haven of male chefs, he gave women a chance to work in one of the finest and best-known kitchens in the country. That just wasn't done at that time.

I had already decided even before the interview that if I wanted to be a good chef some day, I needed to get into a great kitchen with a great chef who could mentor me. I told Fernand I would do anything to work in his kitchen. Unfortunately, "anything" turned out to be a position as either a pastry helper or a salad person. Even to this day, I have never been drawn to pastry like I have to cooking. I love pastry, but baking is a science that demands accurate measurements and discipline—neither of which I seem to do very well. Cooking always seemed to me to be the more creative of the two art forms. So I told Fernand, "No, I don't want to do pastry—I'll be your salad girl," not having the slightest idea what that really meant!

I found out quickly! I worked in the basement near the loading dock area, where trucks would make their deliveries of lettuce and other produce. At that time, there were no pre-made salad mixes like we have today. We did everything from scratch. I washed and prepared salads for thousands of guests each day. It was very cold in the basement during the harsh Chicago winters, and very hot and muggy during the summers. My hands would ache at the end of the day from being in the ice-cold water all day washing and preparing the lettuce.

What I learned was that even the simplest tasks, like preparing lettuce, took skill. I discovered that the best way to clean lettuce is to first take it apart, chop it, and then throw it into the coldest water possible. If you let it soak for a few minutes and don't stir the water too much, you can use your fingers to "fluff" the lettuce so that the dirt and sand just drop to the bottom. Then you gently scoop out the lettuce, and it is perfectly clean.

Chef Gutierrez ran a disciplined kitchen, and I figured out early on that being a good chef didn't happen overnight. It took time and commitment, and you had to pay your dues. But I was also not shy about wanting to improve my skills and get better. I was both anxious and ambitious. I would knock on Chef Gutierrez' door and ask, "Can I come up? Can I do this or that for you?" One time I overheard him say that he didn't have anybody to bone chickens. So I said, "Can I come up and do it for you? You don't even have to pay me for it."

He could have said no, but instead he said, "Come on. You can help," guessing that I'd never boned a chicken in my life. That was his way of giving me a chance. He was right about my lack of experience, but I watched a few of the more experienced cooks and then jumped in. The first few were a certifiable disaster—but I mastered the technique quickly and was boning chickens like a pro in no time!

I was always looking toward the future. I showed up every day knowing that this was the first step on the ladder of my career.

I washed lettuce for over a year, but I knew that I had a future beyond the basement if I worked hard. Every day I told myself, "Tomorrow they might have something else available for me." I was paying my dues. I was always looking toward the future. I showed up every day knowing that this was the first step on the ladder of my career. I had learned discipline and professionalism in the military, and I knew that someday I would move upstairs. It wasn't easy, not interacting with the other cooks and never seeing plates of food, but I never lost faith. Then one day, a pastry position opened up. I couldn't believe that my ascension to the twelfth-floor kitchen was going to be through the pastry department!

I think my coworkers quickly figured out my limitations as a pastry cook. I spent a great deal of time plating desserts, which in those days meant "pulling sugars." My hands went from the cold of ice water and lettuce to the heat of cooked sugar, which was used to make roses. At that time at the Ritz-Carlton, every dessert plate had sugar roses on it. We did a lot of promotions that year—which meant a lot of sugar roses. My fingers were constantly being burned.

In 1985, a young French chef named Emile Tabourdiau from Paris came to do a promotion in the dining room of the Ritz-Carlton. As we worked together on a dessert, he asked me if I was the only Asian in the kitchen. It was unusual enough to see a female cook, but an Asian female was truly a rarity in those days. He had some ideas about some Asian ingredients he was interested in using. "How do you use this? What is the best way to prepare it?" he would ask me. I started working with him on these dishes, and we had a great time. At the end, he asked, "If your chef will let you, why don't you come to Le Bristol in Paris and work with me?"

What an opportunity. I didn't hesitate and told him, "I'll pay my way! I have vacation time, and I'm sure my chef will give me the time. I want to work in your kitchen!" So off I went to Paris for three months, with the blessing of Fernand, to apprentice with Chef Emile. By the time I returned to the Ritz-Carlton, a position in garde manger had opened up, and I was once again given an opportunity. At the time we made cold canapés and appetizers, of course, but we also made pâtés and terrines from scratch, including our own smoked salmon in the cold area. I took the position.

In the mid 1980s, the brunch at the Ritz-Carlton Dining Room was the place to be on a Sunday. We'd have about 300 or 400 guests, and we decorated all of these old-fashioned mirrors with whole poached salmon in aspic. We stuffed the pâtés and terrines with everything imaginable. It's a dying art today, but Fernand was still old school, and I learned to make all of the classics. We put our little twist on everything. One of the great aspects about working in the Ritz-Carlton

Chicago was the tremendous volume. Everything was big—the banquets, the number of covers in the dining room, the café. If ever there was an example of controlled chaos in a kitchen, it was the Ritz-Carlton. When I smoked salmon, I didn't just smoke one salmon; I would smoke 40 to 50 salmon at a time. I did it repeatedly until I mastered it. It wasn't long before I moved up again and became a saucier on the hot line.

> *When you work the line, you have the recipe, the technique, and the plating card, which you follow to the letter if you want to stay in the good graces of the chef.*

My short but passionate apprenticeship in Paris introduced me to the seasonality of food, which would forever change my view of the culinary arts. It was there that I first realized that great cuisine is best built around the ingredients at hand. It was springtime in Paris, so I peeled cases and cases of fennel. In the 1980s French cuisine was still considered king. My cooking had become very westernized as I immersed myself in traditional French cooking and French cuisine. However, at home, away from the kitchens at the Ritz-Carlton, it was very different. There I cooked the dishes that I grew up with in Burma and enjoyed eating my native cuisine—with its Thai, Indian, and Chinese influences. At home, I never really left my Asian roots. But at work, the two cuisine styles never crossed. I kept them separate.

When you're working your way up, you take your direction from the chef you are working under. Fernand was a great chef, but you weren't going to see any bean sprouts or daikon radish in his dishes. When you work the line, you have the recipe, the technique, and the plating card, which you follow to the letter if you want to stay in the good graces of the chef.

It was only when I began working in Singapore in the mid-1990s as Executive Chef at the Pan Pacific Hotel that I really rediscovered my Asian passion and my roots and started to incorporate them into my cuisine in a fundamental way. In Singapore, I worked with a Japanese master chef who introduced me to the traditional kaiseki cuisine. I was immediately in love with it. The beautiful preparation of the dishes was like a fashion show, with one element linked to another. By the thirteenth dish, I was in love. It opened my mind. The ingredients were not new to me. I had used seaweed, salmon roe, wasabi, and soy sauce in the past. But it was the way they were used that drew me in.

Although I had overseen a Japanese restaurant at the Grand Wailea Resort in Maui, Hawaii, it wasn't until Singapore that I think I really began to appreciate the true artistry of Japanese cuisine. I was inspired for the first time to really rethink my style and incorporate the simplicity of ingredients and the complexity of flavors into my more global-style cuisine.

Training

If the only position that's open is in the employee cafeteria, take it. Be the best cafeteria cook there ever was and prove that you can do it.

People come and interview with me for positions all the time. Many have impeccable credentials from the best culinary schools. The truth is, I don't have much turnover in my kitchens, so often the positions that do open up are at the lowest levels. What I learned from my start in Chicago is that there is always opportunity if you make it. When someone comes to me and says, "Oh, I want to be a cook in fine dining," I tell them, "If there is only a position in the employee cafeteria, take it. Work in the cafeteria. Be the best cafeteria cook there has ever been. Prove that you can do it. Own it and showcase your talent. If you do, you'll be noticed."

In most kitchens, even the lowliest "salad girl" will get noticed if she consistently works hard and rises to the challenge. To chefs who want to move up, I say, "When the door's a little ajar, make your own opportunity. It may not be the opportunity or position you were looking for, but if you're talented and a team player and if you show that you have the potential and the desire to learn your craft, the chef will notice you." I am always thankful that I had the opportunity to work every position in the kitchen. I worked in every department, from banquets to the café to fine dining. It made me a better chef.

Times have changed a lot in terms of managing kitchens and developing a staff. Some of this is due to better training and culinary schools, and unfortunately, too much of it is due to the influence of television. In the past, new cooks wanted to be part of the organization. They would come to me and say, "I want to work for a great hotel group. I want to work for the Mandarin Oriental and be a part of something special. I want to come to your kitchen and work with you, learn from you, and develop my craft."

Today, I see young people just out of the top cooking schools, and they come to me and say, "Hey. I've got three or four other people I can work for. I can work for you. I can work for Jean-Georges. I can work for Daniel Boulud. I can work for just about anybody. So what are you going to do for me?" My reply is definitely not what they usually expect. To them I say, "Good luck. Go for it." Fortunately, I know that Jean-Georges and Daniel are saying the same thing. But I would be remiss if I didn't say that I am concerned that the next generation of chefs is not developing the same fundamental skills that we learned as young culinarians.

Too often, in this day and age of the celebrity chef, too much emphasis is placed on where young chefs worked before or what school they graduated from. I think those are important qualities of course, but when I'm talking to a candidate one-to-one, I'm looking for that spark—the one thing that tells me this is someone I should be bringing onto the team. If he or she says to me, "Chef, I really want to work in this kitchen and learn from you. I'll take any position you have if you just give me a chance to prove myself," that person certainly has my attention, even without the best credentials. And it is in those rare instances that I remember sitting in front of Chef Fernand Gutierrez, nervous and scared, but determined to work in his kitchen. I was asking for the same chance that this candidate is asking for right now. But I tell these young chefs, "If you want to learn from me, you must be sincere about it. If you are, then I'll give you my time, and for a chef, time is everything—there's never enough."

When I see the talent and know that the person wants to learn, then at this stage of my career I feel that it is my responsibility to be a mentor and teacher. At the Ritz-Carlton, I had my guardian angels. I had Pascal Vignau. I had Fernand Gutierrez. These were my chefs— the mentors who set me on the right path and taught me the basics, upon which I developed a career. It was a lesson I will never forget.

I always tell new cooks to just take the opportunity and create something out of it. I could have been a salad girl, washing lettuce, for the rest of my life, but I kept moving. My goal was never to be a sous chef or garde manger chef. I was always looking for an opportunity to work the hot line—to be a saucier. At that time, the saucier was king, because French cooking is all about the sauce. So you're at the pinnacle of your cooking career when you became a saucier. It was only after I reached my goal that I realized that I wanted to run a kitchen some day and be the chef.

When someone applies for a job as a cook, I'm not necessarily looking for a specific cutting technique or a certain level of knowledge. I can teach the technical skills. What I want to see is passion and personality—whether or not a person is going to fit into my kitchen. If I see that someone won't be a good fit, then I've learned that I should not waste his or her time and mine. I am also not looking for creativity. Most young cooks think they are more creative than they really are. It's that learning curve they need to focus on. The creativity comes later.

When young cooks are looking for a position and I ask them to make a ham and cheese omelet for me, I don't want to hear, "Oh, I know it's a ham and cheese omelet, but I'm going to put some goat cheese in there instead of ..." That's not what I'm looking for.

I am also looking for style—style is something that you can never teach. It's the intangible element in cooking. For example, if someone gives me a plate with a mountain of food on it, then I know that person doesn't really understand the nature of cooking. But if a cook gives me a plate that may not be perfectly executed but is done with thought and style, then that is someone I know I can train.

Cuisine

A lot of chefs look at the end result first and work backwards. I look at the ingredients first and build upwards.

Whoever first used the words "seasonal cuisine" had to be thinking of me! I live by the ingredients that I have at my fingertips. Although my background and training are in classical French cuisine, I don't do French anymore. My cuisine style is actually similar to Japanese cuisine, but I also don't cook Japanese food. What I did was use French cooking as the foundation, and then, little by little, I started infusing my dishes with Asian ingredients. As my cuisine has evolved over the years, I find that I use a lot of the basic Japanese ingredients—soy sauce, rice, miso, wasabi, daikon, and seaweed. Like the trained Japanese masters, I always keep it simple, with elegant presentation and an emphasis on technique. I love Japanese cooking because it is art on the plate—the confluence of textures, flavors, elegance, and presentation.

What I love about cooking is that it is constantly changing and evolving. For me, the market and the season dictate what I will be cooking. For example, if artichokes are in season, I think, "What am I going to do with these artichokes?" Sometimes I'll be flipping through a cookbook or eating at a restaurant and a dish or recipe will suddenly inspire me. I think, "Oh, this looks good," and then I start moving in that direction. I start thinking, "Maybe I'll make artichoke appetizers, or a carpaccio with artichokes. Or I'll make a salad of raw shaved artichokes." If I decide to shave it, my next question will be, "Who serves shaved artichoke?" I think about the fundamentals of cuisine. Should I base it on an Italian or California style cuisine?" Then I ask, "What goes with shaved artichoke?" I normally love it with really nice parmesan. And I'll need a citrus. Maybe a Meyer lemon or a yuzu. Then I add olive oil to round out the flavor.

Now I have a dish with artichokes that has the saltiness of the cheese and the subtle flavors of the olive oil. But I need a contrasting texture—a crunchy element. So I decide to put a shaved fennel in there. Finally, the dish is starting to come together, and I ask myself, "Okay, now, visually, what else does it need? Oh, I can use baby arugula to provide the color and visual aesthetics." And that's my process for how a dish evolves.

It's a process that can take some time, or it can happen instantly, like a songwriter writing a new lyric or new music. Sometimes it just happens, the words and music are right there and everything flows, and other times I work on it for days or weeks. Sometimes I can clearly see in my mind how the dish is going to work. Other times I know I've found something special but can't put my finger on it yet.

What is it that sparks my imagination? Maybe I'm going to use miso in my dipping sauce or make it into a marinade. It's like playing a chess game and calculating the next move. I'll think about the texture. The look and the flavor of miso is similar to peanut butter, so then I think, what do I make with peanut butter? I use peanut dipping sauce for the satay. So why don't I try to make a miso dipping sauce, not necessarily for chicken satay, but with crudités? Then I'll add it into some of our dishes, usually in small amounts, first marrying it into the marinade or into the sauces. It's basically about layering. I ask, "How can I elevate that particular item, that particular part?" I never know what I'll end up with. Instead, I keep working and experimenting until I get it right. That's how an ingredient like miso can take me in a new direction.

It starts with the taste and then ends with the taste.

Great restaurants are great because they consistently produce outstanding cuisine. But I have learned that I also need to keep the guest intrigued with variety and new dishes. That can be a little bit of a slippery slope, and I have to be careful. When I go shopping or when I go to a food show, I am always on the lookout for something that I'm not familiar with. And when I find that ingredient or item I taste it, because it all starts with the taste. From there, I need to find the best way to incorporate that ingredient into my cuisine. For example, I love Japanese mountain potatoes, but I don't feature them as a main dish. It's not for lack of trying, but the first time I put mountain potato on the menu, my guests reacted in a way that I didn't expect. "Oh, it's slimy!" they told me. "That's the way they are supposed to be," I told them. But I love this potato, so now I put it into a dish with other ingredients. I cut the mountain potato into small pieces and braise them in something like dashi. Then I serve the pieces of potato with a fish dish, like a branzino. In this way, I can layer in the ingredient and introduce it in my cuisine in a way that does not alienate my guests.

Ingredients

The direction of the menu and dishes changes with the ingredients I discover or rediscover.

When I'm learning about an ingredient, I study and taste the individual products first. I'm going to look at all of the different varieties of that ingredient to see what differences I can pick out between producers. I'm looking for a flavor component, a texture. When I look at the ingredient, I may not know which direction I'm going to take until I taste it, and then there's that little bit of inspiration. Something sparks in my head and points me in the direction I need to go. I never arbitrarily say, "I'm going to use this ingredient for this dish." For example, I'll taste different types of miso—white miso, red miso, and a blended version. Then I will taste individual brands. I'll try a mouthful to determine the texture, the grittiness, the saltiness, and the flavors that remain on my palate.

The best chefs know when to stop adding ingredients.

I admire chefs who make beautiful, wonderful dishes with a minimum of ingredients. It reflects confidence and considerable skill to selectively marry just a few ingredients and create a wonderful dish. Too often, chefs today want to open the cupboard and take every ingredient out and try to figure out how to use them all in one dish. "More is better" seems to be the approach. Oh, the dish looks wonderful, and it has great texture and color, and the chef will extol the complexity and composition of the dish. But does it taste good?

Great chefs are artists. Like great writers, they also have to be good editors. And like great painters, they have to know when too many colors detract from the piece. Successful chefs know their limits. They know how to use just enough ingredients to draw out and capture the five senses and then stop.

Sometimes a chef creates something in the kitchen but forgets the customer's point of view. For example, a common mistake new chefs often make is with presentation. They will serve a beautiful seafood soup with whole giant prawns, heads and all. The presentation is beautiful and very elegant, but the guest will say, "How am I going to eat that?" The prawns are so big they will not fit on a soupspoon and the head is still intact. When I create a dish, I always take the guests' perspective and try to appreciate their point of view. What looks wonderful to me may not be appealing to someone sitting at my table. After all, the dining experience is not about the chef—it's about the person eating the cuisine.

Tools

Just give me a knife and I can create something.

My favorite kitchen tool has always been a knife. I think that is a very Asian trait. I've never been drawn to special tools, especially the electronic variety. I don't need a Cuisinart. I don't need a blender. I don't need anything else—just give me a sharp, well-balanced, Japanese-made knife and some inspiration, and I can create good food. I have a great collection of knives that I've gathered over the years, but my favorites have always been Japanese knives.

As a chef, the knife is my extension—this is who I am. I discovered Japanese knives during a promotional event in California. I'd always admired Japanese knives but thought they were too expensive. I was afraid that I would put my knife down in the kitchen, turn around, and it would be gone. However, when one of my chefs de cuisine came into the promotional event with a case of these beautifully balanced Japanese knives and I had the chance to use them, I said, "Oh, I have to have that." I paid $300 for my first Japanese knife, and it is still my favorite to this day. It was only after I started using it that I truly appreciated the value of a great knife.

When you choose a knife, hold it in your hand—get comfortable with it. Once you find the knife that you are most comfortable with, you've found your best friend. Then the knife will speak to you. I use three Japanese knives. The vegetable knife is shaped like a small cleaver and is called a "usuba." I actually use this one most of the time. It takes some time to develop skill with it, because it is not traditionally used in American culinary schools. I have a long slicing knife, a *yanagi* that works well on everything, and a paring knife, which is called "petti knife," for delicate tasks. I carry those three knives with me all the time. Without them, I would be lost.

A Day in the Life

We like to think it's all about the chef, but it really is not. The chef may steer the ship, but the complete dining experience is always the product of teamwork.

There was one time in my career that sticks out as a particularly special challenge. I was the Executive Chef at the Mandarin Oriental Hotel, San Francisco and a member of the Asian Chefs Association and the Asian Chefs Society. Someone from the organization got the idea that we should put together a team for a cooking competition to be held in Taiwan. I was asked to participate as one of five executive chefs representing the U.S. I said, "Oh, Taiwan! I've never been to Taiwan before, so sign me up."

Although the five of us were successful executive chefs, we never worked as a team. We never got together before the competition to practice or learn each other's styles. Each of us was busy running a kitchen and involved with so many projects that it just never seemed like we could find the time. And I think we had the attitude, "Oh, we're pretty experienced—we'll make it work."

So the five of us flew to Taiwan. We treated it more like a vacation than a culinary competition. When we got there, we learned that we were being broadcast by live TV to 11 countries. We were Team USA and entered the cooking arena with red, white, and blue chef's jackets.

In the first round of cooking, we were competing against a Japanese team. We had to prepare five different dishes. It was organized much like the format of *Iron Chef*. We said, "No problem— we can do this," but we struggled, and it was a near disaster. We barely beat the Japanese team—by sheer luck I think. By the second round, with the clock ticking, we were clearly outclassed, and in the end, we were eliminated. I learned an invaluable lesson that day—you may have great individual skills, but without practice and teamwork, you cannot succeed.

Many chefs believe that the only reason someone is in their restaurant is because of their food. That's only half the story.

Dining is a form of entertainment that is choreographed. When properly executed, it provides an unforgettable experience. That experience does not start and end with the food alone. The dining experience is like a symphony. If one instrument is out of tune, it can wreck the entire piece.

Occasionally, I have a guest who did not have a great dining experience. We failed to meet or exceed that person's expectations, and we receive a letter that is less than flattering. After some investigation, we find out that the guest wanted a table by the window with a great view but was given an interior table instead. That guest started the dining experience on a negative note, and of course, from that point on everything was wrong.

The dining experience had nothing to do with the cuisine, but it had everything to do with the entire process. From the time the guest walks into the restaurant and is seated to the time the guest collects his or her coat from the coat check and receives a "goodbye" from the hostess, making the dining experience enjoyable is a team effort. As chefs, we too often think that the success or failure of the dining experience rests with our food, but the truth is, while the chef is steering the ship, it takes a team of people working together toward a common goal to create a truly memorable and great dining experience.

The best thing about being a chef is being able to close the book every night and look forward to the next day.

The wonderful thing about being a chef is that each day I get to reinvent myself and start fresh. Whatever happened the day before, even if it was a particularly difficult day, all goes away when the last burner is shut off and the last pot is cleaned and hung on the rack. Today I start anew. Today I might discover a new product or ingredient and be inspired to create my best dish ever or hire a terrific cook who will someday lead a kitchen. Today I may even change someone's life with my cooking and inspire them to pursue the path that I chose so many years ago. I remember Fernand Gutierrez telling me, "Never look back on yesterday, no matter how good or bad, because tomorrow is always going to be better!"

❖

THIRTEEN

MICHAEL ROMANO

Chef/Partner, Union Square Hospitality Group,
Chief of Culinary Development

Michael Romano joined Union Square Cafe in 1988, preparing his unique style of American cuisine with an Italian soul, and a year later *The New York Times* elevated the USC to three stars. In 1993, Michael Romano became Danny Meyer's partner. Under his leadership, USC has been ranked Most Popular in New York City's *Zagat* Survey for a record seven years. USC also received the James Beard Award for Outstanding Restaurant of the Year in 1997.

In 2000, Michael was inducted into the James Beard Foundation's Who's Who of Food & Beverage in America, and he was named The James Beard Foundation's Best Chef in New York City in 2001.

Michael Romano has co-authored two cookbooks with Danny Meyer, *The Union Square Cafe Cookbook* and *Second Helpings from Union Square Cafe*. Michael opened the Union Square Tokyo in 2007 and Hudson Yards Catering in 2011. In 2013, he published a third book, *Family Table*, in collaboration with Karen Stabiner. He left his post of USHG's Director of Culinary Development in 2013. Michael remains actively involved with USHG's culinary role in Union Square Tokyo, and divides his time between New York and Japan for other projects, including several charity organizations.

Influences

I still have my notes from that meal at Kitcho, which was a complete immersion in Japanese culture, the likes of which I had never before experienced in my life.

I remember precisely the first time I really discovered Japanese food—and it was not in New York City. From 1981 to 1983, I was working in Switzerland for Max Kehl at his restaurant, Chez Max, and I was his chef de cuisine. In 1982, I accompanied Chef Kehl on a trip to Tokyo for a weeklong international cooking competition sponsored by Nestlé involving chefs from 15 restaurants from all over the world—China, France, Italy. America was there in the form of Paul Prudhomme. Max and I were representing Switzerland. This was long before the *Iron Chef* television shows ever came about.

We cooked every day for one week. Every day we were taken by bus from our hotel in downtown Tokyo to the TSUJI Culinary Institute in south Tokyo. Everything we needed was already set up, and we worked on our dishes. Each team had to prepare three dishes: an appetizer, a main course, and a dessert. As we finished our dishes, we were judged by an international panel of judges, one of whom was Craig Claiborne. When the judging was over, everything was packed up and taken back to the hotel, which was in the midst of its grand opening. It all culminated in a live two-hour television broadcast from the hotel, which featured the final cooking competition and all kinds of entertainment. There were singers, and there was a sumo wrestler there as well. We were there being judged, and we had set up tables to display our food.

I was quite busy but still managed to get out for different dining experiences. In the evening, after cooking all day for the show, Max took me to dine with him in several places, one of which was Kitcho, one of Japan's most exclusive traditional restaurants. I still have my notes from that meal, which was a complete immersion in Japanese culture, the likes of which I had never before experienced in my life.

During that week, I asked the Japanese guide I was assigned to take me to simple places where people ate every day. But the experience at Kitcho was so astounding that I can still remember all of the dishes we ate. We were in our own private room, and I was so impressed with the food, the décor, and the hospitality. I loved the fact that the plateware was selected because of the way it matched the seasonal foods being served. This was dining taken to a level of precision and refinement that I'd never before experienced.

And the service! When the kimono-clad server entered the room, she somehow glided from her standing position at the doorway to being seated at the edge of our table, but I never actually saw her sit down! There was only a gradual descent, an utterly graceful movement from door to table.

Once there, I expected her to begin clearing our plates, but instead she simply rested a moment, as if to allow the air she had displaced in the room to settle and for all to be perfectly still and calm. Then, slowly and precisely, she began to gather the items from the table. There was never a sound of the dishes touching. It was so elegant and graceful.

On that first trip to Japan, I also saw how disciplined the cooks were, and how precisely and energetically they carried out the chef's orders. I think the Japanese have a great sense of working with the master and learning and focusing. Everybody was very strongly motivated by what the chef said. The cooks worked quickly and precisely without being cajoled. What the chef said was what they did.

There's a discipline that Japanese chefs have in the way they work, always with an eye toward cleanliness and organization.

Watch sushi chefs. They're constantly wiping down their counter, constantly wiping their blade. And every Japanese restaurant cook does it that way. The chefs are always very aware. They've been taught good work habits and skills. Watch a Japanese cook work with a knife. How many American chefs can pick up a carrot and turn it into a long, paper-thin strip? It seems that just about every Japanese chef can do that. The restaurants and kitchens in Japan function crisply, and things get done in such an orderly fashion. And the attention to cleanliness is amazing!

During the Tokyo competition, teams from 15 competing countries piled into the kitchen to put the finishing touches on their dishes—appetizers, entrées, and desserts, which were to be on display during the live television broadcast of the competition's finale. Chaos ensued as the teams labored to get everything done while working in the limited space assigned to each station. Things were a complete mess. Chefs and assistants were feverishly trying to make the opening deadline. Finally, we all went out for the show. When we returned, the kitchen was immaculate! Everything had been restored to order, and it was as if we had never been there! Very impressive.

Cuisine

I find endless delight and pleasure in Japanese food. First and foremost, because of the way it conveys wonderful, deep flavors with such lightness.

In Japanese cuisine there is great respect for ingredients, which allows them to really shine through. The simplest foods, such as sushi, offer an incredibly pleasurable experience. My cooking philosophy is that food should be basically simple, seasonal, and fresh, and it should delight people. I am a chef who enjoys creating good food to bring joy to others, rather than inventing dishes for the sake of creativity itself. I'm not saying every cuisine has to be authentic and tradition-bound. There's room for creativity and coming up with something new or different. That's why I like incorporating Japanese ingredients into my cuisine. But in general, I don't go in for crazy combinations of things. I don't like novelty or newness for its own sake. I'm not out to wow somebody by the sheer oddity of my food combinations. That's not what appeals to me.

The elements of a dish should flow from one another and should complement each other. For example, our filet mignon of tuna has been on the menu at the Union Square Cafe since 1985. At some point I thought that I needed to change the garnish for the tuna dish and give it an update. What flavors would complement this dish? I had a miso-based sauce that went over the tuna and pickled ginger as a garnish, along with an Asian-flavored vegetable stir-fry. So wasabi came to mind as something that would add punch to it.

It occurred to me that the vehicle for the wasabi could be another of our signature dishes, mashed potatoes. I had made a horseradish mashed potato that I served with a braised short rib, which was not that far away from the kind of flavor I imagined. I wanted something that was at the same time rich and creamy, soothing and easy to eat, but that also had a little bit of heat and punch. The wasabi goes with those flavors. That's done with sushi all the time. So it was a natural step to try it. The whole combination worked quite well, and the customers loved it. That's why it has been on the menu at the Union Square Cafe for a long time.

I was always pushing and trying new things and adding to the repertoire, especially with Japanese ingredients.

When I was Executive Chef at the Union Square Cafe, I had to locate the point between traditional cuisine and a culinary trend. If ultimately trendy, cutting-edge cuisine was "out here," then I was more in the middle. That meant I was going to have a base of dishes that I could rely on, that I knew were going to be well-executed year in and year out and, and which would always be great. Of course, I introduced some new dishes, too. I was always pushing and trying new things and adding to the repertoire, especially with Japanese ingredients. That way my customers got a balance between established repertoire that rotated in and out seasonally and new dishes that entered the menu. I loved it when guests said, "Come on. Bring back the porcini gnocchi! Where's the salmon with corn and balsamic beurre blanc?"

Chefs make a decision, or should make a decision, about what they want to call "their cuisine," or what they want it to be. Not every dish has to be authentic, but if I am going to do a spaghetti marinara, I want the guests to know that I am going to do a traditional one. So people know that when they come to Union Square Cafe, they're going to get spaghetti marinara, and it's going to be a really good version of it. I am not going to call it spaghetti marinara and then have Brussels sprouts in it. If I want to change it, fine, but I let people know somehow that this is my take on it. And if I set my mind to do that, I want to do it in the best way it has ever been done. I want to do it really, really well, with the ingredients the way they should be.

I see the culinary trend leaning to more Asian food.

It would be great if the Japanese government, perhaps at the prefecture-level, got organized in the way that is happening in Spain, and started promoting their products and cuisine. I think that would be big! Lacking that kind of unified expression from the Japanese government, it's going to fall to chefs, culinary educators, and travelers who go there to encourage diners to embrace Japanese cuisine.

Now the focus is French and Italian and Spanish. Well, how about adding Japanese to the mix? I would love to see that! I do see more people getting excited about what's going on in Japan. Japanese chefs are starting to come to the U.S. to teach knife and cooking skills. We need more of these kinds of chef exchanges. But people in the U.S. are still more familiar with Chinese food than with Japanese, so the initiative to increase this awareness of authentic Japanese cuisine and ingredients has to come from somewhere.

Another culinary trend I see, aside from Japanese cuisine, ingredients, and knives, is tableware. When I went to Kitcho the first time, I saw an amazing array of different shapes, sizes, and colors. They matched the dish to the color of the food inside it to create a harmonious effect. In Japan, there is a more intimate relationship between the plateware and the tableware than in the West. But now the trend in the U.S. is to use smaller and more colorful plates. That's another way the Japanese have influenced western cuisine.

Ingredients

When it comes to buying ingredients, which is crucial to any chef, there are differences between products produced and grown here, and those native to Japan.

Playing with different ingredients that require me to use my "sense memory" is a fun challenge. When I'm tasting new ingredients they often trigger, "Wow, this would be good with that." And then I try it. Sometimes it works and other times it doesn't! But experimenting can definitely lead to some fun stuff and interesting tastes.

A Japanese ingredient I use is shoyu, or soy sauce. Soy sauce is full of umami. It's like meat essence without being meat. And it shows up in odd places.

For example, I use it in Italian pasta when I make fresh tagliarini with black truffles. To make the truffle butter, I combine the black truffles with unsalted butter and Parmigiano. Then I drizzle in a dash of soy sauce. It adds seasoning and roundness. It's not the kind of thing you will identify out of the dish, but the dish is definitely better with it than without it. I'll bet they're not doing that in Italy! When I made this dish at the Union Square Tokyo, the chef and cooks didn't say, "What? Are you crazy?" No, they understood. "Yes, of course," they said, "put a little shoyu in it."

But I don't want to play around with an ingredient and introduce it to our guests until I'm pretty sure that it is going to be good. I make the dish and get somebody else to taste it with me. Chefs can get subjectively involved in their dishes and may be a little blinded by their enthusiasm. I might fall in love with the idea, but I'm not really thinking straight. So it's good to have somebody else's palate and opinion. In general, I don't go in for crazy.

Miso paste is another one of my favorite Japanese ingredients. It has an infinite variety of colors, textures, and tastes. Some miso are a very light color, some are chunky style, and some are smooth. Miso is such a rich base. It is a good foundation for other dishes and ingredients. Miso paste has a lot of potential as a replacement for the basic stocks in our kitchens. It can provide the umami dimension to food. It's what chefs use in Japan. I've been eating and using miso paste for a long time at home, and I think it's a great ingredient, really wonderful.

I frequently travel to Japan to oversee Union Square Tokyo. One of the things I most enjoy about my time there is the quality of the basic ingredients, especially the fish. I notice that when I go to my favorite sushi restaurants in Japan, the chefs are always saying, "I got this *uni* from here or this miso from there."

There's a tremendous sense of regionalism in all Japanese ingredients. Hopefully, professional chefs, students, and serious amateur cooks here in the U.S. will appreciate that and buy the best and most authentic ingredients they can find. Sure, you can pick up the cheapest soy sauce on the grocery shelf, but with a little extra effort, it's not that hard to find better ones.

Training

There's something beautiful about repeating the dish, even if you had nothing to do with the creation of it.

We don't need every cook coming out of culinary school thinking entrepreneurially. That's almost a bad thing. Discipline in our kitchen at the Union Square Cafe is a benign and sometimes not-so-benign dictatorship, where the executive chef is the master. What we look for in cooks are deeply ingrained skills. That is what is needed at first. I don't want some maverick in our kitchen who's thinking, "I'm going to do it this way." We want somebody who's going to say to the executive chef, "Yes, Chef, tell me how to do it and I'll do it that way. A hundred times, I'll still do it that way."

If you've got the spark and talent and you want to be an entrepreneur, you do that later, once you've got the basic skills. We don't need that entrepreneur's spirit unless it translates into perfectionism. When I was Executive Chef, I liked to hear a cook say, "I'm going to get damn good at this by focusing and learning my craft." But we didn't need somebody who was already thinking of six other ways he or she could do it when I said, "Do it this way."

When you're coming up as a line cook, you can take in everything for yourself. You learn from your chef, learn from the restaurant, learn from the successes, learn from the mistakes, and soak it all up. It's all for you. In return you give your hard work, and you get paid for it. But when you step up to become the leader of a restaurant—the sous chef or the executive chef—you have to turn around and give back. When you say, "Okay, I'm in charge now," you've got to have something to give back to all those people looking up to you as the leader. If you don't have the life experience, the smarts, or the maturity to guide them and give them something worthwhile, you're not going to last very long.

> *You may even be a good cook with ideas and creativity. But do you have the stability to turn that into a sound business, or are you just going to be hopping around every eight months to the newest restaurant that's opening?*

The Japanese have a different attitude in approaching their craft. I respect and admire the ideals they embody. They believe that in the span of a person's life, it takes a long time to develop deep and mature skills. The Japanese get very, very good at a chosen craft. But they work at it for years.

Tools

Owning the finest Japanese knives is like owning a Ferrari. They require great skill and demand more from the user, but they provide a much more high-performance experience.

In the 1980s, very few non-Japanese cooks were using traditional Japanese knives. Most chefs in the U.S. had their Sabatiers, Henckels, or Wüsthofs. To make an automotive analogy, using these high-quality French and German knives is like driving a Mercedes-Benz. They're solid, reliable, a great investment, and not inexpensive. But owning the finest Japanese knives is like owning a Ferrari. They require greater skill and demand more of the user, but they provide a much more high-performance experience. They reward the user who takes time to master them with great pleasure and high performance.

When I bought my first traditional, carbon-steel Japanese knives in Tokyo in 1982—I still have them to this day, by the way—I had no idea how to use them because I didn't realize how task-specific they are and that the blade is one-sided. I just thought they were the most beautiful and serious tools I had ever seen. And they were much sharper than anything I'd ever experienced. I went back to the shop where I bought them and got a quick lesson on sharpening them because I wanted to keep them that way.

Today you can go into a typical U.S. restaurant kitchen or catering company and see more and more Misono, Suisin, Nenox, Masanobu, or other brands of western-style Japanese knives. For example, I was on a job with our catering company, Union Square Events, and one of the young prep cooks—he seemed to be new and was probably just part-time—asked me to show him how I wanted something cut, so I said, "Okay, let me see your knife." And he handed me a gorgeous, expensive Misono. That was a good sign!

Many American culinary teachers and schools encourage students to buy western-style Japanese knives, but there definitely is not the same emphasis on knife handling and knife skills here as in Japan. Students and professional cooks don't really need traditional Japanese knives unless they're going to be doing tasks specific to Japanese cuisine, like cutting fish for sashimi. In my case, I'm so crazy about all of the knives that I have to have both kinds. Traditional Japanese knives were developed from a specific task. For example, someone long ago said something like, "We're going to eat eel. This fish has these particular characteristics, so we'll need a knife that has this shape to accomplish the task."

When I first bought a traditional Japanese deba, I tried using it as we would use a chef's knife. But it didn't work because it's not meant for that. I was trying to push it through a carrot, and it was not working because the blade is too thick for that. Later I learned that it's for filleting fish.

On the other hand, if someone takes a traditional Japanese knife and finds another use for it in a different cuisine, I don't have any problem with that. I think it's fine if it's efficient, but there's no sense at all in using a tool that makes the work more difficult.

A Day in the Life

What we do in this business is very special, because the end product—delicious and well-cooked food—actually becomes who you are.

My job focus now is on a broader spectrum of tasks that touch all of our restaurants and businesses. I may be cooking at our catering facilities or restaurant kitchens with executive chefs or helping develop new recipes for our much-loved, modern-day hamburger stand, Shake Shack, or designing kitchens for our food outlets, like the one at the New York Mets stadium, Citi Field. And of course, I'm traveling to Tokyo to cook at Union Square Tokyo, where I am the Executive Chef and consult on seasonal menu changes.

Through it all, I continue to be motivated by this wonderful business that I entered nearly forty years ago. It's a delight to watch people enjoying a well-prepared meal served in a wonderful environment of hospitality and conviviality by people who genuinely enjoy bringing these pleasures to our guests. What we do in this business is very special, because the end product—delicious and well-cooked food—actually becomes who we are in a very intimate way. It's a great responsibility we carry and a great privilege and pleasure to be able to do it.

Photo credit: Monika Sziladi

FOURTEEN

MARCUS SAMUELSSON

Chef/Restaurateur, Founder of
Marcus Samuelsson Group

Marcus Samuelsson was born in Ethiopia and was raised by his adoptive parents in Sweden. He studied at the Culinary Institute in Gothenburg, apprenticed in Switzerland and Austria, and came to the U.S. in 1991. At 24, as Executive Chef of Aquavit, he became the youngest chef to receive a three-star restaurant review from *The New York Times*. In 2003 he was named Best Chef: New York City by the James Beard Foundation and has received numerous other culinary awards.

Marcus Samuelsson is the author of several cookbooks, including, *The Soul of a New Cuisine*, the winner of the James Beard Foundation's Best International Cookbook. He is a visiting professor at Umeå University School of Restaurant and Culinary Arts in Sweden and is an advisor to the Institute of Culinary Education in New York City. Today Marcus Samuelsson divides his time between his New York City restaurant, Red Rooster Harlem, his non-profit, Careers Through Culinary Arts, and other charities. His latest book, *Yes, Chef: A Memoir* was published in 2012.

Influences

> *In terms of cooking, the main language in the kitchen—the only language—is good taste and good food.*

When I first started studying cooking in Switzerland, I thought that after I mastered German and French, the rest would be easy. I thought, "Okay, ta-da! I'm learning German now. I'm learning French." But it didn't get easier once I mastered the languages. That's when I realized that language is important. But in terms of cooking, the main language—the only language—is good taste and good food.

Every day our meetings were in German, and the menu was in French. Then I had to communicate back with the guys I worked with in Munich. So it was always this back and forth, back and forth. It was organized chaos, so mistakes happened all the time. And we got yelled at all the time. I think I was cursed at in every language there is—and it always sounded the same. But getting yelled at helped me develop the ability to exchange ideas with people. Now I appreciate all those different curses and insults thrown in my face in all those different languages. I learned that if I wanted to be a chef, I was going to get yelled at a lot.

> *My goal was not to get yelled at, and then I became the guy who told staff, "Don't do this or that," but I didn't yell.*

As a young chef, when my bosses yelled at me, I threw up. I even cried. At that time, I was so young that I didn't really know how to handle it. But the stress always made a big knot in my belly. I would run to the bathroom, throw up, come back out, and work. But I couldn't give up. I was the representative of my family, so it wasn't just about me. No, no. It was also about my mom and my dad and my sister—everyone who helped me get a scholarship to study cooking in Switzerland. That's why, once I got here, I knew that if I got yelled at it didn't matter.

There are some chefs who are natural yellers. Their attitude is, "It doesn't sound like shouting to me. That's just the way I talk." One chef I worked for was like that. He was much older than I was. And he just spoke in one voice—loud! He was screaming all the time. When I came to work, he'd shout, "Good morning!" When he yelled at me to come to his office, I had no idea what would happen. He might say, "I'm sending you … go now." Or it could be, "You did a good job." Or, "Get the hell out of here." It didn't matter. It was always in the same loud tone. At least he was consistent. He came from a different generation. He had a lot of pressure on him every day and just never let his guard down. But he got everything he wanted. We did everything for him, and he did everything for us. There was never a problem with communication. I still think about him to this day.

There was no way I could quit, so I had to figure out ways to hide from the yelling. I joked, "Choose your torture. Which one do you want—the knife or the words?" My goal was not to get yelled at, and then I became the guy who told staff, "Don't do this or that," but I didn't yell.

I'm not a chef who yells. I don't think it's a sign of strength to be a yeller. I don't like to step out of character. I don't like to get angry. If you're angry when you make a meal or angry when you eat it, the food is not going to taste good. If you're angry, you're not focused. You're hopeless in the kitchen. I'm very demanding, but I think there are other ways to show that I am serious.

Cuisine

Cooking is similar to being a fashion designer—I'm always working one season ahead.

When people come into my restaurant today, I can't stop thinking about what we will be doing six months from now. For example, if it's January and we have a winter menu, I'm thinking about the menu for June or July. A menu takes about six months, from concept to starting point. If I'm working on the menu for late spring or early summer, I am probably thinking about that menu when it is snowing outside.

I spend a lot of time developing new dishes for that menu, too. Let's say you are my special customer. I know you love trout, so I'll get the ocean trout from XYZ and the other ingredients from some other place. I form an intimate relationship with the vendors. If it is January, we'll serve the trout with a seasonal vegetable, for example. But if we don't have seasonal vegetables yet, we will use something else like garlic and whatever else we can substitute. We can add some ingredients, and this fish is going to be beautiful.

For me, judging a dish is very internal. I ask myself, how does it taste? How does it look? I watch how my customers react to a new dish. Sometimes when I am developing a dish, I need to serve it three, four, five, six, seven times. By then I have the size right, I have the cuts right. I've settled on doing it a certain way.

Many of the cooks in New York are from other countries, myself included.

In America, many chefs fresh out of culinary school have a big challenge. If they haven't been raised around food and cooking, they can't say, "I know how to do that." No! To really understand ingredients and know what goes into a dish, they need a lot more experience. That's why I think that a lot of cooks who are immigrants do better in our kitchen. Even if they don't have money to go to culinary school, they were raised around food.

Many of the cooks in New York are from other countries, myself included. We grew up around taste—salt, sweet, sour, bitter. We all have different things in our library of culinary knowledge based on the journey that brought us to America. Here people eat potpies or snacks for dinner, or they go to a Pizza Hut. That kind of eating ruins their sense of taste. And they don't break bread together. Getting together to create a meal where everyone has a role—cooking, setting the table, eating—this has been forgotten. So being a cook is not just about the ingredients. It's not just about the cuisine. It's the whole experience.

Ingredients

If you allow yourself to take the time to learn about the source of your ingredients, you can be a great chef.

I think the most important ingredient is water. As a chef, I rely on clean water every day. In my kitchens, we use water for everything, from mixing it with other ingredients to rinsing produce to washing dishes. In Japan, every chef is trained to pay attention to the water. Every chef needs great water to cook great food. If you allow yourself to take the time to learn about the source of your ingredients, you can be a great chef.

One really useful Japanese ingredient is yuzu, and it's popular for many reasons. Some chefs think it is a combination of lemon and lime, but yuzu is neither. People may think that the tastes are similar, but they aren't. Yuzu works so well in cooking and works so well in flavor tests.

But the Japanese ingredient I like most is smoked fish liver. When I went to the Tsukiji Fish Market in Tokyo, I learned a lot about it. I saw how the Japanese care for and preserve the freshness of their fish. I have never in my life seen so many types of fish. I can't even describe my excitement. I've been to fish markets all over the world, but nothing compared to the Tsukiji Fish Market.

Training

Culinary schools are doing a great job of pushing international cuisine ahead. But they're in a transition.

In the past, culinary schools, such as The French Culinary Institute, the Institute of Culinary Education, and The Culinary Institute of America, have focused primarily on French cooking and Italian cooking. Today's chefs want to learn about other cuisines, too. It sounds like I'm not pro-French. I like French cooking very much, but I think the culinary schools need to be open to other cuisines. Now the cooking schools are beginning to recognize the need to include other cuisines and are adjusting their curriculum.

Right now the cooking schools have another dilemma. How can a new chef who has just paid $70,000 for cooking school tuition afford to take a typical nine-dollar-an-hour restaurant job? I don't know what the solution is, but it's very difficult when you do the math. This brings up the question: Who is the cooking school for? In the past this was never the question, because cooking schools were for those people who wanted to learn how to become cooks or chefs and didn't go to college.

Today, the schools have a more diverse group of students. Now many people are attending cooking school because they want a career change. A potential chef might say, "I was a lawyer, and now I want to try cooking." The guy or gal who didn't go to college can't afford to go to cooking school, so he or she goes directly into a restaurant and learns the basics from the other cooks in the kitchen. This is not a bad or a good thing. It's just a different way of entering the profession.

When students graduate, they are told, "You're just at the beginning, the beginning, the beginning!"

In terms of training curriculum, I think cooking schools do a good job of teaching basic cooking skills. They also provide students with great tools. They have the best kitchens, computers, the best libraries with the latest cookbooks, and excellent teachers. Although American culinary schools are good at training, the fact remains that many students are frustrated because they have paid so much money to go to culinary school. Then when students graduate, they are told, "You're just at the beginning, the beginning, the beginning!" And it's true.

For example, the other day I got a phone call from a student and a couple of his friends who wanted to ask me questions about buying a restaurant in their neighborhood. They asked me the type of questions that I would never have asked at their age. But they missed the point about experiencing the journey of becoming an owner/chef. I didn't even know where to start with them. I was completely baffled, so I couldn't reply. These young people think, "It's me, now. Now! Success now!" I don't believe that young chefs like them will succeed in the restaurant business. However, I'm inside the culinary schools a lot, and I see that they're making an effort to change that kind of thinking.

Passion is what we're looking for in the people we hire.

We are very picky about who we hire. How do we choose our people? For me, it's attitude. Attitude is definitely number one. We are looking for a sense of confidence, but not arrogance. In general, I think women are more confident than men. The guys' confidence often translates into arrogance. But I think that if you have the confidence and a true passion, if you really want to go somewhere and if you're humble at the same time, then you can work here. If you're passionate about food, you can be 15 or 50 years old. Age doesn't matter.

At the same time, being a chef is very much like being a blues musician. You can be 65 and seem young or 16 and seem old. Success in the kitchen has nothing to do with age or what you can do. The skills can be learned. Skills come with practice and performing the same tasks every day. But today, most young chefs do not come in with a high skill set, because they lack experience. Passion is what we're looking for in the people we hire.

We're essentially looking for an eighteen-month to two-year relationship. Any commitment less than that is not enough. And the most important communication skill for young chefs in the kitchen is a willingness to share. They have to share everything they know. That's why we pick people who are really committed and willing to put in the time. The chefs who stay with us can be very successful. After they have worked with us, they can go to Sweden, they can go to Japan, they can go anyplace they want. They might even move to Daniel or to Jean-Georges afterwards. We see that all the time.

A Day in the Life

"Why did you do that? We've worked all damn day. Why did you throw all the food out?"

When I was in France, some of the best cooks there were Japanese. Actually, they were the older Japanese guys who really loved being in Europe. They knew Japanese food, and they were highly skilled cooks. At one restaurant I worked in, there was a French chef who always paced back and forth in the kitchen. One day, for whatever reason, the French chef threw out all the prep for that day. Afterwards, when we were all in the refrigerator, the Japanese cook asked the French chef, "Why did you do that? We've worked all damn day. Why did you throw all the food out?"

The French chef answered the Japanese cook by punching him in the belly! But the Japanese cook's stomach muscles were so strong that the French chef just howled because he hurt his hand. I started to laugh, but the Japanese cook never changed his expression and didn't say another word. There was no doubt that the French chef was embarrassed, but so was the Japanese cook because he didn't want to embarrass his boss. I think the French chef almost broke his hand, and all that time I was laughing. We were in the refrigerator, and I knew that I was going to get hit next, and I had no idea what to do. This incident demonstrated where we all were at. In France, I expected this kind of behavior, but the Japanese cook showed the French cook, "You really can't touch me. You're really in shock right now, because you really can't touch me." I don't think I will ever forget that!

❖

Photo credit: Jim Franco

FIFTEEN

SUVIR SARAN

New Delhi–born Chef Suvir Saran has nurtured a lifelong passion for the traditional flavors of Indian cooking, which has led him to become an accomplished chef, cookbook author, educator, and organic farmer. Suvir Saran's approachable and informed style has helped to demystify Indian cuisine in America and has ultimately formed American Masala, his culinary philosophy, which celebrates the best of Indian and American cooking.

Suvir Saran is Chairman of Asian Culinary Studies for The Culinary Institute of America. He leads classes nationwide for audiences ranging from home cooks and fellow chefs to physicians and nutritionists. He has been a featured speaker and guest chef for notable gatherings including Food Network's South Beach Wine & Food Festival and the New York City Wine & Food Festival.

Suvir Saran has penned three cookbooks, and was Executive Owner/Chef at Devi in New York City. At that time, Devi earned a three-star rating from *New York* magazine and two stars from *The New York Times*. It was the first Indian restaurant in the United States to earn a Michelin star.

Influences

I was always doing things for others in the kitchen, even though I didn't think I would ever be a chef.

I grew up in India as a Hindu vegetarian, where the family center was the kitchen. There was no alcohol, no meat, no fish, none of that. When I was four or five years old, I was always in the kitchen while my brother, sister, family, and friends were socializing. When we went to a family friend's home, I would run into the kitchen and ask, "Can I make salad? Can I wash this?" I didn't relate to the other boys. I knew I was different, but the mothers and grandmothers never judged me. They were delighted that this little kid wanted to peel a potato or a cucumber, but they wouldn't let me use a knife, so I washed potatoes and brought food from the kitchen to the table. I was always doing things for others in the kitchen, even though I didn't think I would ever be a chef. I had no role model. The only place where I didn't feel as if people were judging me was in the kitchen.

I wanted to be a painter, so I enrolled in the School of Visual Arts in New York City to study design. In India I had done knitting, sculpture, pottery, but everything at the school in New York was on the computer. I wanted to use my hands, but they had become obsolete. I was unhappy in school and hated my day life. I wanted to become a normal human being, so every night I cooked for 20, 40, even 100 people, many of whom were strangers. Friends would bring six or eight people to dinner, and I was this young Indian cook who made the best Indian food in New York. Instead of going to school, I was home prepping all day. Then in the evening, I hosted parties where I lived, at 90th Street and Columbus Avenue.

One evening after dinner, a guest suggested that I teach a cooking class.

Another guest, Elisabeth Bumiller, a reporter for the Style section of *The Washington Post,* said, "Sweetie, you can't do it for free. You have to charge." So that was the first time I charged. I was about 23 years old.

Cuisine

Do I have to repeat myself like some chefs? No. I do one thing, and then I have to move on to the next. I teach the chefs how to prepare the dish, and I move on and create a new one.

The recipes I made were not the standard ones that people think of when they think of Indian food. These were home recipes. These recipes were passed down from grandmothers to mothers, and I cooked them for my friends. I cooked that way because entertaining people at home is as much about respecting people and their taste as it is about the desire to entertain. Cooking and entertaining are about giving and generosity.

Indian cuisine shines in the home kitchen. It's not a restaurant cuisine. If you are rich or in the middle class, it is an insult to invite guests to a dinner and take them to a restaurant. It means that you don't have the money to entertain at home or you don't value them enough to invite them to your home. At home you have one or two cooks to prepare the meal. Entertaining at home is very prestigious. It's like the Japanese attention to detail, and it's from the home kitchen.

When *Publishers Weekly* reviewed my book, *American Masala: 125 New Classics from My Home Kitchen*, they said my recipes begin at home, unlike other chefs. I'm not a restaurant chef—I'm a home cook before anything else. I don't have a desire to repeat the same dish 25 times. I make it, perfect it, and then I'm finished. I am the traveler, the dreamer. Do I have to repeat myself like some chefs? No. I do one thing, and then I have to move on to the next. I teach the chefs how to prepare the dish, and I move on and create a new one.

I learned about Japanese food when I visited Japan. Once I saw Japanese chefs cook in Japan, I realized that their goal is perfection—to be the best they can be with the best ingredients and the best food service.

There is no disconnect between what the customers are eating and what the chef is doing. The chefs are, at every level, perfection, perfection, perfection. They buy the freshest ingredients, the most beautiful shoyu, the most wonderful mirin. At every level, there is perfection. Japan is about simplicity and harmony. That is the very core of Japanese society.

While visiting the Suntory Whiskey manufacturing plant in Yamazaki, Japan, I saw a French pastry shop with a name that reminded me of Brittany. There is no ocean near Yamazaki, so the idea of French pastries there seemed so out of place, but then nothing is out of place in Japan, so I walked in. The shop, run by a Japanese man and his wife, was perfection beyond belief. I learned that the wife had attended the Escoffier School of Culinary Arts in France, and the husband had studied pastries and baking at The Culinary Institute of America in Napa Valley, California.

The couple came back to their hometown of Yamazaki, where they created this pastry shop that offers every conceivable pastry confection, from madeleines to tarts, better than anyone could imagine—even better than in France. I bought up practically everything, went to the Suntory plant, and then went back to the pastry shop. They had new offerings, so I had to buy everything all over again, but I missed one little cheese pizza. When I said I wanted to buy it, the wife insisted on giving it to me. I said, "No, no, no," but between her lack of English and my lack of Japanese, I accepted her gift. So here in Yamazaki, a Japanese couple was making authentic French pastries to perfection. That speaks a lot about the Japanese mentality.

In Japan, every meal is treated as if it'll be your last meal, so the chefs do it perfectly every time.

I realized that in Japan, I never ate anything that was less than special. The fish I ate in the evening had been swimming in the ocean that morning. I think that local connection is so amazing. In Tokyo, I walked into an unknown place to have cocktails. At first it looked like a fruit stand, but there was a bar at the opposite end of the room. Standing behind the bar in front of a display of antique bottles from around the world were two bartenders in tuxedos. I asked for a martini, or a mojito, or a margarita. The bartenders got the fruit from that stand and, after chopping it, placed it into little Japanese bowls filled with the liquors and squeezed citrus. The ripe fruit in the drink heightened the experience. The cocktails were like poetry, and they were so delicious I could have cried. The Japanese never had cocktails until they learned about them from the West. Now they think of every little thing.

In Tokyo I went to a small tempura restaurant with eight seats at the bar. The chef and the assistant sat on the floor chopping vegetables and then frying them. They were also the hostess and waiters. There were 11 courses, all of which were tempura, and each dish was better than the last. There were thin pieces of ginger dipped into the batter and then fried in the oil. They came out like crunchy little breadsticks. And deep-fried ginger shoots—heaven on earth. The chefs' attention to detail, whether they were cooking or presenting, was incredible.

We visited Chef Ueda's restaurant and watched him butcher a fish. He is a magician with a knife. He had this ease about him, like a performer. It is an art form and a tradition. He took a needle and jabbed it in the fish's head between the ears. When the fish's mouth opened, that's when we knew the fish had died. It wasn't like he was butchering the fish. It was more like he was massaging it. It was done so gracefully.

Ingredients

When I visited Japan, I didn't have to cook to learn about Japanese food. I learned by watching the chefs and tasting the food. I learned that if I use the best ingredients, then I don't have to add 10 more things.

Now, that Japanese sensibility affects everything that I do every time I cook, whether I'm cooking Indian, French, or Italian. The sensibility I learned in Japan is stamped in my mind until I die.

Before I create a new dish, I pick plates that I like. I make up the meal in my head and create dishes that look pretty on the plates. Before I create a particular dish, I might choose a round plate, or maybe a flat one. This dictates how recipes are developed. Different plates and bowls make me think of foods that go with them.

I think tempura and yakitori are my favorite Japanese-inspired dishes that I like to cook at home.

We made a version of yakitori with mirin, shoyu, salt, pepper, and *shichimi*—the seven-flavor Japanese spice mixture—and I slow-roasted them together in the convection oven for three-and-a-half hours at low temperature. As for the peppers, I cut them in half and boiled them until they were almost al dente. I had to bring in some other flavor, so I added some olive oil with soy to the water. Then I grilled the peppers with the skins on. The flavor had permeated through the boiling water. The texture was good, the flavor was complex. I also had carrots that I cooked over a long time. I added more mirin, less shoyu, sesame, salt, pepper, and shichimi. I added a lot to them, so they were spicy.

And I had asparagus, which I ended up grilling. First I let the asparagus sit in water for two hours so they were rehydrated and juicy. Then I brushed them with mirin and shoyu, salt, pepper, and shichimi and put them on the grill. They got crisp on the outside, and when they were caramelized, I put on lemon zest. So it was Italian antipasti with a Japanese twist.

Next I did lobster tail, but instead of a straight butter dip, I made a miso sauce and a little butter. It was perfect—nothing fussy. I put the lobster on the grill with nothing but a little butter and salt and then onto the platter. Finally, I dusted the lobster with shichimi, salt, and pepper, and nothing more. It was all about the lobster. So how can you go wrong? Everybody likes a little spice.

Japanese chefs think about subtle flavors—Indian chefs think about drama.

When you go to an Indian restaurant, you don't order just one dish. There are also condiments, fresh vegetables, and the protein. You never just eat one thing. You eat a complete meal. This is how a Japanese chef thinks, too. All types of ingredients go together to create a complete meal. In that way, we Indian cooks are like the Japanese, because they care for their food but don't give people large amounts of any one dish.

One of the biggest differences between Indian and Japanese food has to do with conception of flavor. I didn't understand the Japanese conception of flavor until I saw the Japanese chefs in action. For example, for a hot pot soup, Japanese chefs combine a lot of beautiful fish and seafood with very savory shoyu and a little rice vinegar. Good quality shoyu has an amazing, rich flavor. Adding kombu and dried bonito flakes gives it layers of flavor. In India, it's the opposite. We have lots of spice, so who cares about flavors?

The ideas regarding food are diametrically opposed. Japanese chefs think, "How can we make it simple?" Indian chefs think, "How can we make it more complicated?"

Many chefs are tempted to persuade their customers to taste a new dish by explaining or saying something positive about the ingredients or the preparation. But customers may not think that exploration is important, so it is better to just give them a chance to embrace the dish. This allows the customer to take ownership. It's not about preaching or selling them on the dish. In many cases, the less said the better.

For example, one evening I had cooked chicken tails for some guests. If they had known what was in the dish, they probably would have said, "I'm not eating that!" When they asked me what the main ingredient in the dish was, I told them it was just some dark meat. They ate it and loved it. When people don't know the ingredients, it's okay. However, these days I do ask people, "Are you allergic to anything? Can you eat beef?" Once they say "Yes, yes, yes," then I can surprise them after the meal by saying, "Well, you've just eaten veal brains or liver," and they say, "Woo-hoo!"

My mission is to not only teach about good ingredients, flavors, and cooking, but to emphasize that it is important for people to pay attention to and be connected to the food that they eat.

As the Chairman of Asian Culinary Studies for The Culinary Institute of America, I travel and teach at large and small cooking schools all over the country. I also work with Harvard Medical School on a program called "Healthy Kitchens, Healthy Lives." This program gives physicians a better understanding of food and nutrition so that when they talk with patients about how diet affects health, both can make better decisions. I also want to educate chefs and other people about the benefits of eating more legumes, like beans and peanuts.

I think anyone going to cooking school needs to do what their teachers tell them, without prejudice and without blinders. It's important to see everything. But students must build on what they have learned in school, because their education doesn't end there. It's just the beginning. It's what they learn outside of school by being mindful every day, every minute, that's important.

Tools

Japanese knives are as amazing as they are beautiful.

My favorite knife is a little one with a bamboo handle. When I use a Japanese knife, it is like magic because it is so sharp. There is no effort. It's the knife doing the work rather than my muscles. A bad knife is an obstacle. I'm thinking about the chopping, not about the next step. What the Japanese have given us through centuries of practice is a perfect tool that lets us dream about our cooking. We dream and keep cooking. The minute I have a knife that's dull and heavy, I think, "Oh God, I still have two more vegetables to chop."

A Day in the Life

"Something's burning!"

Chef Hiroko Shimbo and I were in Minneapolis, at a lovely cooking school. We had just finished teaching a class on how to make home-style Indian apple chutney and had sat down for dinner. That's when I said, "Something's burning!" The students said that everything was on the table, but I said that something was hurting my nose. It smelled like burning cinnamon and ginger. One student ran to the kitchen because she realized that she forgot to serve her dish and that it was still on the stove. She came back into the room with a charred container. Most of the ingredients inside had been burnt to ashes. But remaining in the middle in the bowl were two teaspoons of this beautifully caramelized chutney.

I had a pinch. It was the best chutney ever because of the caramelized sugar. I gave the rest of the chutney to the student and told her this recipe would be in my next book.

SIXTEEN

YOSUKE SUGA

Chef/Consultant

Yosuke Suga was introduced to French cuisine at his father's restaurant, Chez Kobe, in Nagoya, Japan. After graduating from high school, he traveled to Lyon to learn French, then returned to Japan, working savory and pastry stations in hotel restaurants before taking over Chez Kobe four years later. Soon after he met Joël Robuchon and began the ten-year working relationship that has taken him around the world and honed his understanding of French cuisine.

Yosuke Suga began as an assistant to Joël Robuchon. He spent nearly five years beside the chef, working in his laboratory, helping on his TV shows, and traveling worldwide to cook private dinners. In 2003, Yosuke Suga opened the Tokyo outpost of L'Atelier de Joël Robuchon as Executive Chef. In 2006, Suga opened L'Atelier in the Four Seasons Hotel New York, where he worked until 2009. Yosuke Suga worked at Joël Robuchon Taipei until 2010 and then returned to Paris for the opening of the new L'Atelier. In early 2014 Yosuke Suga left Robuchon's team to start his own food lab and restaurant consulting business in Tokyo and Paris. He plans to open a small restaurant in Tokyo, and he has produced an online video program sponsored by Conrad Hotels, "Yosuke Suga's Tokyo."

Influences

I was 21 when I began working in Mr. Robuchon's laboratory in Paris. There were three cooks with him in the laboratory, so I was lucky to get the position, because many cooks worked in his restaurant.

I was born into a restaurant family in Nagoya. My grandfather started a European-style restaurant, where he and my father worked together. About the time that I was a year old, my father also opened a French restaurant, so when I was young I spent many days in the kitchen and came in contact with the chefs. My father had good relations with the people who worked for him, and many guests came to our house. I remember how comfortable it was growing up in that atmosphere. That was what first triggered my interest in restaurants and French cooking.

I first thought about becoming a chef when I was in high school, and I vaguely knew that I wanted to have a restaurant. So off I went to France as soon as I graduated from high school, not to work at a French restaurant but to study the language for half a year. By the end of six months I'd made the decision to become a chef. I wanted to stay in France, but I didn't have the right visa, nor did I have much knowledge about French cooking. I realized that I had to study cooking properly in Japan. So, with my father's help, I got a job at the Hotel Seiyo Ginza in Tokyo, and from there I went to Joël Robuchon in France.

I was 21 when I began working in Mr. Robuchon's laboratory in Paris. There were three cooks with him in the laboratory, so I was lucky to get the position, because many cooks worked in his restaurant. It was like an army. Many of these people worked in Mr. Robuchon's restaurant for two weeks, two days, or a year just so they could study with him.

There weren't too many people who knew about the laboratory or how to get into it, and Mr. Robuchon wasn't looking to hire anyone, but I knew a friend of his. I think the major reason he hired me was instinct. When I first met him he checked everything out—my cooking, my clothes, how I talked, how I cleaned, how I looked at him. I think that's why I got the job.

In the laboratory, Mr. Robuchon had his right-hand person, his shadow, who had worked with him for more than 20 years. This shadow did everything in the kitchen, and I helped him, so I was the shadow's shadow. I worked in the laboratory for five years and learned about food and the customer.

I learned how important the guests are, of course, and also about cleanliness, organization, and perfection. Yes, perfection. Perfection means that you can't be lazy. It means that you need to be in the kitchen all the time and you need to organize your cooks.

Many chefs try to prepare food by themselves, but chefs like Joël Robuchon know how to use their cooks' passion and ability. His cooks make whatever he imagines so he doesn't need to use his own hands. He would explain to me what he wanted, and I would try to realize his idea. Then he would taste the dish. He might say, "Too much garlic," or "Maybe we need to change the herb." When I started working for Mr. Robuchon in 1998, I never thought I could work for the same person for that length of time, but I realized that it was very important to stay with him.

I received many great opportunities from him, and I learned many things, because I listened to him and watched him. He's very old school. It's like that at a Japanese restaurant, too. The mentor is always a very tough guy who continually expects more and more from himself and his restaurant. I was born into a restaurant family, so I had the right mentality, but I wanted to do better, and I wanted to do it in Joël Robuchon's laboratory. So every day I cleaned, cleaned, cleaned—for three years! I even cleaned the bathroom ceiling every day! You don't need to clean the ceiling every day, but I did!

Cuisine

How do I compare Japanese cooking and French cooking? In Japanese cuisine, we don't use much oil or fat. With French food, we use a lot of butter, olive oil, and animal fat—I mean a lot!

However, I do incorporate the philosophy of Japanese cuisine into my French cooking. For example, at the restaurant, we do many tastings with three or so dishes, and I try to include some kind of Japanese-influenced dish with little or no butter, cream, or fat in the ingredients. That's how I let Japanese cuisine influence my French cooking. My food and technique is French, and how I work is French, but my philosophy and culture is Japanese, and my vision is minimalism.

In Japan and France and in China, too, there's a long history of cuisine. We don't really like to try anything new, and we don't do fusion. When I was in Japan, I never put Japanese ingredients in French cuisine. When I was chef at the same restaurant in Tokyo, I never used Japanese ingredients because diners wanted real French food. But here in the United States, a chef is freer to experiment. Some customers and some food critics might say that what I cook here is not really French cuisine. But many guests tell me that our food tastes clean. To me, that means freshness. When customers eat high quality, fresh ingredients, it's easier to digest their meal.

Ingredients

I've said many times that ingredients must speak for themselves.

I use Japanese ingredients in some dishes. For example, I use *amadai*, a Japanese fish that is similar to tilefish. I pan-fry the fish in oil with the scales left on so that the skin gets very crispy. Then I add some yuzu broth and some herbs like shiso. Because I don't use much oil and butter, it tastes light. People think it's Japanese cuisine, but it's really more European. The taste is very Japanese—it's very light and flavorful—but it's not really Japanese cuisine.

I also like yuzu, which is a Japanese citrus. It has a very interesting, strong flavor that is completely different from lemon or lime. I also use some kinds of pickles that you can't find in the U.S. And I like *kinome*, the leaf of the prickly ash tree, whose berries are ground into sansho pepper. The leaves are used as a garnish for many Japanese dishes. Japanese chefs use it a lot because the leaves have a fresh, subtle mint flavor and a tender texture. It's very refreshing. However, it can be challenging to use some Japanese ingredients, because American customers are not familiar with their unique flavors and tastes.

As a chef, I think it's very important to know about the quality of the ingredients. You need to taste good products.

Here in the U.S., and especially in New York City, customers love new food experiences and are eager to discover new tastes and flavors. That's why if you go into the kitchen of any trendy restaurant, you will probably see a lot of Japanese ingredients like daikon, or shishito pepper, or wasabi, even if they are not obvious in the dishes, because people think the flavors are interesting.

Take miso, for example. There are more than 1,000 kinds of miso in Japan. Many chefs in New York use miso, but they don't always choose the best one for the dish. If I go to a restaurant and taste Japanese ingredients in the food, I can tell when the chef didn't understand how to properly use the ingredient. Maybe it's not a big issue because their customers are happy with the food, but if I were that chef, I would try to find someone to teach me more about using particular ingredients.

Chefs also need to know about tuna. Which tuna is the best one to use for a particular dish? It's the chef who decides which one to use because there are differences in flavor and costs. Not knowing the best tuna for the dish can lead to a wrong decision. It is important to know everything about tuna—the good ones, the expensive ones, the cheaper ones, how they taste when they are cooked—everything. Then the chef can decide which one to choose for a particular dish. One kind of tuna might be good for a sauce, but the same tuna in another dish might be too strong. So it's knowledge, not just the recipe, that makes the difference.

Training

Young cooks need to understand that if they keep moving around from restaurant to restaurant, nobody will take a chance on them.

When I was 20 years old, nobody trained me or taught me recipes. I had to observe and absorb them. In Japanese, we say "steal." In France it was the same—nobody told me the recipe or what to do. Mr.

Robuchon never gave me anything written down because I was expected to learn by watching. When I began as a cook, I worked not only to learn cooking skills and technique, but also to understand and to build a relationship and trust.

The mentality of today's young cooks is very different from what it used to be. Now cooks work in the kitchen to make money and to have a day off. They work one year here at Joël Robuchon, at Jean-Georges for a year, and then at Daniel for one year. In the past, cooks knew of Joël Robuchon because they worked in his restaurant. They were not expected to know about other restaurants because there was no Internet, no connections, and no relationship.

But today people talk about a restaurant that's opening in two months that pays very well, and the cooks leave for that job. But even if chefs are smart and learn the technique in just one year, they cannot learn philosophy or patience. Because they are moving around so much, it's difficult to train these cooks and to trust them on a deeper level.

Young cooks need to learn to do more than just make the recipe, but now they expect me to show them everything. "Chef, please show me, please tell me." But this is not the way I learned from Mr. Robuchon. I tell them, "I'm sorry if you want me to teach you—you're learning now, here." I'm teaching cooks exactly the way Mr. Robuchon taught me. He never showed me the techniques, he never "taught" me, but I learned many things from him.

> *Once a cook asked me, "Chef, since I've been in the same station so many months, why don't you move me?" I told him, "Because I don't trust you enough. If you don't want to stay, then quit! That's it!"*

I need cooks I can trust; otherwise I cannot give them more responsibility. In our kitchen, we have five different stations. If I trust

216 · YOSUKE SUGA

a cook, then I'll move them to another station so they can learn more things. But if they're not trying or aren't patient, I won't move them. Young cooks need to understand that if they keep moving around from restaurant to restaurant, nobody will take a chance on them and give them the opportunities they want and need to succeed.

I think—I believe—I hope a cook who works with me can learn something more than technique—how to cook this cake, that fish, or a whole meal. But now in many kitchens, we have to show them exactly how to make a recipe because they don't learn by watching. We have to give them a written recipe with pictures, and then they can make the dish. This is how they learn the restaurant business, but one day, if I open a restaurant, the training will be different.

> *Whoever comes to their restaurant sees everything about the chef by looking at what's on the plate. If chefs only know about recipes, they cannot put their own character into a dish.*

Most young chefs don't try to understand or learn more because, unfortunately, we give information to them all the time. They need to be patient, observe, and learn. If they stay in my kitchen for six months or a year, they can learn how to follow a recipe, but they won't understand Mr. Robuchon or me, because it's not easy to understand how our minds work or what our backgrounds are. Why do we make this dish? Why do we use this sauce?

There are many reasons why we do things, but most young chefs don't realize that. They do the mechanical things, but they don't understand the reasons behind them. When young cooks reach the chef's position, they need to be able to create their own dishes. They need to find a way to make an original recipe because whoever comes to their restaurant sees everything about the chef by looking at what's on the plate. If chefs only know about recipes, they cannot put their own character into the dish.

When I think about cooking a dish, I don't really look at trends. I can't do that kind of cooking because I like simple dishes. Molecular cuisine and using foam are interesting to know about, and I respect the chefs who use these techniques, but this style of cooking is not for me. I always do something that already exists and is simple. I'm not interested in creating a new trend.

Tools

My most important tool is my knife. It is like my hand.

In French cuisine, it is important to have very sharp knives. But sharp knives are also critical in Japanese cuisine. Of course, it's easier to work with a sharp knife, so I always use Japanese knives. In France when I used a French chef's knife, it was always very dull. But over the past several years, French chefs have learned more about knives, and now they use sharp Japanese knives. Before, they really didn't care about knives, but they do now because it's easier to work with a sharp knife.

A Day in the Life

Chefs need to know how to calculate costs—the labor, how much food they need, how much they can pay for ingredients—everything. This is what the chefs need to learn.

As a chef, I'm concerned about the increasing costs of getting high quality ingredients. Beef is expensive, fish is expensive, and wine is expensive. Global warming, pollution, and the growing Chinese and Indian demand for food and wine are just some of the reasons prices are going up. I don't know if customers realize that this is why the prices of the meals have increased so much, but it's going to get worse and worse. This is a real problem for high-end owner-chef restaurants. If the chefs don't use the right ingredients in the future, I'm afraid that customers may not support high-end restaurants.

Restaurant owners and managers care about cost and about numbers, and so they ask their chefs a lot of questions. Chefs need to know how to calculate costs—the labor, how much food they need, how much they can pay for ingredients—everything. This is what the chefs need to learn. They need to be more specific about how to run the restaurant. Owner/chefs may be good chefs—even talented chefs— but if they don't know how to run a business, they will most likely end up closing their restaurant.

At the same time, chefs need to learn how to properly treat their guests. The chef may say, "We can't use this yellowtail because it's too expensive. We have to use this cheaper piece of yellowtail." But the cheaper fish may not please the guest. Then the guest is unhappy and complains, or doesn't come back.

At L'Atelier de Joël Robuchon in New York, I worked with people of many different nationalities—from Mexico, Bangladesh, of course America, France, Spain, and China. For me, it's especially interesting to learn about western culture. For example, I didn't know anything about Jewish foods like pastrami or bagels. In Japan, we didn't have this kind of food and didn't know anything about it. In New York, I've learned about new cultures, and they have influenced my cooking. For a while, I was using pastrami with foie gras and potatoes.

I don't cook Indian food or Bangladeshi food yet, because in Robuchon's restaurant I don't want to do too much fusion. I can't do everything I want to, because there are rules and restrictions. For example, I can't make pizza in the restaurant, So one day, I want to own my own restaurant, and then I can do whatever I want.

Photo Credit: Miya Matsudaira

SEVENTEEN

NORIYUKI SUGIE

Chef, Consultant

After Noriyuki Sugie graduated from the TSUJI Culinary Institute in Osaka and The TSUJI School of Advanced Culinary Studies in Château de L'Éclair, France, he worked at three Michelin-starred restaurants in Bordeaux, including the three-starred L'Aubergade, the one-starred Le Moulin de Martorey, and the two-starred Hostellerie du Vieux. In 1996, he moved to Chicago, where he spent two years as Chef de Partie at Charlie Trotter's, and he then went onto Tetsuya's in Sydney, one of Australia's top restaurants. During Noriyuki Sugie's tenure as Chef and Partner at Restaurant VII, the *Sydney Morning Herald* claimed it Best New Restaurant of 2001.

In 2003, Noriyuki Sugie was appointed Chef de Cuisine of the Mandarin Oriental, New York flagship restaurant Asiate. After four years of rave reviews, and his designation as 2005 StarChefs.com Rising Star Chef, he left Asiate, and in 2008 launched IRONNORI, a restaurant-consulting firm based in San Francisco. Sugie also consults with clients in Asia. He has appeared as a guest chef in the series *Hatchi* and *Hatchi Mix,* and he has also hosted at Breadbar in Los Angeles.

Influences

I learned from Chef Ishinabe that cooking is important to a chef, but so is creating a team in order to nurture the restaurant.

I began working at Chef Yutaka Ishinabe's restaurant in Japan after I came back from France. I was able to see the restaurant overall, not just the cuisine, and learn about how an owner/chef conducts business. He had studied cooking in France but used Japanese ingredients to create his own Yutaka Ishinabe style. I learned from Chef Ishinabe that observing what is going on outside of the kitchen is important in growing a restaurant as well.

Working at Charlie Trotter's restaurant in Chicago also influenced me as a chef. Charlie Trotter was a rugged individual. His cooking was fabulous, but cooking for him was like being on an American sports team. He was the captain or coach. The way he gave instructions and pulled the team together was very different from the French way.

When I first arrived in Chicago and entered the kitchen, I was served a meal. As I ate, I observed the kitchen and the manner in which one of the chefs, David Myers, made his way. I noticed how sharp his eyes were. I had no idea who he was. After a year, we became close friends because I felt we had something in common.

Both Chef Ishinabe and Chef Charlie Trotter emphasized teamwork. But there are some big differences in the way Japanese, American, and French chefs communicate with their staff. In Japan, I was expected to know how to do something without any explanation of how to do it. It was easy, because I was working with people of the same nationality. When I went abroad, there were people from different backgrounds, and there were times when I couldn't get them to understand me. During service there's a need for more communication, otherwise, standards can't be maintained. Instructions are given based on the assumption that everyone has a different mentality.

Working in France is very different from Japan. In France, the team changes about once a year. You work together for about six months, followed by a summer break of about one month. Many people change restaurants around that time. The French chefs have impressive resumes. They have studied at many places. There are no interviews. A single phone call or a recommendation by a chef decides whether you get that next position. To find a position in France, I wrote a lot of letters. I got a lot of information about getting a job there from other Japanese chefs. There was no email in those days—it was all by phone or by mail. I sent form letters in French! If the chef liked what I wrote he or she would contact me.

Once you get into a good restaurant in France, it becomes possible to move to another restaurant. For example, if you work for Chef Joël Robuchon, it means that you have his seal of approval. You work hard to gain the trust and affection of the chef you are working for so that you can be introduced to the next one. That impresses me about the French. When you want to leave a Japanese restaurant, the chef asks you why. But in France, once you give them your best, the chef will introduce you to the next place. You learn and move on. You're encouraged to learn more. This is so different from Japan.

Cuisine

The challenge is for chefs to show their uniqueness.

My goal is to incorporate the strength of Japanese cuisine into my own French cuisine—to add Japanese cuisine and French cuisine together and divide by two. That's my cooking philosophy. For example, in a dish where I need meat stock, I use dashi instead. Consommé becomes a jelly, so I make the same texture using jellied dashi. When making mousse, I make it without cream—I use tofu instead. After studying French cuisine for a time, I have learned a lot about the different natures of French and Japanese ingredients, and I've found natural substitutions. Training in this way has helped me find the direction that I want to take in my cooking. I think many chefs are looking for just that—something to give them direction.

When I develop a menu, the most important thing is to think of the season. Then I decide on one ingredient. For example, if I use a poached egg, or what we call *onsen tamago*, or "hot spring egg," I consider all of the different ways I can use it. I also think about texture, color, and shape, and how these elements tie together. Then I imagine how the ingredient would be heated. In this case, it will be slowly. What kind of sauce will go with it? The egg is soft, so I will need something like bacon to give the palate another dimension. Adding and subtracting such elements build up the menu.

All chefs do this in the natural course of their work, but when it's written down, it's interesting. For example, I write "egg" and draw the different directions it could go: fried, poached, and so on. From there, I think of all of the different things I could serve with it. Some things combine better with eggs than others. Of course, seasonality comes first, then temperature, then the plan for the dish. But I have sketches. They make it easy to understand the menu. When I'm thinking of the menu, I sketch it in my mind.

The next step is eating the dish. First I taste it and decide whether it is flavorful. Otherwise, it can't be served to the guests. The team, including people from different countries, tastes it, too. If I think a dish tastes good but the response of others is not so good, I continue to work on it. I change things and identify what I'm looking for. I try to make the dishes enjoyable for many different people.

Putting the dish into words on the menu can be tricky.

In 2000, when I was executive chef at Asiate in New York City, I was cooking soup every day. Because I had so much leftover lettuce every day, I wanted to make something different—soup using romaine lettuce! It took a lot of trial and error, but I came up with a signature dish—Caesar Salad Soup.

When the guests make the selection from the menu, say chicken, they have a certain image of what the chicken might look like. The dish needs to meet that expectation. Dealing with customer expectations is the hard part. If the taste and expectations of a dish don't match up, no matter whether the dish is good or bad, customers might decide that the restaurant is not right for them. I have to think about how to write the menu so those dishes are easy to understand. The cooking techniques I use are simple, but putting the dish into words on the menu can be tricky.

I think preparing fish is particularly difficult. After meat is cooked, it can rest, but if fish is overcooked it can't be used. It's a delicate ingredient. And there are so many varieties of fish. Meat can have different cuts, but in terms of variety, there's beef and pork, chicken, lamb, and duck—not so many. But there are many kinds of fish. Depending on the characteristics of the fish, a chef decides the best way to cook it and what to serve with it.

Trends in cuisine have been changing, but the dishes that chefs want to make and the dishes that customers want to eat both need to be incorporated into the menu. I think that's important.

Across the U.S., there is also a big difference in menus, taste, and mentality, so I have to research the market in each place. The menus in New York are different from the menus in San Francisco or Los Angeles. So I have to understand the audience.

As a chef, the most important thing is to put forward one's capabilities and to be recognized by the guests. By doing so, the restaurant becomes filled with customers. All chefs have a level that they consider the lowest common denominator. That's a difficult thing to determine. Chefs really need to have an understanding of what they are doing and prepare dishes that the guests will be willing to pay for.

Ingredients

In Japanese cuisine we use ingredients like dashi, katsuobushi, soy sauce, and miso. They add kakushi aji, which means "the hidden taste."

To make dashi, I use katsuobushi—dried, fermented, and smoked skipjack tuna. It's made the traditional Japanese way, but I also like to add dashi powder in the preparation. It's a way to add taste and to bring out the depth of the flavor. I often use a mixture of *iriko* dashi, *kombu* dashi, and *katsuo* dashi that comes in powder form. To the traditional Japanese chef, using dashi powder is akin to being lead astray, but I think it's okay because it adds to the flavor. These commonly used Japanese ingredients come in many varieties, but we need more workshops and information about them so both Japanese chefs and non-Japanese chefs can understand them better and on a deeper level. I think that is important.

Recently, many less-familiar Japanese ingredients have been introduced to chefs in France and America. For example, vegetables from Kyoto, such as *kyo yasai,* and pickled seafood ingredients like *uni, karasumi,* and *konowata.* Some are peculiar to certain areas in Japan and are very limited in availability.

There are a lot of other traditional Japanese ingredients that are healthful and that add a great deal of flavor, too, but I don't think that information about them has been easily attainable in the U.S. For example, *nuka* is a rice bran used for pickling. Japanese pickles are becoming very popular with American chefs and customers. *Natto* is made from fermented soybeans. It doesn't look very good, has a rotten smell, and leaves a strange sensation in the mouth, but it can be used as a kakushi aji, like miso. By applying heat to it, the stickiness disappears, and if you put it into a blender, so does the smell. *Saké kasu* is another ingredient made from the lees after saké has been squeezed from the fermented rice. Japanese chefs get it from a saké brewery in Japan. It's possible to make a dessert like panna cotta or cheesecake and put saké kasu on top. It's a dessert dish using fermented ingredients! I am always interested in seeing which ingredients *ryotei* restaurants, or fine dining restaurants, use and keep on hand.

Training

> *At the TSUJI Culinary Institute in Japan, I learned that French cuisine is called a "plus cuisine"—you keep adding to it.*

When I entered the program at the TSUJI Culinary Institute in Japan, I knew nothing about French cuisine. I think that I was barely able to touch the basics and only on a very superficial level during that one year. I learned about ingredients and the kinds of cooking skills and methods necessary in French cuisine and how to make sauces. There are many time-consuming tasks, such as making stock and preparing basic ingredients, herbs, and spices. I had to study many kinds of wines because the flavor of the sauce depends on the kind of wine used in it. But I also cleaned a lot of pots!

There wasn't much time to actually learn by doing. I had to listen and learn and watch. I was looking at the framework and I was studying it, but I wasn't able to internalize it, because during school hours there were few opportunities to spend time cutting vegetables or slicing meat and fish. I couldn't learn these techniques unless I practiced them many times, so I just had to train myself. I needed to practice at home because the test was preparing the head of a fish, cutting vegetables brunoise so that they looked like tiny dice, and cutting potatoes into the shape of small footballs. I practiced those knife skills for hours because the school tested us on how many we could make within an allotted time.

After finishing my training at Tsuji, I went to school in France because I wanted to learn more about using local ingredients. And I wanted to be where the action was in the kitchen. At the French school, there was a team that executed the menu for the day and then during service raced to get everything done.

> *Restaurant work is a battle with time. Something good has to be prepared within an allotted time. That is the restaurant's service. You can't study how to do service in school. It has to be done live.*

I spent six months at the school and the remainder of the time on-the-job, training at a hotel restaurant in the country. This restaurant served breakfast, and people came there just to eat. It was in a beautiful environment and was a two-star restaurant at the time. The cuisine reflected the natural surroundings and the local ingredients. At first I had to half-peel vegetables and do prep work like cutting tomatoes into squares—really basic things. I was able to do the prep work fairly quickly because I'd been pushing myself to work harder to reach a high level of achievement and also to perform under pressure.

Once I felt that I could do a particular task, I asked for another task, always on my own. After cutting the vegetables, my next task was working with meat—removing the bones, tying it, stuffing it, roasting it, figuring out the number of minutes to cook it and at what temperature. The instructors were watching to see what I was capable of doing. When they asked me to do something, I needed to be able to do it or ask them to teach me how.

> *I think any restaurant must make sure that every detail and every step in a dish is followed exactly, to the point of obsession.*

Traditional French cuisine is created according to a manual. The goal is to create consistency in the kitchen so that the result is the same each and every time. That's how the French think. In America, the result is different, depending on who does it. In Japanese cuisine, there aren't many recipe books except ones for people who make confections. Japanese chefs have their own unique flavorings. The people working for a head chef need to understand these flavorings, the timing, and techniques. There is no manual, so they have to learn by watching and doing and learning the tastes.

While I'm doing consulting work for a client, there are times when I'm unable to be in the restaurant, and the other chefs ask me for step-by-step recipes with photographs so they can maintain consistency. I think any restaurant must make sure that every detail and every step in a dish is followed exactly to the point of obsession.

Tools

I choose a knife according to how it feels in my hand because the knife is an extension of my body.

Knives are an important tool for a chef because they directly affect the quality of the food prepared. When I was an intern, I used western knives, even in Japanese restaurants. When I finally switched to a Japanese knife, I realized how good it was. Japanese knives are made with a combination of determination—or *kiwame*,—and soul, *seishin*. Right now my favorite knife is a custom-made *kodeba* that is very small and fits into my hand. It is the best knife I've ever had for filleting fish the size of a red snapper. I use it a lot. I also have several *yanagi* knives, which I use for slicing fish.

The weight of the knives will differ depending on the material used in the handle and the size of the blade. Choosing the right knife helps a chef become the best possible professional and artisan. I feel strongly about being an artisan and preserving Japanese culture. That's why I like to know how the knives, tools, and tableware I use in my cuisine and restaurant are made.

A Day in the Life

Just having a recipe doesn't mean a chef can make a great dish.

For example, when I was at the TSUJI Culinary Institute, I attended a class demonstration conducted by the school's founder, Shizuo Tsuji Sensei. He and a student created a basic dish in French cuisine called "Sauce Américaine." It is made by removing the shell of a lobster and using the crushed shells in the sauce. Sensei and the student stood side by side and made the same sauce using the same recipe at the same time, but Sensei didn't say anything while they cooked.

When they finished, we tasted the dishes, and their flavors were entirely different. Sensei explained to us why the two dishes were not the same. He pointed out that the way they each sautéed the vegetables, the amount of heat they used, and the order in which ingredients were sautéed, all created a different taste.

EIGHTEEN

TOSHIO SUZUKI

Having great interest in the philosophy of Buddhism, Toshio Suzuki applies his cooking with these influences to his Japanese cuisine. For ten years, Toshio Suzuki studied the concept and history of the Edo style of sushi, the modern style that was developed in the Edo period during the mid-eighteenth century. He then went on to practice the skills of *ikezukuri*, a form of sashimi presentation where live fish are prepared swiftly and presented to the guest while still alive. Suzuki began his professional career at the age of 19, under the guidance of Master Chef Nakanori in Tokyo.

Toshio Suzuki takes an intellectual, spiritual, and scientific approach to cooking. The result is the harmony of umami. Toshio Suzuki opened his restaurant Sushi Zen in New York City in 1983. Since then, he has been serving traditional Japanese sushi and cuisine, with its rich history and philosophy supporting each dish.

Influences

When I was in elementary school, I wanted to become a Buddhist priest so badly, but it was not meant to be.

Postwar reconstruction in Japan was slow, and in Tokyo there was still great disparity among elementary schools in terms of wealth. I just went headlong in the direction the world was taking me. It's still true now. Since my family members were tradesmen, one of my elementary school teachers told me to learn a trade so that I would always be sure to have enough to eat. That's how I got into cooking.

In the late 1960s and early 1970s, Japan was at the peak of its rapid growth. Work was demanding. Although I wasn't dissatisfied with my job on a daily basis, I knew that I would never see the world if I stayed in Japan and worked at one place. It just happened that I had met this cute American girl, and she was very friendly. I thought, "The Americans are such sweet people. Let me go and see for myself." I was 26 or 27. That meeting turned into a chance to break free of my job and come to America.

At that time, I was also hospitalized for one or two days for stress. In the bed next to me was an American, and I discovered that he had the same stress-related symptoms as I did. As we talked, we found that we were kindred spirits. When he asked, "Why don't you come to New York?" it was like adding fuel to the fire. Those two meetings changed my life.

After coming to New York City in the winter of 1972, I started working and gained considerable knowledge of Japanese cooking. At the time, there were really only a few high-class Japanese restaurants frequented by people in the import-export business who wanted to get information about Japan. They were like little communities who kept to themselves. But ordinary Americans had no knowledge of Japanese cuisine other than tempura and sukiyaki. Those were the days before sushi.

During that time, I had a lot of pent-up energy and often felt like getting away. So with New York as my home base, I went all over Eastern and Western Europe. Then I traveled to Asia. Because of the war in Vietnam, I didn't go to China or countries around there. I traveled to a lot of places around the world, came back to New York, and then went away again.

For me, traveling is about self-discovery.

In the North African desert, I saw a traditional tagine pot made of heavy clay. I thought, "How brilliant." It is probably the original tool used for steaming food. I discovered that the people there have great cooking techniques and great wisdom. As I traveled, I often saw similarities in cultures—the way people eat soba in Tibet is similar to how we eat it in Japan. So before I knew it, I had learned many new things about cooking and food. I saw a lot that inspired me. In going to all these places I tasted what it was to have a worldview, but I still returned to live and cook in New York.

Career Path

I felt that if I didn't open a restaurant in the most competitive place in the world—New York City—then I wouldn't truly find myself.

While working at a bunch of different restaurants and watching the customers, I thought to myself, "Next time I'm going to go out on my own." That's how I came to open Sushi Zen. Until then I had always been traveling to seek my own path, and I went to all kinds of churches and temples and did a lot of reading on my own. But in reality, in order to know myself, I needed to challenge myself to see what kind of ability I had.

Religion and philosophy are important when searching for the true nature of one's life, but I think that living here in New York and making a living helped me know "wisdom and determination." New York is, for me, the dojo—the place where I will attain enlightenment. The reason I came here was to search for my own existence. Philosophically, the awareness of spirituality doesn't mean a thing if it doesn't affect us within the actions of daily life. For me, spirituality was practice and performance, not just thought. I thought that it was better if I developed and discovered what was inside me. By building a firm foundation, I had the strength to change direction when I ran into life's tough challenges.

Cuisine

Thinking about ingredients flexibly can lead to important discoveries.

In the early days of Sushi Zen, sushi was still for a very small group of people. Their way of eating, the anatomy of their mouths, and their eating habits were all different from those in Japan. When Americans here ate sushi, it got stuck on the roofs of their mouths. I tried eating sushi the same way as Americans did and it happened to me, too! While I was thinking about how to prevent this, I happened to be making an *uramaki*, or "reverse roll," on a *saiku* (decorative) sushi plate. When my customers tried the reverse roll, they thought it was great, and it just took off. Then I had another idea. I really liked American hamburgers at the time, and I remembered that this place called White Castle had sesame seeds on the buns. I thought, "Oh yeah, that's the ticket!" So I started putting sesame seeds on the outside of the reverse roll and placing the garnish on the inside.

I noticed something about what New Yorkers eat. I happened to pick up on it and further develop it. Just a little change in direction ended up having a huge impact on me. I think that observation and raising questions will always lead to the solution. That experience with sushi was really useful to me when the restaurant was going through hard times.

During the 1970s, I must have come up with 150 different types of rolls. I don't really know, but sometimes I feel like I'm the originator of today's inside-out roll! Maybe yes, maybe no, but many of those rolls that I came up with years ago are now a menu staple at almost every sushi restaurant today, so I guess that is the silver lining or blessing in disguise. Whether I'm happy about it or not, I can't say because the reviews in *Zagat* give the impression that we specialize only in *makimono* rolls. When Sushi Zen first moved to this location on 44th Street off of 6th Avenue in Manhattan, it was tough. We didn't have a big enough advertising budget to dispel that notion, but I am glad that we are so popular.

Although I absorbed all of the different western trends and fashions, I am still Japanese, and I can't remove myself from that society.

I love Japanese culture and history. Over the last 20 years, I've traveled all over Japan to the shrines, temples, marketplaces, museums, and historical landmarks, seeking out the traditional sushi that I was originally taught, and other Japanese cuisine. As a result of offering fish-cutting demonstrations and other Japanese food-preparation workshops through the non-profit organization The Gohan Society, I've been able to get close to some of New York's top chefs and share what I know about Japanese culture and history, as well as my own experiences. In this way, I've found a new path through life.

When chefs make a dish by finding something from within themselves, they become more motivated. My motivation—my mission—is to communicate to people that Japanese culture has a singular uniqueness in the world. And I want every chef to have his or her own philosophy and not be carried away by superficial trends. I believe it's important to look closely and carefully at preparation, ingredients, and customers with one's full attention. For example, making sure that everything is clean is my duty as the person who makes the food. Then, as part of the daily routine, I face the customer with full awareness. I make recommendations by reading the customer's body type and thinking about seasonality, and then I develop menu items, especially for that customer.

Training

At Sushi Zen, we don't have a training manual that explains how to create a dish or a menu.

The chef's inspiration must come from within. At the beginning of a chef's career, it's okay for him or her to just imitate what's being done. However, when chefs make a dish by finding something from within themselves, they become more motivated. For example, as part of a chef's daily routine at Sushi Zen, he or she must make an appetizer. We demonstrate some techniques for not wasting scraps and how to use leftover bits, but it is up to the chef to create the dish—it can be anything. Even if what he or she comes up with is useless, we continue to make suggestions. It's my experience that this chef will discover something as he or she makes the dish. After the dish is finished, I'll take a look at it, and then I'll make it. By trying and watching, that person's capacity grows. Right now, for me, it is really fun to observe these young chefs learn.

I learned this same training technique when I attended the original Sogetsu School of Ikebana to learn flower arrangement. I wasn't even 19 yet, but I found that their ways of teaching really helped me later on. For example, when I opened Sushi Zen, I would make the flower arrangements. Then I asked the manager to do it. In the beginning, learning how to arrange flowers was really hard for all of us. But each manager took a turn. Gradually, all of the managers were able to create their own original arrangements.

In the beginning, the chefs at Sushi Zen base their work on my advice. Then, before they realize it, they become more self-reliant, and the work becomes their own. It's probably a good process for them, and it also serves to grow my restaurant. There's synergy on many levels. I like the attitude that making the restaurant successful is not just up to me alone. We all make it happen. I guess it's a Japanese way of thinking.

After work on New Year's Day we do a big cleanup in the restaurant, from the floors to the utensils, the cookware—the whole environment. We clean the entire place.

New Year's Day is the day that sums up the entire year, so we follow this Japanese tradition. We clean everything, from the cutting boards to the utensils to the refrigerator. This approach to training may look very tough, but young chefs need the structure of it. Today's young people tend to lack that spirit of self-reliance. Self-reliance is something you have to see for yourself, and must attain on your own. As chefs, they have to ask themselves if they are really doing this work for the art of cooking or if they're doing it because they think New York is a temporary home. If this work is just one part of their life, then making a living, as a ritual, feels like a kind of punishment.

Tools

We honor tools. Among the most important is the hocho, the all-purpose utility knife.

Each chef purifies his own knives and cutting boards with his own salt and saké to show gratitude. We chefs have the samurai spirit in our minds, so we always sharpen and polish our knives with care. We do it alone and each of us does it differently. When we perform the ritual, we are also "burnishing the heart," so we can cut and slice and chop with skill.

The way a chef sharpens his knives is very revealing. If the chef rests the knife on top of the cutting board while sharpening it, the entire character of that person is projected. I say to myself, "Oh, I get it—this chef is one of those who are probably not going to be around here for long." It's one way I observe people. Just like a highly esteemed warrior, part of what makes a chef is how much care he or she takes with the knives and how they are sharpened and used. If a knife is not sharpened correctly or is not used in the right way, then it is useless in Japanese cooking. That's really why this knife ritual should be done by each person in his or her own way, because each person has a different attitude and spirit.

A Day in the Life

In business, I have had some really terrible times.

When Sushi Zen was still on 46th Street, we came close to bankruptcy. I was in denial about it, but it was the decision handed down by the American judge that saved me. Even after so many years, I recall him saying, "We are here to protect your business." I still get emotional when I think about the words of that man. They changed my view of human nature and got me through the really hard times.

If it weren't for my bonds with friends and their support, I would not be here today. During those hard times, I do not think that I had the determination to say, "I'm going through with this." I have been helped in so many ways by so many people. It is the individual things that people have said and the encounters with them that have kept me going. The truth might be hidden inside a "bad outcome" or a "good outcome." I am aware of the people and events that created my path, and now I am extremely grateful.

I am filled with gratitude to be in New York every day. New York has the depth of heart and is the Zen temple and the spiritual dojo of my life. It is home to the masters and teachers who have guided me and showed me my existence and potential. The bonds with these people mean I'm not alone. New York helped me recognize anew the beauty of Japan. As a chef I interact and chat with customers—not just with Americans, but with people from around the world. If I have visited a country where the customers live, I feel an affinity with them and a desire to create something special for them based on my experiences there. This is the most amazing and joyful thing. It is the motivation that has gotten me this far.

❖

NINETEEN

SHINICHIRO TAKAGI

Owner/Chef, Zeniya, Kanazawa, Japan

Born in Kanazawa, Shinichiro Takagi completed his bachelor's degree in commercial science at Nihon University. After serving his apprenticeship at Japan's top kaiseki restaurant, Kyoto Kitcho, he returned to Kanazawa to run Zeniya, an eatery opened by his father. Takagi prepared a special dinner for an event in the U.S. co-hosted by the Consulate General of Japan and the Ishikawa Prefectural government to promote Ishikawa's refined Kaga cuisine. Takagi has been a guest chef at hotels and events in Japan and abroad, including the U.S., Germany, and Hong Kong.

In 2009, Shinichiro Takagi was appointed Chairman of The Real Japan Ishikawa Project Committee. Takagi has been a guest chef at many international cooking venues, including The Napa Valley Reserve, The Hong Kong International Film Festival, the Hotel Blauer Bock in Munich, the Consulate General of Japan, and as a member of Japan's team for Worlds of Flavor at The Culinary Institute of America. Takagi is dedicated to spreading Ishikawa's traditional culinary culture abroad, believing that Japanese cuisine is, in essence, an aggregate of regional dishes.

Influences

From an early age, my parents took my brother and me to many kinds of restaurants, mostly in Kanazawa and the Ishikawa Prefecture, but sometimes in Tokyo, Osaka, and Kyoto, too.

One day when I was eight or nine years old, I asked my father, "Can you make sashimi?" He said, "You know I am a chef, so why do you ask me that?" I had never seen him make sashimi, so I wondered if he could make it. At that time, my father had several chefs working in his restaurant so that he didn't have to do all of the cooking by himself. He said, "Okay, I will show you. Let's go to the restaurant."

On the way to the restaurant, we picked up a small, live fluke. When we got to the restaurant, he killed it and prepared sashimi for me. It took about 30 minutes, and it was beautiful! Then he said, "Why don't you taste it?"

After I took a bite, my father asked me, "Did it taste good?" I couldn't say yes because it didn't taste good. I told him, "It's too fresh. The texture is good, but its taste is not so good. It's not cold enough for sashimi." My father just laughed. That was the first time I tasted sashimi prepared by my father. In fact, I think he prepared meals for me only two or three times.

From an early age, my parents took my brother and me to many kinds of restaurants, mostly in Kanazawa and the Ishikawa Prefecture, but sometimes in Tokyo, Osaka, and Kyoto, too. We didn't really talk too much about the food, but even though I was only 13 or 14 years old, we shared wine or saké during dinner. I think he thought I was too young to learn actual cooking techniques or about the presentation of this cuisine, but he tried to teach me how to appreciate the meal and enjoy the restaurant.

For a kid in high school, it was almost impossible to understand how one plate, even if it was 200 years old, could cost more than 100,000 yen!

When I was in junior high and high school, I worked four or five nights a week in the restaurant, from 6 p.m. to 9 p.m., washing dishes. My father used very old dishes and tableware, so I had to be very careful with them. Sometimes he asked me, "Do you know how old this plate is?" I said I didn't know. "It's more than 200 years old. And do you know how much these kinds of plates and tableware cost?" I had no idea. But for a kid in high school, it was almost impossible to understand how one plate, even if it was 200 years old, could cost more than 100,000 yen!

Serving food on antique tableware, even in the best kaiseki restaurants, was rare in Japan. But my father's hobby was collecting antique dishes. He believed that the dish was a kind of canvas for the meal. He was very serious about his tableware collections and how cuisine looked when it was served to his guests. His said, "I try to prepare great meals, and they need to be served on beautiful dishes."

Going to the U.S. as a high-school exchange student was one of the greatest experiences in my life.

In 1986, when I was just 16 years old, I spent one year as a foreign exchange student in upstate New York. I learned to speak English and experienced an entirely different food culture. After I came back to Japan, I finished high school and moved to Tokyo to go to college, but I hadn't thought about being a chef. I wasn't particularly interested in cooking, but I loved to eat foods from all over the world.

I'd go to French, Italian, and Chinese restaurants as often as possible. Since I was a college student, I didn't have much money, but

I always went to the best restaurants I could afford. That was my hobby.

Career Path

I thought that maybe this was an opportunity to decide which way I should go regarding my career, so I said, "Okay, why not?" It was at that moment that I decided I wanted to be a chef.

Unfortunately, in 1991, when I was a freshman in college, my father suddenly passed away. That's when my mother took over the restaurant. Then, in 1993, when I was a senior in college, one of my father's best friends, Mr. Yamashio, came to visit me from Hong Kong. When I was driving him back to the airport, he asked me, "Are you going to take over the restaurant?"

I didn't say yes, I didn't say no. I just mumbled, "Hmm." But to my surprise, my father's friend interpreted my response as a yes. He called me a couple of days later from Hong Kong and told me that he had arranged for me to have a job interview at Arashiyama Kitcho, Japan's most famous kaiseki restaurant. I was shocked because Arashiyama Kitcho didn't interview inexperienced people like me for an apprenticeship, but Mr. Yamashio was one of their best customers. He owned one of the most prestigious banks in Hong Kong, so he easily arranged an interview. I thought that maybe this was an opportunity to decide which way I should go regarding my career, so I said, "Okay, why not?" It was at that moment that I decided I wanted to be a chef.

Mr. Tokuoka told me that at 24 years of age, I was too old. It was too late for me to become a chef.

I had the interview with the President of Kitcho, Mr. Tokuoka, and his son, Kunio-san. But President Tokuoka told me "no" for two reasons: first, he said that he didn't take chefs from other restaurants because those chefs always went back to their own restaurants. And second, he told me that Kitcho didn't take amateurs who graduated from college and didn't have any cooking skills. Mr. Tokuoka also told me that at 24 years of age, I was too old. It was too late for me to become a chef. That response made me almost give up getting into Kitcho.

After the interview, I telephoned Mr. Yamashio in Hong Kong and told him that the interview didn't go so well and asked what I could do. He suggested that I ask some other important Kitcho customers for their help. I knew I couldn't ask them, but maybe my mother would. She called Mr. Murai, the chairman of Asahi Beer, Mr. Takanashi, the past chairman of Kikkoman, and finally, Mr. Toda, one of the most famous antiques dealers in Japan, and asked them to recommend me for a job at Kitcho. They all answered, "Why not?" Here is how they did it.

First, Mr. Murai, Mr. Takanashi, and Mr. Toda made separate reservations on different days at Kitcho so they could each talk privately to Mr. Tokuoka. It was Mr. Tokuoka's custom after dinner to go into the private dining rooms to ask the guests how they liked their meal. Of course, Mr. Murai, said, "We had a great, great time. Oh, by the way, why don't you help Shinichiro Takagi-san?" When Kitcho first opened, I think Asahi Beer was one of its biggest sponsors. For Mr. Tokuoka, there was no way he could say no, so he said he'd think about it.

A couple of days later, Mr. Takanashi visited Arashiyama Kitcho and had dinner. After he praised Mr. Tokuoka's meal, Mr. Takanashi

said, "I know a young guy from Kanazawa. Please help train him."
Mr. Tokuoka asked, "Is this about Takagi-san?" A few days after that,
Mr. Toda dined at Kitcho and afterwards asked Mr. Tokuoka, "Why
don't you hire this guy from another Japanese restaurant?" Mr.
Tokuoka said, "Are you talking about Takagi-san, too?" Well, after
that, it was done. I got a job working at Arashiyama Kitcho.

*Mr. Tokuoka told me that the best way to learn how to cook is
by watching.*

Working at Kitcho was very tough, because it was a busy
restaurant and the days were long. Six days a week I woke up around
5 a.m., took a train and arrived at the restaurant just before 6 a.m.,
worked until about 1 a.m., took the train back to where I lived for a
few hours of sleep, and then went back again to the restaurant.

At first I didn't prepare dashi or anything like that. That came later.
In the beginning, the order chef taught me how to position the knives
and pots so that everything was ready for the chefs when they returned
to the restaurant with their ingredients from the market. After I
distributed the ingredients to the hot station, the cold station, and other
prep areas, I started with very basic preparations, such as washing and
cutting vegetables. I didn't have a position at a particular station.
When the restaurant opened for lunch or dinner, I worked to support
whichever station needed me. Sometimes I worked for the chef
preparing vegetables, and sometimes I worked for the chef making
sashimi or other main dishes. I did all of the basic kitchen duties, and
of course, I constantly washed and cleaned things.

When I started working at Kitcho, Mr. Tokuoka told me, "You
don't have to learn how to cook Kitcho's cuisine. You can learn here
what you cannot learn at your family's restaurant." But at that time—
and I'm not really sure why—I wanted to learn how to cook kaiseki

cuisine. Mr. Tokuoka told me that the best way to learn how to cook is by watching, because it's very easy to forget if the order chef just tells you how to do something. Besides, Kitcho was too busy for the chefs to stop what they were doing to teach me. I learned through watching so I would never forget.

When a few of the order chefs who had worked there for a year or so left suddenly, I had to do a lot of the basic jobs by myself. After 10 months, because my arrangement was to work at Kitcho for two or three years, Mr. Tokuoka gave me the opportunity to go to the market with him. This was very special, because usually an apprentice had to spend several years working exclusively in the kitchen before doing that.

After that, I went with Mr. Tokuoka to the market every day for about two hours. We went to the fish shop, the seafood shop, and a couple of produce shops. He showed me how to choose fish, vegetables, fruits, and other ingredients. If I asked him, "Why did you choose that one?" he might explain but not always. Sometimes he asked me, "Which one do you like?" This was like a test. After I chose something, he often said, "Oh? You have to learn a lot more." But he always gave me a chance to think for myself. That was his way of making his point and his way of teaching me.

I had been at Kitcho for two years. It was a hard job but a great experience and helped prepare me for an even bigger challenge—running Zeniya.

When I took over running Zeniya, there was an older executive chef who had worked there since my father's time. One day he asked if he could quit because he wanted to open his own restaurant in Kanazawa, and I couldn't say no. This was a real shock, because I was too inexperienced to be an executive chef. So I went to Osaka to see an old friend of my father with the hope that he could help me find a replacement executive chef. He introduced me to the executive chef at a large Osaka restaurant. Over dinner, the chef and I talked about Zeniya and the position. I had hoped that he would introduce me to a great chef who would want to take the job. But then he asked, "How old are you? Why don't you do it yourself?"

I said I was 29 but didn't have even close to the 10 years' experience it took to be considered for the position as an executive chef. The chef said, "Go back to Kanazawa right now. Starting tomorrow morning, go to the market and pick up the fish and vegetables, and make the menu by yourself."

I was so disappointed. On the two-and-a-half hour train ride back to Kanazawa, I couldn't figure out any other options, so I did what he told me to do. The next morning I went to the market, bought ingredients, and wrote my first menu as Zeniya's executive chef. I was scared. I wondered if I could do it. That kind of thinking lasted a couple years, but it never stopped me from going to the market every morning.

Ingredients

I go to the market each morning without a menu in mind and look for the highest quality ingredients available. Different days, different hours, and even different weather affect what I buy, so I create a different menu every day.

I have no set daily menu at my restaurant. Whatever ingredients I choose for that day change the entire menu—even those items I prepare in advance, like pastry.

And, of course, I have to think of our guests. Some guests come from Kanazawa. Some guests come from Tokyo, other regions of Japan, or from countries in Asia. Some guests come from New York

City or Europe. Everyone wants to enjoy Kanazawa's famous crabs, squid, and other local ingredients. So I prepare the local fish, seafood, and vegetables to match the tastes and expectations of my guests—and maybe surprise them, too, with unique meals that showcase our region's wonderful local ingredients.

Training

Young chefs applying for a job should say, "I don't know anything, but I'd like to work at Zeniya because I want to learn."

Over the years, most of the new chefs who have worked at Zeniya went to the TSUJI Culinary Institute or other culinary schools in other countries. Some of them were from the Ishikawa Prefecture, but most came from cities like Tokyo or Yokohama. When I interview young chefs for a position, I always ask, "Why do you want to work at Zeniya?" Some say their teacher in culinary school recommended Zeniya. Some say that they saw a picture of Zeniya's cuisine in a magazine and they thought it was beautiful. Others don't know why. ("Thank you very much. Good-bye.")

What is most important during the interview is the person's attitude. I always watch young chefs' faces to get a sense of their attitude about food, cooking, and work. Recent graduates from culinary school know little about the restaurant business, so they need to communicate a passion and a desire to learn. Young chefs applying for a job should say, "I don't know anything, but I'd like to work at Zeniya because I want to learn." That is the attitude I look for. I don't need to hear how knowledgeable they are—only how passionate they are.

If a chef's attitude is wrong, even if they are experienced, I won't hire them. For example, when I asked one chef why he wanted to work at Zeniya, he tried to impress me with all his knowledge about our cuisine by explaining why this ingredient matched with that saké, and so on. Of course, if I'm looking to hire an executive chef or sous chef, I will ask about his prior jobs, technique, and those kinds of things, but even an experienced chef needs to show that he works well with others. I've found that chefs like that guy who tried to show how smart he was can be very difficult to work with. I told him that I didn't think Zeniya was right for him and suggested that he look for a job in another restaurant.

> *I always think about how I can make each person into the best chef possible.*

I don't care if a chef is Japanese or from somewhere else. I have many chefs working at Zeniya who are from other countries. For example, last year I had a young female chef from Germany, plus young chefs from Italy, Israel, New York, Korea, and Singapore. I don't know how they found out about Zeniya, but they chose to work with us over many other Japanese restaurants. That is reason enough for me.

As the owner-chef, I feel that I have a responsibility to make them into good chefs. Yes, I am paying them to work for me, but I think of it as an honor to have them as part of our team. That's why I always think about how I can make each person into the best chef possible.

Some new cooks want to be an executive chef in a big restaurant or a big hotel. Others want to be the owner-chef of a small restaurant or take over their family's restaurant. Some don't know or haven't yet decided on the kind of restaurant that will make them happy. It is impossible for me to know what will make them happy, but I can introduce them to a good restaurant and good cooking techniques. I also hope that when they leave Zeniya, they take with them good memories and knowledge of the particular things that they wanted to learn. It is not easy to learn Japanese cuisine—or any cuisine—in a short time, but if they feel that they have found what they came for, that's enough for me.

Cuisine

The most important skill of a chef is to never stop thinking about how to make the guests happy.

There are many ways to please restaurant guests. One way, of course, is to prepare the best meals. But this is not all. The smiling faces of the wait staff make guests feel welcome and comfortable. A beautiful wine heightens the taste and enjoyment of the food. To understand what makes guests love a restaurant, I need to identify the things that please me when I go to a restaurant. Without understanding these elements, it is impossible for me to create a completely fulfilling experience from the moment the guests enter Zeniya to the time they leave and we wave good-bye to them outside the restaurant. I want our guests to feel happy that they dined here so they will come back again. That's our goal.

To give food demonstrations overseas always makes me so excited.

There are many chefs and other people outside Japan who are interested in Japanese cuisine, especially our traditional kaiseki cuisine. And so it has become my duty and honor to not only explain the traditions of kaiseki internationally to non-Japanese audiences, but also to demonstrate how to prepare and present it. Many Japanese chefs cook abroad, and some of them think, "This is a foreign country. This is the United States. This is Hong Kong. This is Shanghai. I have to do something special for foreign people." But most of the international chefs, dignitaries, and Japanese food lovers who attend my cooking demonstrations want to see and taste examples of Japan's traditional kaiseki cuisine. Preparing menus for international restaurants is a challenge.

> *I needed to understand the restaurant customer's expectations, mood, dining experience—everything—and then I came up with a personalized menu.*

A Day in the Life

> *Opening a restaurant in Seoul, South Korea was a big challenge for me and my team.*

Before I created the menu, I stayed there for several weeks. I needed to understand the restaurant customer's expectations, mood, dining experience—everything—and then I came up with a personalized menu. I had to develop my basic menu and try to adjust it to Koreans' tastes, but that didn't mean that I was going to use chili pepper or kimchee.

Fortunately, one of the chefs I sent to Seoul to be the executive chef had worked beside me at Zeniya for seven years, so he knew I was always changing the menu for the guests, and he knew what I wanted to do at the new restaurant. Also, we had three Korean chefs work at Zeniya to learn how we do things in the kitchen before they went to work in the restaurant in Seoul. They spoke Japanese very well and understood how Japanese people think. It was easy for me to communicate what I wanted them to do when they moved back to work in Korea.

JAMES WIERZELEWSKI

Corporate VP of Food and Beverage,
Rotana Hotel Management Corporation,
Abu Dhabi, United Arab Emirates
Past Executive Chef, Marriott Marquis,
New York City

As a 16-year-old, James Wierzelewski began a two-year internship at the historic Pfister Hotel in Milwaukee. From there, he spent a decade with a hotel restaurant innovator, Hyatt Hotels, working his way up to Executive Chef. During these years, James Wierzelewski opened several new restaurant concepts for the rapidly expanding Park Hyatt brand at locations across the United States. In 1991, James Wierzelewski began working abroad and apprenticing with several renowned chefs, including Chef Roland Durand at the two-star Michelin-rated Le Pré Catelan in Paris and Chef Michel Husser at the two-star Michelin-rated Le Cerf in Alsace, France.

James Wierzelewski has opened seven new hotel restaurants in the past 15 years. He was the Executive Chef at the New York Marriott Marquis, and Harrods, London; and was the Director of Kitchens at Fairmont Singapore and Swissotel, The Stamford. His philosophy is "Dining out is not just about the food or beverage. It's about hitting all of one's senses. Customers want an overall dining experience that leaves them with a lasting memory. That's 'eater-tainment.'"

Influences

I have always seen travel as part of life's journey and an opportunity to learn.

In the late 1980s, I made my first jump out of the United States. I went from the Hyatt in Waikiki, where we had a couple of different teppan tables and a sushi bar serving some westernized Japanese dishes, to Miyako Restaurant at the Hyatt Regency on the island of Saipan. Saipan, a tiny, beautiful island about 120 miles north of Guam, is a popular vacation spot for Japanese tourists, so we incorporated a lot more traditional Japanese elements into our restaurant philosophy and concepts there. We even had quick-service noodle bars along with full dining, as well as teppan, but there was still a western slant. Unlike the Hyatt in Waikiki, all the chefs in this restaurant were from Japan except me. I was the Executive Chef.

When I stepped into this kitchen, there were 10 or 15 chefs who spoke a language I didn't know. Without a translator, I couldn't speak fluently to any of the chefs in the kitchen. Everything was done through translation. But I could see the chefs understood the differences in menus. I saw a great sense of respect and understanding for Japanese tradition. Each person there played an important role in that kitchen, whether it was preparing hot food or cold food or working at the sushi bar. And among them, they had their own rankings. As a westerner, I tried to see the hierarchy of the kitchen and also understand and respect their principles.

The methods for making the sushi, the sauces, and the most important ingredients in any Japanese restaurant—the cooking of the rice and prep of other side dishes—were rooted in Japanese tradition all the way. All of the beverages, tableware, and food products for the restaurant were from Japan. In terms of influences, I have always seen travel as part of life's journey and an opportunity to learn. The job in Saipan was no exception.

Cuisine

I believe that food should be simple enough to be understood, yet unique enough to be marketable. Marketable in this case means, "Hmm, that sounds okay! I'll try it."

When I worked in Asia, I committed myself to not being one of those chefs who bastardized traditional cuisine. I'm going to take the time, slow it down, and understand the reasons behind the culture's food. Then when I present a dish, I'm going to do it in a way that is stylish and modern. To summarize my philosophy of cuisine, I believe that food should be simple enough to be understood, yet unique enough to be marketable.

I see uncomplicated layers of flavor as the key to a successful meal. When I think about Japanese cuisine, I think about the successes we had with the guests at the New York Marriott Marquis. When customers can eat through a dish and hit uncomplicated layers of flavor, that's when you know you've won them over. On the other hand, it's no good if the flavors are too overpowering or over-blended or if the menu description leaves the customers confused about what the dish is.

My food style has Asian influences and Asian techniques and principles, but my palate isn't 100% Japanese. I think a Japanese-inspired meal should also represent various cooking methods, from simmered dishes to grilled dishes to raw food; from marinated food to soups to the pickled items. For me, the ideal is seeing those elements layered in the food. That's very important.

My restaurant concepts have a clear identity so that a server can explain them to the guests in a few sentences. I want them to walk away nodding, "I see it. I hear it. I feel it. I got it!" Restaurants at the Marquis are not ultra modern. At the same time, they are not traditional either. They are somewhere in the middle, so when I want to introduce a new dish to the customers, the challenge is twofold. First, the menu verbiage has to be carefully crafted. How a dish is depicted on the menu is very important, because it creates expectations for the dining experience. Second, the dishes or ingredients have to be recognizable—balanced with a little bit of the unknown, simple enough to be understood, but unique enough to be marketable.

There is more exploration with appetizers, smaller portions, or first courses than with main courses. When the restaurant launches a course or a new dish for the public, I want to make sure that the guests will have a bigger comfort zone in the $30 entree price point. Then we can be a little bit more avant-garde, a little bit more daring, a little bit more fun in packaging smaller plates for the appetizer menu.

I believe that going out to eat should be an "eater-tainment" experience, not entertainment.

I'll give you an example of a Japanese-inspired appetizer that is simple enough to be understood, yet unique enough to be marketable. I take white miso and combine it with tahini paste, sesame paste, yuzu, and Japanese mayonnaise to make a creamy dressing that has a different flavor than western mayonnaise. Then I grill some asparagus and toss it with this white miso dressing. Next, I take sesame oil and a little seasoning and put it into the ice cream machine until it freezes. I mound up warm grilled asparagus with the creamy white miso dressing, put little bits of this sesame ice cream off to the side, and then top it off with finely diced onions that have been slowly cooked down in soy sauce so they are caramelized and sweet. It is creamy, oniony asparagus and sesame oil—and a marketable appetizer that is easy to understand, taste, and enjoy.

I think that most Americans don't have the respect for food that the Japanese do, so I focus on the marketability of food and the "hyper-positioning" of my cuisine. By hyper-positioning, I mean food as it relates to a dining experience. I believe that going out to eat should be an "eater-tainment" experience, not entertainment. That means there should be a lot of things working to make that experience memorable, because the memory is the only thing that's going to ensure repeat customers.

I'm the kind of guy whose food radar is always up. I want to know what kinds of Japanese cuisine other than sushi rolls Americans want or might be willing to eat. So when I go into a Japanese restaurant, I watch to see what dishes and from what categories people are ordering. Using this information, I place two or three dishes from each category on the menu. I look at marketing these dishes in a way that makes them acceptable to the western palate by offering them in smaller tastings.

At the Marquis, if the dish didn't sell a certain number of portions, we took it off the menu and tried a new dish. If it did sell, we did it for awhile until we found out that some guy down the street was doing it, too. Most culinary trends don't last long. They come and go. When somebody else does it, I say, "Okay, let's get off of that and move onto something else."

Ingredients

When it comes to ingredients, I want to know their origins and how they were produced. I know how to use my products, so I don't want to be taught what to make with them.

I get a lot more value out of a product if I learn how it was made. The more I understand it, the quicker I will be able to find a use for it. While I do culturally inspired cuisine that's rooted in tradition, I'm also a fan of altering the composition of a dish without substituting traditional ingredients. Fusion to me means that I use yuzu instead of lemon juice because yuzu has a very distinctive flavor. I also believe in using specific brands. The brands for miso differ greatly—some are saltier, some are thinner, some are thicker, lighter, darker. Once I get used to a brand, I want a reliable source where I can always get it.

For example, the concept of the Vix Restaurant at the Hotel Victor in South Beach, Miami was based on what I call "four palates," one of which was Asian. That was where you'd find my Japanese-inspired dishes. I got most of the Japanese ingredients from a Japan-based vendor in Miami called Mutual Trading. But I didn't know the Japanese names for a lot of ingredients, so I couldn't get on the phone and tell the sales rep exactly what I wanted. Instead, I said, "I'm coming down. We're going to walk up and down the shelves, and I'm going to tell you what I'm looking for."

In New York, I also found reliable and helpful sources where I could buy traditional Japanese ingredients. What was so great about Japanese vendors like Mutual Trading and some others, too, was that most of the time I could go there, look up and down the shelves, and get the exact same stuff that I once had flown in from Japan. Once the reps knew what I was looking for, they wanted to do business with me. When the company got in something new, the rep said, "When I saw this, I thought of you. You're always looking for something different, and here's what we've got."

What chefs need to do with Japanese food is take four, five, or 10 products—miso, oils, vinegars, rubs, or marinades—and bring them to the customer in a variety of dishes.

Making Japanese ingredients recognizable and approachable is what I recommend that small Japanese food manufacturers do to sell more of their ingredients or products to western chefs. Take soy, for instance. I'm making a dish with soy, but I want to do something different with the ingredient that will leave an impression on the guest. Instead of having bottled soy on the table, I use dehydrated soy salt that a waiter can easily grind onto the guests' salad, appetizer, or main dish using a cheese grater or spice grinder. A simple and inexpensive item like shaved soy salt can have a memorable impact on customers.

Here are some of the Japanese ingredients that I think we will see more of in the future. The first is miso. There are so many different forms of miso, several of which we use every single day here. I think miso is going to be around forever. And we'll see more wasabi oil as part of a dressing or on light greens. Just a drop will do! Chefs will sprinkle it over a piece of fish or other dish. Plus, the smoke temperature of this oil is beautiful—it doesn't burn quickly like a high-grade olive oil does. I can float it on top of a soup if I just want the essence, but it washes out quickly when eaten. Finally, I'll guarantee you that we will see soy salt used in a lot of restaurants in the next year or two. And mark my words—a waiter will come to the table and grate something over a noodle dish or a salad and when asked, "What is that?" he'll say, "It's soy sauce."

I believe in the philosophy of bringing food out to the table to broaden its acceptance.

To expand their market, Japanese producers and restaurants need to do what the wine industry has done well—have experts talk about their products and educate their customers. I believe in the philosophy of bringing food out to the table to broaden its acceptance. Remember 20 years ago, when you ordered wine by the glass? It was either white or red. Today, at fine restaurants, when you order wine by the glass,

264 · JAMES WIERZELEWSKI

the server brings you the glass, tells you a little about the wine, and asks, "Would you like to try it?" You sip, enjoy the moment, and then say, "Oh, that's great, please pour me a glass!" As a result, wine sales have greatly increased. If Japanese food manufacturers encouraged chefs to use their products in unique and memorable ways like this, their sales would soar.

Training

> *When American chefs understand the Japanese chef in his station, they'll see that he's happy doing the yakitori, the noodles, or the cold station prep, and he's not trying to become the next sushi bar guy.*

Chefs trained in Europe and Asia learn their craft through structured apprenticeships and techniques that have been passed down from generation to generation. But most chefs trained in the United States who work in big hotels don't learn that way. And there's a different attitude, particularly among the younger western chefs who want everything in a snapshot. They say, "Don't make me look for anything. Don't make me research a dish. Don't make me double-check." As an Executive Chef in a large hotel, I needed pictures, step-by-step bullets, not a lot of verbiage, a conclusion, and, finally, a couple of reminders like, "Make sure you do this or that." It's sad to say this, but if some of my chefs have to turn a page on my recipe, I've lost most of them. At the Marriott Marquis in New York City, I had a 260-man team. People came to work there for a lot of different reasons, but I still needed the end result. That's in my fiber, my culture, and my character. So I expected my staff to give me 110 percent or find another job.

I think young American chefs need to learn from Japanese chefs who have perfected their craft. When they understand the Japanese chef in his station, they'll see that he's happy doing the yakitori, the noodles, or the cold-station prep, and he's not trying to become the next sushi bar guy. Within the Japanese kitchen, there is this culture. Within the culture, there's a respect for process and position, but with rigidity can come some limitations.

For many Japanese chefs working at the Marriott Marquis, the hardest thing for them to understand was that they didn't have to work within the same boundaries as they did in Japan. For some of these guys, that was the first job they'd had in the States. They did what they knew. When they were asked to do something different, it was hard because it wasn't in their comfort zone.

I've found that Japanese chefs are concerned about hierarchy and respect based on age and sex. For example, if I have three traditional Japanese chefs who are five or 10 years apart in age, I might ask the youngest to make me a new dish. He is going to ask the oldest chef, "Should I do this or not do this?" That's the hierarchy and respect. The older chef has the experience.

When I'm working on an Asian-inspired dish with Japanese chefs, we approach it from two different angles. Mine is results-oriented, and theirs is process-oriented. They go through a process that involves hierarchy and respect. I say, "I don't care who makes it. Let's just get it done." These differences in perspective make working together a little cloudy.

I think that for Japanese chefs to make it in the States, they need to be willing to step up and lead. They don't have to reinvent, just lead. They can take a traditional dish and experiment a bit with their presentation and vessels. They need to be a little bit more playful for western clients. I'm not talking about having some beautiful sashimi and sushi on a platter. That's beautiful and certainly appreciated, but there are a lot of other traditional Japanese vessels—those beautiful gold-inlaid plates, ceramics, and lacquer ware—that can play an important role in making a new or unfamiliar dish more approachable for the western customer.

Tools

I love to see traditional Japanese tools, and I really appreciate and admire chefs who know how to use them.

There's a right knife for every job in the kitchen. That's my philosophy. The end result is important to me, including the texture, the look, and the finish. And I need the right tool to get that result. For example, I often use a bowl that's ribbed inside. When I put an ingredient inside it, it gives me that texture and that grind that I want. When I'm cleaning octopus or fish, I put it in the bowl and rub it lightly, the way I do when I have sand on my feet. That gentle rubbing lightly tenderizes or texturizes the outside of the fish. I also like Japanese ginger graters.

I love to see traditional Japanese tools, and I really appreciate and admire some of the chefs who know how to use them. In America, everybody wants the new, the flashy, and the trendy. In the Japanese culture, the best tools are handcrafted. They have been handed down and do their jobs efficiently.

A Day in the Life

The closer I can get my chefs to the source of the ingredients and to the origin of the cuisine, the more they will walk away with, and the more the restaurant will benefit.

When I was at the Marquis in New York City, I took six of my chefs and cooks to Boston to visit the oyster beds. Why? Because I wanted them to be able to work on the raw bar in the restaurants. I knew that if they had to open oysters and clams all day for a month, they would complain. They would say "Chef, you've got to let me do something else. I'm wasting my time opening oysters all day." But if I asked them, "How do oysters reproduce?" or "If I put five oysters in front of you, can you tell me their species and where they are from?" they'd all say no.

We went out to the beds in flat-bottom boats and started pulling up scallops. The chefs held scallops the size of a pencil eraser. They were just little specks, and out in the open air, they were bouncing all around in their hands, hundreds of these little scallops. None of those chefs had ever seen anything like that.

Then we reached into the water and got a bigger scallop and some oysters. We were shucking them and slurping them and tasting that salty water right on the boat. I guarantee you that these cooks and chefs gained a new appreciation for and an understanding of shellfish. They learned about different varieties, their characteristics, and what to look for.

The point is, the closer I can get my chefs to the source of the ingredients and to the origin of the cuisine, the more they will walk away with, and the more the restaurant will benefit. I know they have passion, but they don't know what they don't know. They need somebody to show them. That's why, after seeing those little scallops bouncing in their hands and picking the oysters out of the water, their understanding was completely different. As a leader, I put those oysters and scallops into their hands and let them see and taste them. I know that those experiences will stay with them for a very long time.

❖

TWENTY-ONE

BARRY WINE

Restaurant Consultant, Past Owner/Chef,
The Quilted Giraffe, New York City

Envisioning an American restaurant that would be equal to the best restaurants of Europe, Barry Wine taught himself to cook and opened The Quilted Giraffe in New York City in 1979. The restaurant's success served as the first blow to the prevailing belief that only French cuisine should be served at fine restaurants. *The New York Times* hailed The Quilted Giraffe as "perhaps the most extravagant and innovative restaurant in America." Private farming of vegetables, fine dining take-out, and loyalty to in-season ingredients were early innovations. Barry Wine is often credited with initiating tasting dinners, the use of artistic dishware, and the blending of Asian flavors, preparation, and presentation techniques.

Barry Wine's extensive study and expression of Japanese culinary techniques seeded his celebrity in Asia. The restaurant sold its lease and closed in 1992. Since then, Barry Wine has planned and built a highly acclaimed executive dining club for Sony and has also consulted on hospitality matters for owners of iconic office buildings.

Influences

I guess Nouvelle Cuisine was what we were doing, but our tasting menus for Nouvelle Cuisine looked Japanese.

The Quilted Giraffe started in New Paltz, New York in 1975 as a really simple restaurant. At that point, I was a working lawyer, and I had never been to Japan. My wife, Susan, had an art gallery, clothing store, and toy store—separate little businesses in one tiny store. In order to get more business, we said, "Let's have a restaurant, and we'll get ladies to come for lunch and go shopping." The name came about when, coincidentally, somebody came into the art gallery and said, "I want to do an exhibition of my quilts," and the quilts had pictures of giraffes on them. So we bought all of the quilted giraffes and hung them on the walls. It was kind of simple. I mean, not sophisticated. It looked like a children's nursery.

The Quilted Giraffe didn't have any Japanese influences until after 1983, several years after we moved to New York. Before that, I had been to France and saw this thing called a "tasting menu"— degustation is what they call it. A tasting menu is many courses served in small portions. That was one of the things that The Quilted Giraffe pioneered. We were probably the first restaurant to serve a tasting menu in America. Not even the French restaurants here were doing it.

A tasting menu is very difficult to do. In a typical meal, the customer gets two or three courses. With a tasting menu, you're giving them 10 courses, so you're cooking a lot of food! Timing is very important, and with respect to timing, the smaller the ingredients are cut up, the faster they cook. At The Quilted Giraffe, I was doing that to make multiple courses, but the dishes started looking Japanese because of the way the ingredients were cut. I was always interested in dishware, and I liked the way Japanese food was presented in magazines. I guess Nouvelle Cuisine was what we were doing, but our tasting menus for Nouvelle Cuisine looked Japanese.

In 1983, there were many Japanese in New York, buying real estate, eating and drinking wine, and wanting to learn about everything American. Many were guests at The Quilted Giraffe. One day a Japanese customer said to me, "Your food looks Japanese. Why don't you go to Japan, and I'll introduce you to some people. You'll get to see some Japanese restaurants." So that's how the Japanese influence at The Quilted Giraffe came about.

I was lucky, because my first day in Japan I met Mr. Shizuo Tsuji, founder of the TSUJI Culinary Institute.

Tsuji-san took me to Kitcho, the most famous kaiseki restaurant in Japan. The food, the service—everything at Kitcho—became the standard for The Quilted Giraffe. That day I also met the son of Akio Morita, who was co-founder of Sony Corporation and whose family had a miso business in Nagoya. It wasn't until later, maybe in 1986 or 1987, that I met Mr. Sumihara and his "extended family," who belonged to a new religion called Tenrikyo. They were probably the ones who taught me the most about Japanese culture. I became very close with them. I visited them many times when I was in Japan and incorporated what I learned at The Quilted Giraffe.

On one occasion, Mr. Sumihara arranged for his daughter, who was extremely interested in food and cooking, to come to New York and do a 10-course kaiseki dinner party for about eight of the most important people that he knew. She brought her own dishes for the dinner, and when it came time to go back to Japan, she left me all of these very beautiful, beautiful dishes! So that was one of the things that got me started using Japanese dishware. Soon after that, I started going on trips to Japan to buy dishware.

Cuisine

We thought having a coffee was part of dinner, and we didn't want guests to try to save $2.00 and not get coffee.

In 1975 in New Paltz, a complete dinner at The Quilted Giraffe was $9, and you could buy Château Lafite by the glass. We had a special wine night on Thursdays, and we'd sell glasses of wine for $3.50. After we moved to New York in 1979, the price on the first menu, I think, was $22.50. We always served a complete prix fixe dinner—never à la carte. I didn't believe in it. I wanted everyone to have the real experience. We didn't want them not to have an appetizer even if they thought they wanted to be cheap. We even included coffee in our dinners, whereas in most French restaurants with prix fixe dinners, coffee was an à la carte extra. We thought having a coffee was part of dinner, and we didn't want guests to try to save $2 and not get coffee.

Once we were in New York, we were busy, and customers would all say it was very good. At the beginning, critics didn't say it was very good. Food critic Mimi Sheraton first gave it one star in *The New York Times*, and Seymour Britchky called it "poor." But the customers always really, really liked what we were doing, so we raised our prices every six months or so and went from $22.50 to $27.50 to $35 to $45 for a kaiseki dinner. I'd come back from a trip to Japan and say, "When we open next week, let's be $55 this time." We were almost testing how high we could go, and by the end, a kaiseki dinner was $135. In 1991 or 1992, that was really a lot of money. Finally, by 2000, the other restaurants got up to that price, but I was there in 1992. That was a lot at the time, but there was no resistance.

The Quilted Giraffe started to have a reputation with the Japanese that it was the place to eat because it was fusion—in a nice way.

The Japanese could bring the Americans there and say, "Look what we do." And Americans could bring the Japanese and say, "Look what we do." It was a good setting for business. I never left the restaurant. I was there for almost virtually every meal and touched every plate when it was going out. So I could serve and I could invent at the moment. The Quilted Giraffe was fun and sexy in the way that no other restaurants were, and by and large, very few restaurants are today.

Our signature dish, the Beggar's Purse, and truffles were two of the things that made the restaurant very sexy and profitable.

The Beggar's Purse had two benefits. One was financial. It was very expensive. Beggar's Purse was essentially $50 a bite added onto a prix fixe menu that was already $75, so that made for a $125 dinner. But I gave you more value, because I gave you more caviar for your $50 than any other restaurant in the city. And I did that with the truffles as well. The other benefit—the other half of all of this—was sex appeal. The Beggar's Purse was a mini crepe filled with cold caviar and crème fraiche, covered with warm melted butter and sitting on a beautiful, three-tier or a five-tier candelabra that a waiter carried into the dining room. You had to put your hands behind your back and eat it without a napkin in just one bite.

In the later days we used handcuffs, but at the beginning it was just no hands. Then we took a picture at the very moment that you were eating your Beggar's Purse. When you saw the camera, if you were out with your girlfriend or your wife, you'd say, "You've got to have caviar! You've got to have caviar! What do you mean? You don't want to do caviar?" This was just the opposite of what you'd say in another restaurant: "You want caviar? It's $50!" But in this case, because of the sexiness of it, everybody wanted everybody else to have it.

With the fresh truffles, I'd say, "Tell me when to stop." Of course, nobody ever took too much, but I wasn't counting the slices. And everyone knew that the best way to eat a truffle was off the top of a wife or a girlfriend's hand! And all of this was going on because people were having fun—it was a performance. We got four stars.

My goal was to blend constant change with consistency.

The menu constantly changed. If you ordered a kaiseki dinner from me, I never served you the same meal or the same dishes twice. By consistency, I mean that each meal at The Quilted Giraffe was always four stars. That I learned from Kitcho. Even if a guest said, "I had this or that last week, and I want the same meal," I wouldn't give him or her the same meal and would create some other dish. If one person was having a kaiseki dinner and somebody else at another table ordered a kaiseki dinner, each got a totally different dinner with totally different dishware. That's very difficult. Communication in the kitchen was very important.

Today, when you order the chef's choice tasting menu and you look around the room, everybody's eating the same dinner. That's the chef's special, but it's not very exciting. That's not creating a dinner just for you. I would make it a point to do something for you. For example, if a Japanese customer told me he came from Kyushu, then I would give him dishes from Kyushu. If another customer were wearing a red dress, I would give her only dishes that went with her dress.

Training

In those days, there were no professional management classes for restaurant owners, and there were few professionally trained non-French chefs or cooks.

The only well-trained cooks had been in French restaurants, but they were trained to cook for the shelf. They weren't trained to innovate. They were trained that Dover sole had to come with a boiled potato cut a certain way with parsley on top. We were breaking away from the French model. Nobody had any idea what I was talking about or what I was trying to do. I had 14 cooks working in the kitchen, but nobody knew what we were trying to do. Today, a chef who has worked for Daniel and then goes to work for Jean-Georges has been taught the new non-French manner of running a restaurant, of cooking in a restaurant. But back in the early 1990s, it was totally groundbreaking.

In the French restaurants, there was no management in the dining room. There was the French maitre d', who was a glorified waiter who got tips. Right? Isn't that what you did? You would slip him $25 for your table or $20 when you left. So a maitre d' by definition isn't a manager. At that time, nobody was trained to be a manager. Today, when you go to Daniel or Jean-Georges or any restaurant, you'll see four or five managers on the floor who have been trained by the restaurant to carry out the restaurant's vision. Like the cooks, they have worked for somebody else and have learned what it means to be a manager, not a tipped employee. In the beginning, all restaurant employees were tipped employees. I changed that, too, at The Quilted Giraffe. I eliminated tips and just added an 18 percent service charge to the bill.

Ingredients

At one time, believe it or not, in New York restaurants there was no fresh foie gras, and there was no arugula.

Foie gras came in a can from France. It wasn't until 1981 or 1982 that we were able to get fresh foie gras. The same thing is true of arugula and fresh raspberries. When we were in the Japanese mode, people were beginning to import fresh fish from Kagoshima, the capital city of Kagoshima Prefecture at the southwestern tip of the Kyūshū island of Japan. Do you know the word for direct shipment by air from Japan? "Expensive"! It leaves Kagoshima yesterday and it gets to us today. But nobody, not even the sushi restaurants in New York, did that.

Today, you go to a sushi bar and they say, "Oh, we have fresh fish from Japan. It's very expensive." Well, I was bringing fish in then. I remember a fish called *ishidai*, meaning "rock" or "stone." There were also the *sawagani* crabs. They are small crabs, about as big as the first joint of your thumb, usually grilled and served whole. We'd put the live sawagani into a martini glass, and then I would tell the guests, "Only men from Osaka are brave enough to eat it while it is still alive! You have to bite it before it bites you!" We called it a "popcorn-y crab." So we were doing those kinds of things. This was just totally unheard of in America at the time.

I was having fun and so were my customers, but they were also learning about Japanese food.

You couldn't bring wasabi into the United States until very recently. Wasabi was always a big issue. So when we came back from

Japan, we hid it in our suitcases. It is exactly the same story with saké. There was no fancy saké in 1989, 1990, or even 1992. There were the big bottles of the cheap saké, but no small brewery stuff. I used to go to Japan and bring back a suitcase of 10 bottles of fancy saké. Then in the restaurant I'd make a big deal out of it. I'd say, "Oh, I'm giving you the real stuff." We were the first ones selling premium saké.

On the fifteenth anniversary of The Quilted Giraffe in 1990, my friend, Mr. Sumihara, decided to give us a good present. He sent 15 barrels of taru saké by air freight. True taru saké is fresh and unpasteurized, so he had to deliver it quickly because it would otherwise spoil. And he made a special label with the Statue of Liberty that said, "New York, the Statue of Liberty, The Quilted Giraffe and Kikusui," which is a brand of delicious saké.

So we had 15 barrels of taru saké—you know how big a barrel is! It's like a keg where you have to take a hammer and break the top. These 15 barrels wouldn't last more than a month. Because it was fresh, we had to drink it, and it wasn't refrigerated. During that time, I was always inviting people to come drink saké. Sometimes at the end of the night, if there was a little bit left in the barrel, I would take the barrel up to a Japanese restaurant and bring them fresh saké. That was special.

One of the first non-fish Japanese ingredients that came from Japan was Kobe beef. It actually came from Matsuzaka, a region in Japan most famous for kinds of beef with a high fat-to-meat ratio. That was one of the ingredients that we had, before today's American kind of Kobe beef. In those days we had real Kobe beef. And we bought *fugu*, the Japanese blowfish famous for its potential toxicity, from a man at Restaurant Nippon. He was very famous. We were his only non-Japanese customer. The fugu was frozen and already cut, so there was no risk. I bought a license from him to sell it. We even used the dried fugu fish tail. When you put it in saké—it's called "hirezake"—it burns and gives the saké a distinct taste.

At that time, we were all learning about Japanese cuisine.

I wasn't intentionally studying Japanese cuisine during that time. But I learned. One time a Japanese customer called me to the table and said, "Oh, this is perfect. This is the mountain. This is the river and the earth." It was mashed potatoes with a little sauce. Then I learned the fish had to be swimming upstream. A fish can never be placed downward on the plate. The fish always goes up, with the head to the right. An American chef working in the kitchen would say, "Put the fish to the left." It would never occur to him to face it the other way. What did we know about presenting food the Japanese way? A dish would be upside down, but it was on a pretty plate. It looked good this way, and it looked good that way. But to the Japanese, it had to be "this side up." So I learned that, and so did the people who worked for me. I don't think any of them had ever been to Japan.

I was good at cooking, but it wasn't a dream of cooking. It was a dream of having a great restaurant.

I learned to cook on the job at The Quilted Giraffe, but nobody taught me what I had to know about creating the dishes. I invented it. These were all new concepts that were invented at The Quilted Giraffe. I learned as it was happening. This is where service came into it, and it was one reason why the prices at The Quilted Giraffe got to be what they were.

I decided that the customer wanted and could afford a flawless dinner. In order to do that, I didn't want to have bussers. I had only wait staff, because that gave the guests a better meal. I could teach the wait staff what I wanted, and I expected a higher level of performance from them. I was paying the wait staff more per hour than I would pay a busser. In order to justify that and be able to do it, the price of dinner had to be higher in my restaurant than it was at other four-star restaurants. Ours was $75 and theirs were $58.

A lot of this has more to do with economics than is clear on the surface. Every restaurant owner thinks he or she can tell the wait staff exactly what to do. One restaurateur I know has the most beautiful complicated employee manual that lists what every person is supposed to do during a shift. Each thing has to be checked off. Somebody has to go to the bathroom every 15 minutes and sign his name showing that he was there. A lot of things like that.

I wanted it to be the $75 meal, because I wanted it to be as good as Kitcho in Japan. I wanted that kind of standard.

Of course I showed the wait staff exactly how I wanted things done, but I'm talking more philosophically. I policed and "beat the horse" to make sure that the customer got his $75 worth. At $58, the customer's expectation was not as high as at $75. So I was always walking a tightrope. Could I give them the $75 meal? Everything was feeding that. I wanted it to be the $75 meal, because I wanted it to be as good as Kitcho in Japan. I wanted that kind of standard. If you think of the French maitre d' who insults you—that was the French experience. Some people went to those restaurants for that experience. But I was going to give customers a different experience. And my experience cost $75 to produce.

What does it cost to serve you this dinner? I used a crystal glass that cost $22—that was Hoya at the time—and every night the wait staff broke six glasses, because that's what happens in a restaurant. At other high-end restaurants they are breaking $8 glasses and I was breaking $22 glasses, but I wanted to use $22 glasses because I wanted customers to feel the difference. I was more focused on the customer experience than making a larger profit on that $75.

I didn't send a waiter to the table to say, "How is everything? How's your fish?" That was always happening at other restaurants, but at The Quilted Giraffe, the waiter would say, "We hope you're enjoying your dinner." Of course, the fish was always good. There was just no question that the fish was good. It couldn't not be good— what we were buying, the care we were giving it, treating the ingredients before we served it, cooking it, bringing it to the table fast so it wasn't cold. You couldn't get cold food at The Quilted Giraffe because it was out of the pan, onto the plate, and, "Hurry up and take it to the table!"

You'd go to a French restaurant and the dining room stunk! It smelled like Sterno.

Before the 1980s the only French restaurants were French and only French. Of course, there was just the maitre d' who looked down his nose at you. The menu, which maybe you could read—maybe you couldn't. But what went with French cooking was cooking that I called "for the shelf." The cooks put it in a copper pan and put it on the shelf. The waiter comes with a little trolley—the guéridon—and says, "Give me that copper casserole." Then he takes it in the dining room and, for effect, flambées it—that is, plays with it—and then lets it sit above a rechaud, or can of Sterno. This is not so long ago— honestly, this is 1980! No foie gras. No fresh raspberries. No arugula. But Sterno in the dining room!

One of the first things that The Quilted Giraffe changed was how fast food was served. Food came out of the kitchen already on the plate as opposed to it sitting on the shelf. That was unheard of in a fancy restaurant. The Quilted Giraffe's style was out of the frying pan, onto the plate, to the table—and it was fast! I was always yelling, "I'm getting mad! Where's the waiter? Take it! Take it! Don't look at it. Carry it away. Get it to the table now!"

Pacing was an extremely important part of our restaurant service. The Quilted Giraffe believed that there should be 10 minutes between courses. You got your appetizer 10 minutes after you ordered, and then another course every 10 minutes. If you were having a kaiseki dinner, a multi-course dinner, or a tasting dinner, then we allowed seven or eight minutes between courses. We had digital clocks in the kitchen—today you see them but at the time they were new, so the cook would know how long he or she had.

We were serving only 100 people. The Japanese always ordered the tasting menu. They'd sit down and say, "Bring me the tasting menu." Or they would tell a guest, "Oh, you've got to have the tasting menu." We used to call it "American Kaiseki." That was the phrase.

Asian food is a trend. It's well underway, and it's not going to stop.

Over the next five years, you'll have American sushi chefs. Today, there are almost no ingredients in Japan that aren't here, too. And there are almost no preparations that aren't here. There might be some super sophisticated ones that require knife skills, such as the *hamo*, or the pike eel, with 120 cuts. When you eat hamo in Japan, you're impressed that this fish has a lot of bones and that the chef can make exactly 120 cuts in each fish. In Japan, customers say, "Oh, isn't he a great chef? Look how good his knife skills are!" Do you get that in New York? No. But is it important? No. We're not interested in the chef's skill when we go to a restaurant. We're interested in our experience as a customer. That's a big difference.

Japanese people who come here to open their restaurants have the skill, but they don't understand the way that the American customer enjoys food. And vice versa. I think an American restaurant that goes to Japan makes a mistake by trying to be too Japanese. An American restaurant, doing American food—this is what the Japanese find interesting. If American restaurants go to Japan, they should be American. Japanese restaurants here need to understand that for Americans, eating is an experience. It's not to congratulate the chef on his or her skills. Of course, some American chefs who open restaurants think they are going to be congratulated for their skills. Those are the restaurants that fail, too. Showing off in a restaurant doesn't matter. The most important thing to know is what the customer wants.

Today, people say, "I can remember what I ate when I went to The Quilted Giraffe, and it was the best meal I ever had." This relationship with the customers kept it at the top for a long period of time. Plus, it was a nice thing to be the best. Maybe you remember Sparks Restaurant, the steakhouse. The owner was named Pat Cetta—he died a long time ago. But he taught me something. When somebody tells you, "This is the best meal I've had," the right thing to say is, "Well, somebody has to be the best, and we're glad that you think it's us."

A Day in the Life

I thought, "Isn't this wonderful for world understanding?"

I was doing a Japanese cultural festival in New York and invited one of Japan's most famous chefs and restaurateurs, Kiyomi Mikuni, to do Japanese food. I thought, "Isn't this wonderful for world understanding?" Meanwhile, he'd made a side deal with an American woman who was on camera speaking Japanese on Nippon TV, to film him while he was here for the festival.

Chef Mikuni brought a camera crew with the plan that they were going to film him, and the whole thing was to be set to music from Rocky! This was an hour show they were filming. The theme was:

"The Japanese chef challenges the American chef to a fight." The goal was to find out who had the better food. Since I thought we were doing something else, I couldn't understand why he was acting as if he were training for a fight. The crew filmed him running in Central Park. Then they filmed him standing at the stove in the kitchen shadow boxing, and then getting a bloody nose. He invited me and some people from the Four Seasons to be on the show. A bunch of the French chefs came, too, and there we were—on camera for Japanese television. It was silly, but Kiyomi Mikuni brought a lot of new Japanese ingredients to New York. That was just another day in the life of a chef in New York.

TWENTY-TWO

LEE ANNE WONG

Chef/Consultant

Lee Anne Wong is an American chef, and was one of the last four contestants on the first season of Bravo's *Top Chef*. She was the culinary producer for the show's next six seasons, where her duties included sourcing and styling the ingredients, and determining the creative challenge, budget, equipment restrictions, and time limits.

After graduating from The French Culinary Institute and working at Aquavit and Jean-Georges Vongerichten's Restaurant 66, she became the Executive Chef of Event Operations at FCI, a position she held while participating in the *Top Chef* competition. She has appeared on many food television programs including *Food Crawl with Lee Anne Wong,* and Food Network's *Chopped* and *Iron Chef America,* among others. She was also the chef-consultant for the film *No Reservations* (2007), and participates in many fund-raising events.

In December 2013, she moved to Honolulu to open Koko Head Cafe, which opened its doors in March 2014. Her first cookbook, *Dumplings All Day Wong*, was published in 2014.

Influences

Working at Aquavit was when I first started taking a serious interest in Japanese food and ingredients.

When I was 12 years old, my family visited the Philippines for my cousin's wedding. My uncle Tony took my brother and me to a sushi restaurant somewhere in Quezon City. It was my first time eating sushi, and my uncle dared me to eat the entire ball of wasabi. He put me up to a $100 bet, and of course, being a kid, I wanted to impress my older brother. So I popped the whole thing in my mouth and swallowed it with water. I didn't chew it. My uncle ended up forking over $100. I had a very bad stomach ache the next few days. And that was my first introduction to sushi, but also the last for a while, because there wasn't much sushi in upstate New York.

I started cooking when I was 20 or so. I was taking classes three nights a week at The French Culinary Institute in New York City and bartending to pay the rent. The first month at FCI felt right, so I contacted career services and asked for a list of local restaurants to contact. Aquavit, a Scandinavian restaurant, was listed under "A," so I called and asked if the restaurant was looking for interns or part-timers. I knew that Aquavit was a famous restaurant and had seen its owner, Marcus Samuelsson, on TV. What amazed me was that after I called, Marcus personally called me back! That surprised me! When I talked to Marcus on the phone, I said I wanted real restaurant experience—fine dining experience. He invited me to come in.

Career Path

I did whatever they asked me to do that first day, and they asked me if I wanted to come back the next day. Of course, I said yes!

On my first day at Aquavit, I met John Kingsley, the sous chef; and Nils Norén, the Chef de Cuisine. Kingsley asked me to turn a case of artichokes, which, thankfully, I had learned in culinary school the week before. So I went through the case of artichokes with my little paring knife. My hands were on fire and quite sore by the end of it. It was a test. I showed them how I did the first case, and then Kingsley said, "Yep, do the rest."

Aquavit was a Scandinavian restaurant, but we used all kinds of Asian ingredients. We used yuzu from Japan. We had different kinds of sesame oil, different types of soy sauce from China and Japan, curries, lemongrass, limes—ingredients that I had never experienced.

Japanese food is a feast for the eyes.

In terms of Japanese sushi, my first epiphany was at the restaurant Ichimura. It was a tiny place on Second Avenue and 53rd Street in New York City. I didn't speak any Japanese, so I sat at the bar and ordered the "omakase"—chef's choice. It cost about $100 and was the first traditional omakase I'd ever had. I started with my appetizers, and then I had the sashimi dish, clear soup, and vegetables. Then I had the cold fish dish, the hot fish dish, and so forth. From where I sat, I could see everything—fake plastic bamboo things and everything wrapped up in plastic wrap.

The fish in front of the chef was in a box on a tray. When he lifted the lid, I could see that everything in there was perfect. I had never

288 · LEE ANNE WONG

tasted fish so good because the chef flew in his fish daily from the Tsukiji fish market in Tokyo, and from Norway. It was the freshest sashimi, and also the best sashimi, I had ever eaten. At that time, spending $100 on dinner seemed frivolous, particularly since I was a line cook making only 11 bucks an hour. It was an expensive meal, but it set a standard for me. I would never again enjoy cheap sushi.

I remember after that first day at Aquavit, I begged Marcus to let me keep working the line, but he put me in pastry, and I didn't want to work in pastry. I didn't want to be pigeonholed because I was a girl, and the only other girl in the kitchen at the time was in pastry. I told him, "I don't want to do pastry!" Then Marcus asked me, "Where do you want to be?" I told him garde manger. He said, "Careful what you ask for."

Garde manger is—no joke—the toughest station at Aquavit. I didn't realize it at the time, and I spent a year in that position. During my time at Aquavit, Marcus and Nils asked me to write menus and then sat down with me and reviewed my ideas, which they didn't do with everybody. Eventually, they gave me a position managing in the cafe kitchen. I put the weekly specials on the menu, which is a huge opportunity for a line cook.

I spent almost three years at Aquavit and came out being a good line cook.

I learned a lot from Marcus and Nils, but I wanted to see if being a private chef was better, so I went to a special employment agency that placed culinary staff with wealthy families. It became very clear after a short time that this kind of work was not for me, so I then went to the career services department at The French Culinary Institute. The director told me that Jean-Georges Vongerichten was opening a Chinese restaurant in Tribeca and he needed a cook, so I said, "All right."

Taking that job was a step back. I had been a big dog at Aquavit. I was there for almost three years and knew every station, how to do everything, and how to run a crew. As the day cook at Jean-Georges' new restaurant, I was put on the hardest station with a female partner who ended up becoming my archenemy. Everyone was climbing over each other's back to get the sous chef position—I'm not into that. I would show up at six in the morning, and sometimes I would be there until 10 at night rolling scallion pancakes. I was there a couple months and realized that I needed to get out of there. I wasn't making much money—maybe $11 an hour. I quit the day we got reviewed. It was really tough, but it was the best decision I ever made.

Working at the FCI changed my culinary career. Hands down and no regrets.

I went back to FCI again and asked if they had anything freelance for me. They were between executive chefs in the amphitheater, so I came in and assisted a new chef, who ended up getting married and pregnant two weeks after she took on the position. The FCI liked my work, so they offered me the job. It was a big decision for me—I was about 27. I wondered if stepping away from the restaurant kitchen to work at a culinary school was the right decision. It ended up being the best decision I ever made.

Being the Executive Chef of Events at the amphitheater enabled me to work with every guest chef that came to the school. One of my responsibilities was to coordinate a chef demonstration program, so I got to work with every guest chef who visited. I set up demonstrations, ordered the food, tested the recipe, coordinated guest chefs' car service, and made sure they had everything they needed. I also got to work with the FCI deans, including Alice Waters, Jacques Pépin, Jacques Torres, and one of my favorite mentors, André Soltner, on a regular basis. I learned so much just standing next to these culinary legends and talking with them.

I worked with anywhere from 5 to 12 guest chefs every month—sometimes even more. I had to learn how the guest chefs wanted things done. I asked questions like, "What is your thought process behind this?" I learned their recipes and techniques. It was a great time for me to be a sponge, because each day was different and I was learning something new from different people. While I was doing that, I created menus at events and for our private clients. I planned all of the food for graduations and wine classes with Andrea Immer-Robinson. No menu was the same, and I never did anything twice. And that's the way I work now.

> *There has been a shift within America's culinary industry, and that shift is moving more towards the locavore philosophy—a purity of ingredients. And who has been doing this kind of cooking for centuries? Japan.*

I spent six years in that position at The French Culinary Institute building up the amphitheater. It was during that time that I discovered the restaurant Ichimura, which became my favorite Japanese restaurant in New York. I met Chef Tadashi Ono and Owner/Chef Eiji Ichimura, who gave a demonstration about sushi and Japanese cuisine—the first of many demonstrations of Japanese cooking at the FCI. The demonstration was so traditional and so amazing—the students at the school had never seen anything like that before.

Japanese cuisine wasn't at the forefront of cuisine back then. It wasn't as modernized and popular as it is now. In fact, the culinary world hadn't paid much attention to Japanese cuisine, because for the past several decades the focus had been "Spain-Spain-Spain" or "France-Italy-Europe." But recently, there has been a shift within America's culinary industry, and that shift is moving more towards the locavore philosophy—a purity of ingredients. And who has been doing this kind of cooking for centuries? Japan.

That's why we invited the Japanese TSUJI Culinary Institute, along with 10 top chefs in Japan, to come to FCI for a conference to focus on Japanese cooking techniques and ingredients. It was wonderful to be able to learn about Japanese cuisine in an educational forum in New York City.

People think that the Top Chef shows are scripted—they're not.

While I was at the FCI, I became one of the first contestants on *Top Chef*. It was interesting, because there was no TV show like it. It was fun and weird being thrown into a house with the other contestant chefs. I had lived alone for many years. Then, suddenly, I was living in a house with 11 other crazy adults and kids, but it was a very positive experience. There's a lot of work that goes into the show, and the challenges are real. The time limits to cook are real, too. My training at the FCI helped me get through the series. I knew I could learn something from everybody in the room, so I kept an eye on what everybody was doing. I tried to present myself in the best fashion and represent the FCI without losing my own identity.

It's very rare that you get the opportunity as a chef to cook your food and then have the best criticism thrown back in your face on a regular basis. When food connoisseurs like Tom Colicchio gave me direct feedback about what was right and what was wrong, I sat there and nodded. He knew a lot more about food than I did, which is why he was successful in business and why I was sitting on the other side of the table.

I was on *Top Chef* the first season. I made some lifelong friends and learned a lot. Then I became the culinary producer and traveled with the show for four years. When I wasn't working on the show, I was at the FCI. It was very strange for me because people at the FCI thought that I was on vacation, when in reality I was working 60 days straight for 16 to 20 hours a day. It was crazy. I would come back from shooting the show and go back to the FCI feeling tired as a dog and physically burnt out.

I finally had to make a decision to quit my position at the FCI. I left in January 2009 because I was going on the road with the show for another five months. While filming the show, I lived in other cities for months at a time—Miami, Aspen, Los Angeles, San Francisco, Hawaii, Las Vegas, New Orleans, and Puerto Rico. We would stay for a couple weeks or a month at a time and experience their local foods.

It was great to see the world that way, but after a few years, there were times when I was bored and unhappy. We had just finished a series, and we were doing a spin off, *Just Desserts.* I had turned into this machine cranking out shows, and that was something I didn't want to be a part of anymore. I made a decision to come back to New York. I don't regret my time with *Top Chef* for a second. It was an amazing opportunity to connect with the industry in a different way. But now I am committed to living in New York.

Cuisine

I've cooked it all because I love it all so much, but I especially love Japanese food, and that's why I'm leaning more toward Japanese cuisine.

People often ask, "What types of cuisine do you specialize in?" As a chef, I'm in the process of branding myself. I'm trying to figure out my identity. And I want that identity to include Japanese ingredients and technique. I'm familiar with all types of European, African, and

Indian cuisines, and all different kinds of Asian food. I trained in classical French cooking. I worked at a Scandinavian restaurant. I opened a Chinese restaurant. I worked in the Caribbean for a month. I've cooked it all because I love it all so much, but I especially love Japanese food, and that's why I'm leaning more toward Japanese cuisine.

Not long ago, I was down in South Beach for an event called Access House, a managers' party. It was only for chefs. The industry was invited, but no press or media were allowed in. Everyone came to relax in a safe, very exclusive haven. I had the honor of cooking there one of three nights. The first night, I did my version of the marriage of Japanese and French cuisine.

For my burger, I dredged fresh shiitake mushrooms and stewed them and seasoned them with soy, mirin, and sugar, slicing them into the mixture. I then cooked down some red onions and caramelized them. Then I deglazed them with red wine, saké, and miso and folded that in. So it was a red onion red wine miso jam.

Next I made Parmesan fricos, or what they call "cheese crisps" in America. I made my fricos with real Parmesan cheese and *tougarashi*, or chili pepper, blended with flour and a bit of water. I baked them on a sheet tray so they would be super crisp and thin wafer crackers. The burger was all about umami, so I used salt and pepper, the soy and sweetened shiitake mushroom mixture, the red onion miso jam, and some mayonnaise with shiso. I won best burger for the night, and it was rated best burger for the weekend at Access House.

Despite the many Japanese restaurants I have visited, and as much as I love the food, I didn't know anything until I set foot in Japan.

The most eye-opening experience in Japan for me was seeing the entire food culture and how different it is from American or western food culture. Everywhere you look in Japan—left or right—you see food. It's ingrained in Japan's culture, its history, and its heritage. Everything about Japan's food is connected with nature and seasonality, and the chefs take great care in how they handle their food, including the way it is grown and transported. Even the way the food is displayed plays into the chef's idea of hospitality. *Irasshaimase* means "welcome," and I feel that spirit exists everywhere in Japan and easily translates to its food. Japanese chefs aren't so different from any other chef in the world. The disciplines are pretty much the same, but I am inspired by their training and the way they think about food.

Food is seasonal in Japan. Certain types of fish and vegetables are on a menu during the winter but not during the summer, not only because of the lack of availability, but also because chefs in Japan have a commitment to using the same seasonal ingredients. The perfect examples of this were the dishes for the many kaiseki meals I had when I was there in the summer. Every kaiseki menu was exactly the same, no matter where I was in Japan. The finest chefs in Japan were all doing the same dishes. They were all making the mountain vegetables, the clear soups, and the *ankake*, or thickened sauce.

I didn't really understand it at the time, but now I can understand why the Japanese chefs do this. I was so in awe of everything they did, but it took a while for me to realize why. At one point I thought I might be getting sick of kaiseki. But I told myself, "Lee Anne, you don't know when you're going to be in Japan and have this experience again. You have to love it."

Ingredients

Chef Takagi told me to touch the skin of the squid, which was still alive. Its skin was blue! He explained, "That's how you know the squid is fresh—by touching it, whether it's alive or not."

While I was in Kanazawa, Japan, Chef Shinichiro Takagi from Zeniya Restaurant gave me fish-buying and butchering lessons. He took me to the Oumicho Fish Market and talked about how he buys fish and what he looks for. There are hundreds of fishmongers there, but Chef Takagi introduced me to a guy who, he said, had the freshest fish. Chef told me to touch the skin of the squid, which was still alive. Its skin was blue! He explained, "That's how you know the squid is fresh—by touching it, whether it's alive or not."

Now when I go to a fish market in New York, or wherever I am, I know what to look for. I know the basic rules. But I still want to learn more from a Japanese chef on a deeper level. To achieve a true understanding of the Japanese philosophy, I would need to literally stand side-by-side with a Japanese master the way I did at culinary school and hang out with him, talk with him in the kitchen, and get to know his story. Until I understand what it takes to become a master, I'll never fully understand everything that's going on and how to perfect my craft.

I'd love to train with a master chef like Yoshihiro Murata, the author of *Kaiseki: The Exquisite Cuisine of Kyoto's Kikunoi Restaurant*, as well as with that 19-year-old kid who's putting out that banging bowl of pork ramen at Ippudo Restaurant in Kanazawa. Young or old, these chefs are masters because they can take a few ingredients and enhance them by highlighting their best attributes. It's not just a bowl of ramen—it's the best bowl of ramen on earth! Whatever that kid did with the pork bones and that little extra pork fat on top, I want to learn that technique from him.

Training

People used to say, "Go to cooking school to stay out of trouble and to stay out of jail." Now it's a glamorous thing.

Culinary school is necessary, but there are certain misconceptions that come with it. It takes a couple of months to adjust the attitude of a young chef out of culinary school. I was a smart ass. I thought I knew everything. It took me a year or two to learn respect for my fellow cooks and respect for my job. Young chefs are going to learn almost everything they need to know at their first job. I think they come out of culinary school with a lot of bravado and think that they are ready to take on the culinary world, but they don't realize that they are going to spend the first couple years on the line, sweating it out in line or as a prep cook.

There's no easy way to the top. Becoming a professional chef is not about TV. Young people see *Top Chef* and watch Food Network. They think, "Oh that's great. I want to be famous and be on TV." But that's not the reality of it. It's not enough to think, "I cook for myself every day, so maybe I'll go to culinary school and be on *Top Chef*." People with this attitude would come to open casting calls for *Top Chef* and say, "I watch Food Network and cook every day. I read *Bon Appétit*. And that's why I want to be a chef."

That's not going to be enough.

Being a professional chef is about discipline and a willingness to work and learn until the day you die. There's always somebody out there who can teach you something new. For me, it is Japanese cuisine. I'm so delighted to have discovered an entire culture that I can dedicate the rest of my life to finding out about. This is not something I can learn in the next year or in five or even 10 years. It's going to take a lifetime to learn and immerse myself in Japanese cuisine.

Tools

My knife skills increased dramatically once I learned how to work with a petty knife.

I remember my first Japanese knife. I started using Japanese steel over 15 years ago and I still have it. It is beat as hell, but I still love it. It's my most important tool. It's an extension of your arm. Since then, my collection has grown exponentially. I honestly haven't bought German steel since then. German knives are metal poured into a mold, but in Japan, knife makers are still hand-forging steel. When I was in Sakai City and met the famous knife maker, Mr. Doi, I was amazed to learn that this old man in his 80s has been standing in front of a fire for more than 60 years of his life, hammering steel as part of a three-man "orchestra" that creates the most spectacular knives in Japan. These men are so sweet and so humble about what they do, but they are so serious that they can do it blindfolded. It is their craftsmanship and the heritage of knife making that make these knives so special.

What is it about a Japanese knife that's different for me? I'm a female, I'm Asian, and I've got tiny hands. I trained with a giant German chef's knife that was almost the size of my forearm. It was awkward. During my first two years at Aquavit, our sous chef tried to teach me really good knife skills, so I invested in my first Japanese steel. At the time, a Japanese knife was like a Rolls Royce, but I wanted to make sure my knives were on point. My Japanese knife was sharper, thinner, and lighter than the German knives.

For the most part, the petty knife is my every-day knife. I have big slicers, chef's knives, and others, too, but I opt for a petty knife over the bigger knives because it's small and my hands are small. I can do fine work with it. I can bone things with it. The petty knife was a revelation when I discovered it. My knife skills increased dramatically once I learned how to work with a smaller knife.

A Day in the Life

Everybody who worked at Aquavit did everything in their power to see if I would quit.

When I first started cooking at Aquavit, I wanted to learn how to cook, but there was a point where it was unbearable for me. I was getting yelled at every single day by the executive and sous chefs. One day when I messed up really badly, the executive chef really let me have it. I kept asking him how to fix it, but he kept at me. Finally I said, "Can I talk to you for a second?" I told him, "I like working here. I want to work here, and I want to learn. I'm not learning anything when you talk to me this way. I'm sorry I messed up, and I will always admit it when I mess up. But unless you tell me how to fix it, you're not doing your job, and I'm no good to you anyway."

We never had a problem after that. We came to an understanding, and he never yelled at me like that, ever again. It was such a big thing for me because I've worked in a lot of kitchens. I see the way chefs treat their cooks. I want to be in an environment where my chefs are willing to stop and talk it out with me and help me understand why something doesn't work, not yell at me. Fortunately, the executive chef gave me that opportunity. And I think it's important to create a bond with your first mentor. He was that mentor to me. He taught me a lot. I'd lie down in front of a bus for that guy—as long as he doesn't yell at me!

Years later he admitted to me that they yelled at me every day just to see if I would quit. It was really mean, but I really wanted to cook. And now I can say to him, "Aren't you glad I didn't?"

❖

GLOSSARY OF JAPANESE INGREDIENTS AND TERMS

Abura-age A deep-fried rectangular tofu pouch

Amadai Japanese fish that is similar to tilefish

Amazake Sweet rice saké with no alcohol

Bonito flakes (Katsuobushi) Dried, smoked, and shaved skipjack tuna

Chawanmushi Japanese egg custard that dates back to the fifteenth century

Daikon Japanese white radish

Dashi Japanese stock made from kelp and dried bonito flakes (*see* **Katsuobushi**)

Edamame Green soybeans in the pod that are boiled or steamed and served with salt

Enoke mushrooms Long, thin, white mushrooms popular in Japanese and East Asian cuisine

Fugu Japanese word for "blowfish" or "pufferfish." The dish prepared from it that is famous for its potential toxicity

Funazushi Fermented sushi, pickled plum, and pickled daikon

Gari Pickled ginger

Hamo Pike eel

Hatcho miso Dark, robust, strong, chunky, and extremely rich and salty miso made only from soybeans

Hinazushi Traditional pickled fish

Hirezake Hot saké in which the dried fin of the fugu fish has been steeped and then served

Hone sembei Small, crisp bone crackers

Iriko dashi Traditional dashi prepared from dried anchovies or sardines

Ishidai Popular fish in Japanese cuisine; also known as "knife jaw," or stone perch

Ishiri Fish sauce made from fermenting squid guts and salt for up to three years

Ishiyaki Traditional Japanese type of cooking where dishes are cooked on heated stones

Junsai A perennial aquatic plant, the unfurled leaves of which are covered in a slippery, transparent jelly

Kabayaki Grilled eel

Kaiseki (kaiseki-ryori) Traditional multi-course Japanese dinner; collection of high-level cooking skills and techniques

Kakushi aji Japanese concept which refers to hidden tastes in food

Kani miso Liquid extracted from the head of a crab, baked into a paste, and eaten with rice or as a side dish with saké

Kansha Aspect of Japanese food culture that means "appreciation." Compels the full use of food, water and other resources

Karasumi Salt-pickled mullet roe

Katsuobushi Steam-processed bonito fillets dried to wood-like hardness and shaved into flakes; referred to as bonito flakes; one of the two essential ingredients in making dashi, the other being kelp.

Kinome Leaf of the prickly ash tree, whose berries are ground into sansho pepper

Kombu (konbu) Dried giant kelp (seaweed) used in Japanese cooking

Konka iwashi Sardine pickled in rice husk

Konowata Pickled sea cucumber entrails

Kuro edamame Known as "black edamame" considered tastier than regular edamame. Actually light brown-green in color.

Kuzu Stable thickening agent that is clear and has no taste

Kyo yasai Traditional vegetables from Kyoto that have unique shapes and vivid colors and are rich in nutrition

Makimono (makizushi) Vinegared rice, fish, or other ingredients rolled into a sheet of nori, soy paper, cucumber, rice or other ingredients. Usually cut into six or eight pieces—a single roll order.

Mirin Sweet cooking saké; thin, golden-colored syrup

Miso Thick paste and cooking staple used for sauces and spreads, pickling vegetables or meats, and mixing with dashi soup stock to serve as miso soup. Produced by fermenting rice, barley, and/or soybeans with salt and the fungus *kōjikin*, the most typical miso being made with soy; **Genmai miso** (made from brown rice and soybeans); **Kome miso** (made from white rice and soybeans); **Mugi miso** (made from barley and soybeans); **Natto miso** (made from ginger and soybeans); **Soba miso** (made from buckwheat and soybeans).

Mushimono Traditional Japanese method of cooking by steaming vegetables, meat, chicken, or fish

Nanakusa Harvesting of the seven edible wild herbs of spring

Natto Fermented soybean paste

Neba neba Japanese reference to sticky or slimy foods, often referring specifically to boiled okra

Nimono Traditional Japanese method of cooking by poaching, usually vegetables

Nori Dried, paper-thin seaweed sheets used to make sushi and other Japanese dishes

Nuka Rice bran used for pickling

Nukazuke Japanese pickle made by fermenting *vegetables* in rice bran (nuka)

Omakase A Japanese phrase that means, "I'll leave it to you." It is used in restaurants to entrust the selection of dishes to the chef

Onsen tamago Hot spring egg, or slow-boiled egg

Ramen Chinese-style wheat noodles often served in a meat- or fish-based broth

Sado (Chado) Japanese tea ceremony involving the ceremonial preparation and presentation of green tea

Saké Traditional rice wine used for drinking and cooking

Saké kasu Ingredient made from the lees after sake is squeezed from fermented rice

Sansai Foraging for wild vegetables

Sansho Ground spice made from the pods of the sansho tree

Sashimi Japanese delicacy consisting of very fresh raw fish or meat, thinly sliced

Sawagani Japanese river crabs, or freshwater crabs

Shichimi (shichimi togarishi) Collection of seven dried and ground spices and ingredients used as a seasoning agent

Shirako The sperm from cod, anglerfish, monkfish, or fugu

Shiso Perennial herb from the mint family used primarily as a garnish, either whole or chopped

Shottsuru Pungent regional Japanese fish sauce made from the brine of salt-pickled fish

Shoyu Brown, pungent, salty soy sauce made from a fermented mixture of soybeans, wheat, salt, and aspergillus mold. It is a primary ingredient in Japanese cooking.

Soba Dried buckwheat noodles

Sushi Cooked vinegared rice combined with seafood, vegetables, and other ingredients. Ingredients and forms of sushi presentation vary widely, but the ingredient which all sushi have in common is rice.

Takiawase A mixture of vegetables, each simmered separately and then combined when the dish is served

Tanmi The subtle, natural flavor of an ingredient

Tekka-maki Rolled sushi that is meant to be eat quickly and easily

Tempura Dish of seafood or vegetables that are battered and then deep fried

Tofu Also called "bean curd." Made from dried soybeans that are soaked in water until soft, then crushed, boiled, and separated into pulp and curds or milk. The warm curds are combined with a coagulant, cooled, and molded into solid cakes.

Tsukemono Traditional pickles usually made from vegetables, such as daikon, cucumber, and eggplant

Udon Wheat noodles

Udonko High-gluten flour

Umami A pleasant, savory flavor known as the "fifth taste," in addition to salty, sweet, bitter, and sour

Umeboshi Pickled plums

Uni Salt-pickled sea urchin roe

Uramaki Type of sushi in which the rice is on the outside of the roll

Usukuchi shoyu Lighter, thinner, saltier type of soy sauce.

Wasabi Root similar to horseradish grated into a fine, pale-green paste and used as a spicy condiment with a strong flavor like hot mustard or chili pepper; typically accompanies sashimi, sushi, and other traditional Japanese dishes.

Washoku A traditional way of preparing Japanese food. Literally, it means "harmony of food."

Yakitori Skewered and grilled chicken, meat, and vegetables

Yuzu Citrus fruit used in cooking that adds a bright fragrance to soups, simmered dishes, pickles, relishes, and sweet confections

SELECTED COOKBOOKS OF PARTICIPATING CHEFS

Elizabeth Andoh

Washoku: Recipes from the Japanese Home Kitchen, by Elizabeth Andoh, 2005

Kansha: Celebrating Japan;s Vegan and Vegetarian Traditions by Elizabeth Andoh, 2010

Michael Anthony

The Gramercy Tavern Cookbook by Michael Anthony and Dorothy Kalins, with a history by Danny Meyer, 2013

David Bouley

East of Paris: The New Cuisines of Austria and the Danube by David Bouley and Melissa Clark, 2003

World Cuisine United States of America by David Bouley and Jean-Georges Vongerichten, 2005

Eddy Leroux

Foraged Flavor: Finding Fabulous Ingredients in Your Backyard or Farmer's Market, with 88 Recipes by Tama Matsuoka Wong with Eddy Leroux, foreword by Daniel Boulud, and photography by Thomas Schauer, 2012

Nobu Matsuhisa

Nobu: The Cookbook by Nobuyuki Matsuhisa and Robert De Niro, with a foreword by Martha Stewart, 2001

Nobu Now by Nobuyuki Matsuhisa, 2005

Nobu West by Nobuyuki Matsuhisa and Mark Edwards, 2007

Nobu Miami: The Party Cookbook by Nobuyuki Matsuhisa and Thomas Buckley, with photography by Masashi Kuma and forewords by Daniel Boulud and Ferran Adrià, 2008

Dashi and Umami: The Heart of Japanese Cuisine by Nobuyuki Matsuhisa, Kiyomi Mikuni, Heston Blumenthal, Pascal Barbot, 2009

Nobu's Vegetarian Cookbook by Nobuyuki Matsuhisa, with photography by Masashi Kuma and forewords by Jean-Georges Vongerichten and Eric Ripert, 2012

Ben Pollinger

School of Fish by Ben Pollinger, 2014

Eric Ripert

Le Bernardin Cookbook: Four-Star Simplicity by Eric Ripert and Maguy Le Coze, 1998

On the Line by Eric Ripert and Christine Muhlke, 2008

A Return to Cooking by Michael Ruhlman and Eric Ripert, 2009

Avec Eric by Eric Ripert, 2010

Michael Romano

The Union Square Cafe Cookbook: 160 Favorite Recipes from New York's Acclaimed Restaurant by Danny Meyer and Michael Romano, 1994

Second Helpings from Union Square Cafe: 140 New Favorites from New York's Acclaimed Restaurant by Danny Meyer and Michael Romano, with photographs by Duane Michals, 2001

Family Table: Favorite Staff Meals from Our Restaurants to Your Home by Michael Romano and Karen Stabiner, with a foreword by Danny Meyer and photographs by Marcus Nilsson, 2013

Marcus Samuelsson

Aquavit: And the New Scandinavian Cuisine by Marcus Samuelsson, 2003

The Soul of a New Cuisine: A Discovery of the Foods and Flavors of Africa by Marcus Samuelsson, 2006

Discovery Of A Continent - Foods, Flavors, and Inspirations From Africa by Marcus Samuelsson, 2007

New American Table by Marcus Samuelsson, 2009

Yes, Chef: A Memoir by Marcus Samuelsson and Veronica Chambers, 2013

Suvir Saran

Indian Home Cooking: A Fresh Introduction to Indian Food, with More Than 150 Recipes by Suvir Saran and Stephanie Lyness, 2004

American Masala: 125 New Classics from My Home Kitchen by Suvir Saran and Raquel Pelzel, 2007

Masala Farm: Stories and Recipes from an Uncommon Life in the Country by Suvir Saran, Raquel Pelzel, and Charlie Burd, 2011

Lee Anne Wong

Dumplings All Day Wong: A Cookbook of Asian Delights From a Top Chef by Lee Anne Wong, 2014

Index

bushido, 98

C

Cardoz, Floyd, 125–126
caviar, 273
Charlie Trotter's (restaurant), 222
cod sperm (shirako), 68
Colicchio, Tom, 291–292
colors, xvii, 6–7, 113–114
Comme Ça (restaurant), 97
communication, 93, 148, 188–189,
    194, 222–223
competitions, 169–170, 174
Cooking and Hospitality Institute of
    Chicago (CHIC), 156
crab, 66–67
creativity, 117
Culinary Institute of America, (CIA)
    12-14, 37, 83, 192, 197, 200,
    205, 243
customers
    dining experience, 103, 168,
        170–171, 175, 253, 257, 278–
        280, 281
    expectations, 170–171, 225, 254
    treatment of, 84, 93, 253

D

daikon, 9, 71, 164, 213
Daniel (restaurant), 81, 83
dashi, 12, 23, 37, 52-53, 70, 116,
    148, 166, 224, 226, 248
David Myers Cafe, 97
Delouvrier, Christian, 124–125
dishware, 179, 245, 271
Dōgen Zenji, xvii, xxi
Drew-Baker, Kathleen, xx
Ducasse, Alain, 125
Dufresne, Wylie, 46–59
    Alder (restaurant), 47
    awards/reviews, 47
    background, 47–48
    career path, 48–50
    cuisine, 52–54

on ingredients, 50–51
tools, 56–57
on training, 54–56
wd~50 (restaurant), 47, 54–55,
    57–59

E

eater-tainment, 257, 260, 261
edamame, 51
Edo Period, xix
Edo style, 233
educational programs
    CHIC. See Cooking and
        Hospitality Institute of
        Chicago
    CIA. See Culinary Institute of
        America
    Externships/internships, 83
    in France, 77
    FCI. See French Culinary
        Institute
    Gohan Society, The, xiii–xiv, 29,
        130, 238, 317-318
    "Healthy Kitchens, Healthy
        Lives" program, 20
    ICC. (Formerly FCI) See French
        Culinary Institute
    ICE. See Institute of Culinary
        Education
    limitations, 190–191, 193, 296
    A Taste of Culture, 3, 11
    training styles, 13–14, 77
    TSUJI Culinary Institute. See
        TSUJI Culinary Institute of
        Osaka
    variety of, 27–28
enoki mushrooms, 10

F

farmers, 25, 35, 82, 101
The Fat Duck (restaurant), 57
fermentation, xxi, 24
fires, 94–95
fish. See also specific types

About the Authors

Saori Kawano

Saori Kawano founded Korin Japanese Trading Corp. in New York City in 1982. Korin is the premier supplier of traditional Japanese knives and tableware to prestigious hotels, restaurants, cooking schools, and serious amateur chefs across the U.S. and the world.

Saori Kawano has been recognized by and participates in many food industry organizations, including the James Beard Foundation, the International Association of Culinary Professionals, Women Chefs and Restaurateurs, the Foodservice Consultants Society International, City Meals on Wheels, National Minority Business Council, Euro-American Women's Council, and others.

In 2005, Saori Kawano launched The Gohan Society, a non-profit organization fostering U.S.-Japan culinary and cultural exchange. Through The Gohan Society, she brings together professionals from culinary institutions, journalism, and publishing, the restaurant and restaurant supply industries—as well as others who love Japanese food—in order to develop exchange programs.

Saori Kawano has been featured in dozens of prestigious food, hospitality, and business-related publications, programs and blogs in the U.S and Japan including: *The New York Times*, *Crain's New York Business*, *Fortune*, *New York* magazine, and the *Los Angeles Times;* as well as *Newsweek Japan*, *Yomiuri,* and *Asahi*, Japan's largest national newspapers. Saori Kawano has also been featured on *Martha Stewart Live,* PBS's *Discovery Channel,* NBC's "Sunday Morning," and several other nationally broadcast programs in the U.S. and Japan.

Contact Saori Kawano at 212-587-7021, saori@korin.com, www.korin.com, or www.gohansociety.org

Don Gabor

Don Gabor is the author of the best-seller *How to Start a Conversation and Make Friends,* plus twelve other books on business and interpersonal communication skills. His books have been published by Simon & Schuster, Random House, Prentice-Hall, and McGraw-Hill, and have been translated and published in more than 27 editions, including Japanese, Chinese, German, and Spanish. He is also a ghostwriter and writing coach for people who want to write, traditionally publish, and self-publish books.

Don Gabor is a professional speaker and was a media spokesperson for Frito-Lay, Grand Marnier, and Sprint. He has been a member of the National Speakers Association since 1991 and was the 2010–2011 President of the New York City chapter. As a frequent media guest, Don Gabor's books have been featured in hundreds of print, radio, and television interviews, including "A Few Minutes With Andy Rooney," *The New York Times, The Wall Street Journal,* and others. *The New Yorker* called Don "a gifted conversationalist."

Don Gabor founded Conversation Arts Media in 1991, a communications consulting company. He shows professionals from all disciplines how to grow their credibility and revenues through strategic networking, public speaking, and book writing. He has presented workshops to FM Global, GenRe, the Professional Association of SQL Servers, Marriott Hotels, and many other companies, associations, and colleges. Don Gabor has been working with Saori Kawano and Korin since 2002 and is a member of The Gohan Society's Advisory Committee.

Contact Don Gabor at 718-768-0824, don@dongabor.com, or www.dongabor.com.

Additional Resources

Please visit www.gohansociety.org for free additional materials including:

- *Chef's Choice*: Tips and Quotations
- *Chef's Choice*: Culinary Student Study Questions
- *Chef's Choice*: Reading Club Discussion Questions
- *Chef's Choice*: Media Kit
- … and much more.